Papers on Language Acquisition, Language Learning and Language Teaching

Edited
by
Henning Wode

1804
NULLA DIES SINE LINEA

JULIUS GROOS VERLAG HEIDELBERG

CIP-Kurztitelaufnahme der Deutschen Bibliothek

Papers on language acquisition, language learning
and language teaching / ed. by Henning Wode. –
Heidelberg : Groos, 1983.
    (Studies in descriptive linguistics ; Vol. 11)
    ISBN 3-87276-260-5
NE: Wode, Henning [Hrsg.] ; GT

ISSN 0171-6794
ISBN 3-87276-260-5
© 1983 Julius Groos Verlag, D-6900 Heidelberg
Satz und Druck: Beltz Offsetdruck, D-6944 Hemsbach

General Preface

Studies in Descriptive Linguistics is a series intended to supplement the *International Review of Applied Linguistics (IRAL)*. The series contains anthologies of articles and also monographs dealing primarily with the description of English, German, French, Russian, and Spanish; some other languages may, however, also be dealt with.

The descriptions concern more particularly the grammatical, semantico-syntactical and pragmatic levels of the languages involved, including discourse analysis. Occasionally, however, the phonetic-phonological level will be taken into account. Contrastive studies, studies in error analysis and in first and second language acquisition are also included. Furthermore, there are volumes concerned with the descriptive implications of particular models of grammar, e.g. case grammar and systemic-functional grammar.

Thus the series *Studies in Descriptive Linguistics* attempts to reflect the latest developments in the description of natural languages within the framework of language teaching. It will be of interest to students, teachers, and language-material writers.

Dietrich Nehls

Dedication

fœ mɔda

Preface

This volume brings together a number of papers dealing with various aspects of the study of language acquisition and language learning. The intention is to overcome barriers imposed by restrictions in the accessability of both publishing sources (journals, conference reports, working papers) as well as languages. Therefore, all papers are in English. Those originally written in German have been translated.

The papers originated between 1970 and 1980. They derive from long-term investigations which began 1968 at the University of Freiburg and which were continued since 1969 at the University of Kiel. The essential theme is the nature of man's language learning system, i.e. the ability which allows human beings to learn, and to be taught, natural languages. This ability is unique to human beings; it is species-specific; and very likely biologically endowed, i.e. innate. One of the major concerns throughout these papers is to show that learning a foreign language in the classroom via foreign language teaching is by no means totally different from mastering a language in natural situations. Foreign language teaching must be integrated into a comprehensive view of language learning which includes all types of language acquisition.

I have abstained from large scale editing. Printing conventions are harmonized. The text of articles which appeared in journals has not been altered. This leads to a small amount of repetition concerning technical matters, like the design of the Kiel project and the progress made at the respective dates of publication. Apart from reasons of copyright, it was felt that by retaining these passages the reader was provided with an outline of the development of the project. I am grateful to the publishers for the permission to reprint the articles. Specific acknowledgements are found with each article. All references have been amalgamated into one comprehensive bibliography.

Throughout the development of my thinking on language learning I have gratefully benefitted from the assistance, encouragement, and criticism of my students, collaborators, and colleagues, notably Sally Allendorff, Jens Bahns, Ocke Bohn, Hartmut Burmeister, Sascha Felix, Dietrich Lange, and Detlef Ufert. Thanks for help with the preparation of the manuscripts are due to Christina Borck, Juliane Brohmann, Jack Daugherty, Gesche Jach, Jutta Kaulbach, Wolf Kursawe, Andrea Peter, Nina Twork, and Thomas Vogel.

University of Kiel   Henning Wode

Contents

Preface

Part I

A NEW APPROACH TO THE STUDY OF LANGUAGE LEARNING

Introduction

In the past, research on language acquisition of whatever type, i.e. first language learning (L1), second language learning (L2), bilingualism, etc., was focused on individual types. For example, Jakobson's classic study (1941) proposed universals of language acquisition for phonological acquisition. But, in fact, Jakobson dealt only with L1 acquisition, and to some extent with L1 bilingualism. It never occurred to him to also look at phonological acquisition in the classroom or at the relearning of phonological systems. Similarly, traditional foreign language teaching, notably error analysis of various sorts, has almost exclusively been carried out in strict isolation from, and in disregard of, the study of the other types of language acquisition, for example, L1 acquisition. The recent upsurge of research on naturalistic L2 acquisition allows us to begin to broaden the gap by looking at parallels between L1 and L2 acquisition. However, it seems necessary to push on and to investigate all types of language acquisition if a clear understanding of those cognitive capacities which enable human beings to learn natural languages is ever to be gained. The goal must be to develop an integrated theory of language acquisition which brings within the scope of one integrated theory all types of language acquisition. This theory should enable us to state within a systematic overall framework the commonalities as well as the differences among the various types of language acquisition.

The result of the papers in this volume is that a theory of language acquisition cannot be regarded as merely a special instance of a general learning theory, Piagetian, behavioristic or whatever. The description of how human beings learn languages requires a special learning theory that is integrated into man's overall cognitive functioning only on a higher level.

Article no. 1 of part I was the first in which such goals were considered — tentatively, of course. It was written in 1972. It turned out in the research which took place since the early 1970's in Kiel and elsewhere that most of the issues which were to capture the interest of L2 researchers were already stated or raised in this paper, notably: a typology of acquisitional types; language acquisition and the development of cognition and of man's perceptual processing abilities; nativism vs. behaviorism; parallels between L1 and L2 acquisition; the universals issue; individual variation among learners; L1 transfer in L2 acquisition; age and the critical period hypothesis; the importance of insights from naturalistic L2 acquisition for foreign language teaching; the effect of socio-cultural variables; and the disappointment about the fact that presently available linguistic theories are so ill-suited to describe learner utterances. Above all it is argued in paper no. 1 that the impact of teaching procedures can only be assessed adequately, if the students' natural contributions via their natural language learning abilities are given proper consideration. The provocative question is: do the students learn in spite of, or because of, the teaching methods?

The second article of part I was written five years later. It expands some of the topics about foreign language teaching mentioned in the first paper and it already reflects empirical findings as of 1976. It is stressed in particular that learning a language in the classroom should be made subject to developmental investigations, i.e. emphasis should be placed on the student as a learner rather than on the teacher and teaching, as has been the dominating approach in the past.

NATURALISTIC L2 ACQUISITION: ISSUES, GOALS, AND PERSPECTIVES*

Henning Wode

0 Purpose

How do people acquire a second language (L2) or even additional ones without the help of schoolroom instruction at a time when the first language (L1) has already been mastered either completely or partially? How, for example, do children of migrant workers pick up German from their playmates? How do their parents learn German from their German co-workers? How do immigrants and their children acquire the language(s) of their host countries? There is no justification at all for the lack of attention which questions of this sort have attracted to date from researchers on language acquisition. This paper is intended to call attention to this kind of language acquisition. It will be termed *naturalistic L2 acquisition.* It seems to me that insights can be expected which will be of great importance for foreign language teaching, for psychology, and for linguistics, to mention just a few disciplines.

The aim of my discussion is to review the existing literature on naturalistic L2 acquisition in order to identify the major issues, so that a research programme can be developed for the investigation of these questions[1].

In this paper the task will primarily be approached from a linguistic point of view. After all, the linguistic aspect is (still) most central for investigations on language acquisition. This will become clearer from § 3. I proceed as follows: First, naturalistic L2 acquisition will be allocated its place within a theory of language acquisition (§ 1). Some terminological distinctions are introduced in § 2. In § 3 I briefly discuss the state of development which research on language acquisition has reached to date. I review those topics and approaches which have proved expecially fruitful for this kind of research or which have primarily occupied researchers. As an example of the kind of empirical data that are presently available I briefly review the L2 as well as L1 acquisition of negation in English (§ 4). Some conclusions of a more general sort are presented in § 5. Included will be a survey of those issues for which linguistic investigations on naturalistic L2 bilingualism can, I hope, contribute valuable evidence.

1 Naturalistic L2 Acquisition within a more General Language Learning Theory

The topic of naturalistic L2 acquisition/L2 bilingualism arose from attempts to devise a (linguistic) theory of language acquisition. The central problems to be solved include
1. How does one learn a first language?
2. How does one learn several languages?

a) if one has been exposed to several languages from birth?
b) if one learns a second or third language at a point of time when the first one(s) has/have already been mastered completely or partially?
3. How does one acquire a language under naturalistic conditions?
4. How does one do so if exposed to schoolroom foreign language instruction?
The topic of naturalistic L2 acquisition is posed by point (2b) in conjunction with point (3).

2 Some Terminological Distinctions

The term *language acquisition* is used here as a cover term for any type of mastering a language. It will become clearer later on that it is usefuld to have such a cover term. It is quite intentional that the term *acquisition* is used. Terms like *learn/learning* are avoided because they are most familiar from SR-experiments in experimental psychology. This technical use of the term *learn/learning* does not apply to many aspects of the language acquisitional process(es). For example, Braine 1963 observed utterances like (1) with an English-speaking child at the age of 1;8 - 2;0[2]:

allgone shoe
allgone vitamins (1)
allgone egg

These utterances were instances of a productive construction type of the child. Which properties of English or of the speech surrounding the child could possibly have functioned as *reinforcement* in the sense of SR-theories? Such word order patterns are not current in English and they therefore cannot function *in toto* either as a stimulus or as a reinforcer. The inadequacy of SR-explanation is even more drastically highlighted by the acquisition of negation (see § 4).

The term *model* refers to the structure of the language to be acquired and/or to the structure of the linguistic item of this language (word, construction, etc).

The *first language* (L1) is the one acquired first. This tautological expression is to stress the chronological aspect. The first language is not necessarily the one which a speaker prefers, or which he speaks best if he commands several languages.

Multilingualism refers to the command/acquisition of several languages. *L1 multilingualism* refers to the phenomenon of exposure to several languages from birth. If a second language is mastered after the first one has already been acquired completely or partially, then this type is called *L2 acquisition/L2 bilingualism* (L2).

Human beings can learn languages in various external situations, for example, with the help of school instruction. This is *tutored language acquisition,* either *tutored L1* or *tutored L2 acquisition.* The latter type is familiar as *foreign language teaching;* the former type may occur as *speech therapy.*

If no formal instruction is applied then language acquisition proceeds under *naturalistic conditions*. In general, this applies to L1 acquisition and L1 multilingualism. It is also possible, however, in L2 acquisition, and by no means rare. Naturalistic L2 acquisition can be observed, for example, with the children of migrant workers who acquire German from their playmates; with adult migrants who have to acquire the host language from their native co-workers; with immigrants, refugees, etc.[3]

3 Naturalistic L2 Acquisition and Linguistically Oriented Language Acquisition Research

In § 3.1 I briefly summarize those areas which have so far been the major concern of researchers of language acquisition. Topics and approaches which have proved to be particularly fruitful are surveyed in § 3.2.

3.1 Domains of research

Past research is concentrated in two areas. One is L1 acquisition, notably child language acquisition. To be more precise this is L1 acquisition under naturalistic conditions, in most cases monolingual, more rarely multilingual.

The second area of interest is foreign language teaching, i.e. tutored L2 bilingualism or L2 multilingualism. The main concern here has been teaching methodology and, especially during the past decade, the development of technological devices helpful in the classroom. I think that the problem of how to evaluate the effectiveness of teaching methodologies including the technological devices has not been solved as yet in any satisfactory way. One type of approach to this problem of evaluation can be seen in the many experiments in which the achievements of different groups of subjects which have been exposed to different teaching methodologies are compared. This, however, is but a fairly superficial sort of evaluation. For example, there tend to be no explanations offered as to what exactly it is that language teaching methodologies actually achieve. Do they speed up a development that takes place anyway? Or is it possible to optimize the structure of this language learning process with the help of teaching methodologies in the sense that its natural course of development is changed, perhaps, in that students jump certain developmental stages, or that some stages can even be eliminated? Or do teaching methodologies achieve nothing at all?

These provocative questions cannot be answered at present, due to of lack of comparative data, i.e. we lack information about the acquisition of a second language under naturalistic conditions. The mastery of a second or a third language in a natural setting has not yet captured the attention of researchers. The phenomenon as such is by no means rare, as already indicated in §§ 0 and 2. The cases mentioned there clearly indicate that L2 bilingualism can very likely be acquired in a natural setting at all age levels, although it is also well known that, in general, the results become increasingly unsatisfactory as a function of age. I argue in § 5 that such global assessments have to be made much more precise by reference to the structural area involved in such unsatisfactory results.

3.2 Methods and approaches

3.2.1 Linguistic approaches: language as a system

As for the methodological insight to which the upsurge of research in language acquisition during the 1940's is largely due, this is primarily the realization that a human language must be regarded as a sign system, although structured in highly complex ways. The acquisition of a language, therefore, means the acquisition of structures and not just mastery of isolated words or sentences. This insight inevitably leads to the central question behind the research on language acquisition: How does the system of the target language develop in the mind of the learner?

This is the point where the central impact of linguistics for any integrated theory of language acquisition is most obvious. Of course, in addition to linguistics, contributions have to come from psychology, sociology, education, and other disciplines. Linguistics, however, must be central because it is this discipline which identifies and describes the structures of the target language as well as the structure of the learner's utterances.

3.2.2 The universalist hypothesis and developmental sequences

Jakobson (1941) was the first to pursue, develop, and make more precise, the linguistic approach to language acquisition, although he limited himself to phonological acquisition. On the one hand, he suggested that language acquisition was subject to universal regularities that could be described within a linguistic framework. This is the universalist hypothesis. On the other hand, Jakobson suggested that language acquisition follows a chronologically ordered sequence of developmental stages. There is an implicational relation between these stages such that stage Y cannot be reached unless stage X has already been reached.

Today, it has become a basic assumption that L1 acquisition follows ordered developmental sequences, although it is still one of the major goals in present day research to identify these sequences. We are probably still very much at the beginning. Similarly, the universalist hypothesis is still very much an open question. No doubt, striking parallels between different languages can be pointed out. However, these commonalities primarily relate to early stages of development (see, for example, Slobin 1970 for early syntactic-semantic parallels; E.V. Clark 1973 on lexical development; Jakobson 1941 on phonological development). In addition, the respective phenomena have not always been observed with every speaker of a given language. According to Slobin 1970, Bowerman, for example, found pivot structures[4] only with one of the two Finnish children which she observed.

Jakobson's claims about phonology have been repeatedly criticized as empirically false (see, for example, v. Raffler-Engel 1970).

3.2.3 Developmental sequences as a function of the structure of the model and/or cognitive-perceptual prerequisites.

Some of the limitations inherent in linguistic methodology become apparent if one considers to what extent developmental stages may be determined by the structure of the model. The fact that the sequencing of the acquisition of the linguistic structures is, in fact, determined quite crucially by the structure of the model has been reconfirmed also by more recent studies. For example, H.H. Clark 1970 attempts to show that children acquire the lexical structures of English in such a way that they master the unmarked before the marked elements.

But to what extent are cognitive-perceptual prerequisites involved? After all, the child has to recognize the linguistic structures in the model before he can proceed to master them. This presupposes specific abilities of a cognitive-perceptual sort. Very likely the child has to acquire some of these in turn. In any event, there are probably some phenomena involved which function as prerequisites for the mastery of linguistic structures.

The problem of language development and cognition is today discussed more frequently in terms of cognitive-perceptual development as a basis for language development. Although this problem is in the forefront of interest among researchers, we are still very much at the beginning. We lack reliable techniques to isolate the linguistic as opposed to the cognitive-perceptual variables. Some impression of the sort of insight that may be forth-coming can be derived from Slobin 1973.

Furthermore, it seems to me that investigations into naturalistic L2 acquisition may provide us with evidence for the issue of cognitive-perceptual requisites in ways which are beyond the possibilities of investigations of L1 acquisition. If certain cognitive variables are acquired via the L1 and if they are claimed to cause the late appearance of certain linguistic structures, then it is no longer possible to argue that similiar linguistic structures are acquired late in L2 because of the lack of appropriate cognitive prerequisites. One such example will be discussed in § 5.2.2.

3.2.4 Explanatory hypotheses for language acquisition

No other problem has been debated more hotly in recent discussions than the search for explanations of the *how* of language acquisition. How does one acquire linguistic structures? The discussion has centered around three approaches:

a) Behavioristic: Learning a language is achieved via conditioning, analogous to how a dog, a rat, or a dove ,,learn" something in animal experiments. (for example, Skinner 1957, Staats 1971).

b) Nativistic: Languages are learned via some species-specific, hence genetically given

8

acquisition device. This device contains — genetically — linguistic categories as, for example, sentence, subject, predicate. (Such views were advocated particularly within the generative-transformational framework, e.g. Chomsky 1965, and notably McNeill 1970a).

c) Cognitive: Language is seen as a reflex of cognitive development in two respects: on the one hand a child is not likely to want to express anything which is beyond his cognitive-conceptual state of development. On the other hand, certain cognitive abilities are required in order to enable the learner to recognize the structures of the model, if they are to be learned and reproduced — even if in not target-like ways (see Slobin 1973).

Strictly speaking, the cognitive approach is not an explanation about the *how* of language acquisition. The cognitive approach specifies prerequisites for it. As far as I can see they are compatible with both behavioristic as well as nativistic explanations.

This means that it is still an open question how to explain language acquisition. Nobody can seriously doubt that any child is biologically endowed in a species-specific way to acquire human languages. The real question, therefore, is how much is genetically pre-programmed. Unfortunately, such discussions regularly drift off into fruitless global polarizations.

It seems to me that the question of how languages are acquired has to be posed in a more differentiated way, namely by determining which structural areas may be acquired, for example, behavioristically and which not. Morphophonology is, if at all, very likely more suitable for behavioristic than for nativistic explanations. The reverse seems to hold for large areas of syntax, as the acquisition of negation will show (§ 4).

In any event, the issue of how to explain language acquisition is, ultimately not a linguistic problem. Linguistics can only provide certain primary data to be interpreted by psychologists, and, perhaps, by other disciplines[5].

4 Naturalistic L2 Bilingualism

On the one hand, it seems reasonable to carry out the investigations on naturalistic L2 acquisition within the framework of the major issues which pertain to language acquisition in general and as outlined in § 3. On the other hand, the peculiarities of L2 acquisition must also be investigated.

One might hypothesize — as has been done repeatedly (for example, Corder 1967) — that L2 acquisition proceeds like L1 acquisition: an identity hypothesis. According to this hypothesis one would expect to find with L2 speakers who acquire, say, English as L2, those and only those structures which occur when children acquire English as L1. On the other hand one might assume — if for no other reason than for the sake of this argument — that L2 speakers make use of the linguistic knowledge which they have already acquired via their L1, perhaps in such a way that they modify their respective L1 structures step by step in the direction of the target L2. In certain extreme cases one might find, for example, constructions from one language with the words from the other. This would be an interference hypothesis.

To check either hypothesis, it would be necessary to compare the L1 developmental sequences and the respective developmental structures with those of L2 acquisition. To illustrate, I single out some syntactic aspects of the acquisition of negation in English. In addition, a few observations relating to other structural areas are added. Since the L2 speakers to be cited for comparison have Norwegian as their L1 (see § 4.1.3) I offer a few hints about differences and commonalities in the negation system of both languages.

4.1 The Acquisition of Negation in English

4.1.1 Negation in English and Norwegian

My remarks are limited to positional properties of *not* ~ *-n't* for English and *ikke* for Norwegian, respectively. In English *not* ~ *-n't* are placed after the finite auxiliary. If ther is none, *do*-support is required. This also applies to inversion.

In Norwegian *ikke* is placed after the finite verb, irrespective of whether it is an auxiliary or a full verb. If the direct or indirect object is a personal pronoun, it is placed between the finite verb and *ikke*; if it is a noun, *ikke* is placed directly after the finite verb. In the same way, i.e. depending on whether the subject is a noun or a personal pronoun, the subject is positioned differently in cases of inversion.

The word order patterns are:

English (2)

a) Subj $\begin{bmatrix} do \\ AUX \end{bmatrix}$ not ~—n't V...

b) $\begin{bmatrix} do \\ AUX \end{bmatrix}$ not ~—n't Subj V...

Norwegian (3)

a) Subj $\begin{bmatrix} V_{fin} \\ Aux_{fin} \end{bmatrix}$ ikke....

b) $\begin{bmatrix} V_{fin} \\ Aux_{fin} \end{bmatrix}$ ikke Subj (N)....

c) Subj $\begin{bmatrix} V_{fin} \\ Aux_{fin} \end{bmatrix}$ pers. Pron. ikke ....

d) $\begin{bmatrix} V_{fin} \\ Aux_{fin} \end{bmatrix}$ Subj (pers. Pron.) ikke ....

4.1.2 L1 acquisition[6]

For the L1 acquisition of English three major developmental stages have to be envisaged according to Klima & Bellugi 1966[7] and as summarized under (4).

External position of neg (initial or final):

a) no singing song   (4 I)

   no money

   no heavy

   no sit there

   no Fraser drink all tea

b) touch the snow no

   book say no

In general, the negative morpheme is *no,* more rarely *not.* In most cases neg is placed initially, rarely at the end, but never within the constituent S which follows or precedes *no/not.*

   neg S (yntagma) ~S neg

   no   no

   not

Internal placement of neg in S:

a) he no bite you   (4 II)

   I no want envelope

b) that no Mommy

   there no squirrels

   that not ,,O", that blue

c) don't leave me

   don't wake me up .... again

d) I don't sit on Cromer coffee

   I don't like him

e) I can't catch you

   we can't talk

In sentences or their precursors, neg is now placed after the subject and in front of the predicate, or what are later to become subject and predicate. *Can't* and *don't* are still monomorphemic. They are variants of neg. *Do* and *can* are not yet produced without *—n't.* In negated imperatives neg is placed initially:

```
Subj   neg   Pred
       no
       not
       can't
       don't
neg   VP
don't
```

The rise of AUX: (4 III)

a) Paul can't have one

   I didn't did it

   you didn't caught me

   that was not me

   I am not a doctor

Now the auxiliaries are acquired. *Don't* and *can't* are now bi-morphemic as required by the target:

```
Subj   Aux   neg        X
             not ~ –n't
```

4.1.3 L2 acquisition

As for the L2 acquisition of English negation, I rely on the work of the Norwegian scholar Roar Ravem. He is one of the very few whose reports can be used for systematic evaluations concerning naturalistic L2 acquisition.[8]

Ravem observed how his two children, Rune and Reidun, acquired English in Edinburgh under naturalistic conditions. Their L1 is Norwegian. Rune, the boy, was six and one half years old, the girl three years and nine months, when the family moved from Norway to Scotland.

So far, Ravem has reported about the acquisition and development of negation, wh-interrogation and certain aspects of the auxiliary verbs (Ravem 1968, 1969, 1970).

For negation, see Ravem 1968, and in particular 1969. Unfortunately, Ravem did not date the examples from his children in such a way that it would be useful to raise the question of the chronological sequencing of the acquisition of the various structures.

I have separated the evidence for the two children. Since it is not worthwhile to attempt to specify the developmental sequence I simply list a few examples for each of the structural types observed with the children. Those structures which are comparable to L1 acquisitional ones are marked by appropriate Roman numerals. Developmental types not observed in L1 acquisition are discussed separately. Glosses are added only if provide by Ravem.

4.1.3.1 Rune

With Rune, comparable examples for the L1 stage (4 I) are lacking. As for stage (4 II) see:

II a) I not like that (5)
   the teacher not come (i.e. didn't come)
   I not looking for edge
   b) it's not ready yet
   c) no don't do that
   d) I can't see he
   oh, I mustn't do something now
   he's not take a bath
   I haven' take all ....

Rune's examples for stage (II b-d) (5) are difficult to classify because they already look target-like as far as negation and the development of AUX is concerned. They could, therefore, already be assigned to stage (III) (4). On the other hand, Ravem 1969 insists that *don't* and *can't* were monomorphemic when first recorded. Unfortunately, the examples are not distinguished by him in accordance with this suggestion.

Another utterance which might already be target-like is the following:

   one is not crying (6)

There is no directly corresponding L1 evidence for the following exhaustive list (7):

   a) I don't will more (perhaps (II d) (4)) (7)
   b) so that we not will (perhaps (II a) (4))
   c) I will not more
   d) /dis/ have not boots − the car − /dis/ have round „hjul"
   e) first we haven't a TV − and so we have one
   f) I see not to twelve, „men" to eleven (i.e. I didn't watch TV till 12, but till 11 (last night))
   g) say it you not to daddy?
   h) like you me not, Reidun?

It seems that in (7 a-b) *will* functions as a full verb. (7 c-f) with neg after the verb is reminiscent of (3 a) of Norwegian, and (7 g-h) of (3 c-d). The utterances (7 g-h) are taken from Ravem 1968, p. 183.

What is surprising about this evidence is that only a relatively small number of the structures is suspect of being due to the influence of the L1. The overwhelming majority corresponds to early structural types from L1 acquisition. The utterances might have been taken from Bloom 1970a or Klima Bellugi 1966: Where did the boy get them from? His parents? No, because his father has a brilliant command of English. His playmates? Certainly not, because children around the age of six are well beyond such a stage of development. Or does the boy reduce target utterances of his environment in a systematic way such that he deletes auxiliary verbs and retains neg plus the following VP? Hardly, because what would utterances like (8) be reductions of?

> I don't will more
> so that we not will[9]
(8)

Above all, it is highly unlikely that the parallels between the acquisition of English as L1 and L2 should be accidental because similar parallels can also be found with Ravem's second child Reidun.

4.1.3.2 Reidun

Ravem did mark Reidun's examples on negation chronologically as to months and weeks of contact with English (e.g. 3;2 means 3 months, 2 weeks of contact). But the initial development is also lacking here so that the question about the developmental sequence cannot be posed in a detailed way for Reidun either. Therefore, the examples are grouped according to the structural types, as with Rune. Ravem's dates of occurrence are added in brackets.

I a) „ikke" – not here; not there (4;1)   (9)
     not ready (4;1)
     „ikke har" this one, „men" this one (3;2)
     „ikke gå" to Gillian afternoon (3;2)
     no, not this one (3;2)
     not like it now (4;0)
     not go off (I don't want to get off your foot) (4;2)
     no, no like it – no, not like it (4;4)
     not broke it again (I mustn't break it again) (5;2)
     no, not Mummy said that (in response to: you are four years old) (4;4)
     no, „ikke" Mummy „skal til London" (4;4)
     not Mummy „skal til London" (I don't want her to go to London) (4;4)
     not I have a butterfly (4;4)

II a) I not this way (I don't want to jump this way/like this) (4;1)
     „jeg" not like this one (4;2)
     „jeg" not like it (4;2)
     „jeg" not like fish (4;2)
     I not build house (5;0)
     I not like it (5;1)

II c) don't touch (3;3)
   don't do that (4;0)
   no, „ikke" do (4;1) (perhaps I a)
   not take me — mine — not take mine (5;0) (perhaps I a)

II d) I don't like it (in response to: what? don't you like it?)
   I don't know
   I haven't see this afore

II e) „jeg vil ikke har" this one (I will not have/I don't want...) (3;2)
   I can't „slik" (3;2)
   „jeg" can't find car (4;0)
   I cannot have this one now (4;4)
   you can't have this one back (6;0)

Reidun, like Rune, occasionally places neg after the verb.

„jeg har" not bird on (I haven't got a card with a bird on/I have   (10)
   a card without bird(s) on) (4;0)
I have not butterfly (4;4)
„jeg har" not more fish (4;4)
now I /ə/, got not more (4;4)
I haven't long piece (of bacon) (6;0)

The following examples cannot be assessed properly in developmental terms:

we no(t) don't walk (6;0)   (11)
that can I read — no — but that can't I read (6;0)

As far as syntax is concerned, the next example looks target-like:

Dolly „er" not here (4;0)   (12)

Reidun shows more interference with Norwegian than her brother, in particular lexical interference. But with her, too, the majority of the examples — and they were not listed exhaustively here — can be matched with comparable L1 types. In addition, as with Rune, the interference type with neg after the full verb (see 7 c-f) is also found. Rune's interference-like utterances such as (7 g-h) which were reminiscent (3 c-d) of Norwegian were not noted for Reidun.

5 Conclusions

As far as the topic of naturalistic L2 acquisition is concerned, the evidence from both children is structured quite similarly. Ravem's material about the acquisition of English wh-interrogation and about the auxiliaries provides additional evidence which is also quite similar. And so is the material in Huang 1971. All this evidence makes it very unlikely that the parallels that have been identified are purely accidental. Rather, it seems that what is involved are regularities which should be investigated systematically. Below I attempt to propose some points which may be useful for deriving working hypotheses which can be applied to (some) of the problems outlined in the initial sections of this paper.

5.1 Identity or interference hypothesis?

Neither of the two hypotheses outlined in § 4 can be totally disposed of at the present time. After all, both children in Ravem's study employ structures which one would expect for L1 acquisition, but there was also interference. In fact, one interference type occurred with both children. The identity hypothesis does not explain the structural type with neg post-posed to the full verb, because this type has not been observed so far for the L1 acquisition of English. The interference hypothesis offers no plausible explanation for the appearance of the types I-II. After all, the types under I and some of those under II could not have been heard by the children in their environment. One uncertainty remains, however. It is at present not known whether similar or perhaps the same structural types as found in English appear when Norwegian is acquired as L1. If this is the case, then there would be additional options for interference to occur so that the interference hypothesis as developed in § 5.3.2 would have to be expanded.

As a consequence, it seems that future research should bear both hypotheses in mind. In addition, two languages L_i and L_j should be investigated both for L1 and L2 acquisition. This way it would be possible to decide whether those structures which cannot be explained by interference relate to the L1 acquisition of L_i or L_j.

Both hypotheses need to be enlarged on in several respects. I start with the identity hypothesis.

5.2 Tightening the identity hypothesis

The striking syntactic parallels between L1 and L2 acquisition should not mislead one to conclude in a global way that parallels can be envisaged for the L2 acquisition of all structural areas of a given linguistic system.

Such a sweeping claim must surely be modified with respect to, amongst other things, the age of the speaker, and the structural area to be acquired. Moreover, one can not even guess at present whether the developmental sequences are the same (more details in § 5.2.2).

5.2.1 Language acquisition and age

There is a widespread view — and it is probably not totally incorrect — that adults acquire a second language easier and faster if they can have recourse to foreign language instruction. Children, however, master a second language faster under naturalistic conditions. Perhaps there is a critical period during which the language acquisitional process remains fully applicable under naturalistic conditions both for L1 and L2 acquisition. Its applicability decreases as a function of increasing age. But it seems necessary to be more precise with respect to time as well as with respect to the linguistic structures involved.

As far as L1 acquisition is concerned, the acquisition of certain syntactic-semantic areas is not completed by age ten, or possibly above (see C. Chomsky 1969, Kessel 1970). Phonological acquisition, on the other hand, notably the acquisition of distinctive features, should be accomplished earlier. Large scale empirical investigations on phone acquisition in English, such as Olmsted 1971, point to an age range of 4;0-6;0 and possibly a little later. According to the same sources, the acquisition of the vowels seems to be completed slightly earlier than of the consonants. The important point, however, is whether the language acquisitional processes and their regularities vanish after one language has been acquired; or whether these processes remain applicable/available for later use, for example, for L2 acquisition. It is possible that here, too, a differentiation according to structural areas may be necessary. This is indicated by the familiar type of L2 speaker who has mastered syntax, semantics, morphology, and other structural areas of the respective L2 brilliantly even at a relatively advanced age, but whose phonetics are still poor although he may have spent more than 10 years in the respective L2 environment. [10] Young speakers are said to cope much more successfully with phonetics[11]. However, the experimental evidence is in itself somewhat contradictory (see., for example, Asher/Garcia 1969 vs. Olson/Samuels 1973).

5.2.2 Developmental sequences for L2

Unfortunately, Ravem's data are not detailed enough to lead one to venture hypotheses about the details of the developmental sequences for L2 acquisition that is for the chronology of the developmental structures. That there are parallels between L1 and L2 acquisition is more than likely. But, what exactly constitutes the parallel(s)?

a) Do the same structures appear in L1 and L2 acquisition without the developmental sequences being the same for L2 and L1?
b) Do the same structures appear in L1 and L2 acquisition with identical developmental sequences?
c) Concerning points (a-b): Do all or only some of the L1 developmental structures occur in L2 acquisition?
d) Concerning points (a-c): Are there different parallels depending on the structural area concerned?

That at least some L1 developmental structures should also occur in the L2 acquisition of structural areas other than negation is indicated by Ravem's observation concerning Reidun: Adam, an American boy of the Brown study, initially did not understand *why*-questions, i.e. causal questions (Brown 1968, p. 286f.). In this case, one could have argued that Adam still lacked the concept of causality as a cognitive prerequisite. However, at the beginning Reidun did not understand English *why*-questions either, as her answer to Rune indicates (13) (Ravem 1970, p. 35).

> Rune: why do you put the telephone on the front seat? (13)
> Reidun (3;2): yes

The girl had long ago mastered the concept of causality for Norwegian. Very likely she could not activate this information for L2 acquisition. Instead she went through a developmental process within which it was one and a half months later than the above example, i.e. five more months of contact with English, that she understood *why*-questions. Her difficulty was not that she lacked the cognitive concept. She couldn't identify the concepts or the semantic category, respectively, within the L2. This implies that investigations about naturalistic L2 acquisition will throw light on the acquisition of decoding strategies segregated, as it were, from the cognitive concepts.

In any event, as far as the L2 acquisition of decoding is concerned there are even fewer reliable data available than for the acquisition of encoding. It may be possible that, under certain conditions, the relationship between age and the speed with which L2 acquisition proceeds for decoding is the reverse of that for encoding. Asher&Price 1967 found that, in an experiment, adults learned to understand Russian much faster than children.

5.3 Tightening the interference hypothesis

What impact does the state of development which the learner has reached in his L1 have for his L2 acquisition? It is very likely that, at least for certain age groups, interferences proper will have to be distinguished from L2 regularities which derive from the state of L1 development that the speaker has reached due to his age.

5.3.1 Impact of the learner's state of L1 development

Christian 1971 reports about a child who used pivot constructions in his Gujarati (L1) and had some rudimentary inflections. In his English (L2), inflections were lacking but pivot constructions did occur. This might imply: Only such structural types will appear in the L2 which are no more complex than those already acquired for the L1. In addition and in support of the above, one can frequently hear parents report that their child quickly advanced to the stage of development which L1 children of the same age group normally attain for the respective language (for example, Métreaux 1964/65; Kenyeres 1938; Valette 1964). It remains to be determined whether it is age in the absolute sense or the state of development which the learner has reached in his L1 which is crucial in these cases.

5.3.2 Interference

Theoretically one might assume several interference relationships from L1 and L2:

a) from the L1 as spoken by the adult environment of the L2 speakers;
b) from the state of development of the L1 as acquired by the L2 learner so far; or
c) from the early developmental structures which the L2 learner went through when he acquired his L1.

Point (a) seems to be unlikely. There is no proper evidence for point (c). As for point (b) Ravem's children seem to indicate that, possibly, only specific L1 structures may lead to interference.

As can be gathered from the survey in § 4.1.1 Norwegian, but not English, has the word order pattern with neg after the full verb. In addition, Norwegian has different positional relationships for personal pronouns as opposed to nouns (see (2-3)). Rune and Reidun both use the interference type neg after the full verb in their English. As for the interference type personal pronoun in front of neg (recall (3 c-d)) there are only the two examples (7 g-h). They are Rune's. With Reidun this interference type is not indicated in the published material. Ravem 1969, p. 9, expressly points out that his children did not normally use this interference type. This type was marginal. In accordance with this there are examples like (14) from Reidun, but none like (15).

a) not like it now   (14)
b) no, no like it
c) „jeg" not like it
d) I not like it

a) * „jeg" like it not   (15)
b) * I like it not

This evidence is all the more surprising since both children already had these word order patterns in their Norwegian.

It seems important therefore for future investigations to pay attention to such interference types. It may be quite possible that it will turn out that such types of interference should be interpreted rather as a phenomenon of (over-) generalization.

5.4 L2 acquisition and explanatory hypotheses about language acquisition

Those difficulties which SR-theories have so far not been able to overcome with respect to L2 acquisition (recall § 2) seem to impose themselves in much the same way for naturalistic L2 acquisition. The L2 structural types I-II are clear indications of this. After all, which aspects of the target structures should function as reinforcement with respect to the structures I-II?

The relationship between cognition and language acquisition will have to be reconsidered. As for general cognitive prerequisites for L2 acquisition, there is no reason why *why*-questions should have been mastered by Reidun as late as they were (§ 5.2.2), or why, for example, Huang 1971 found the same developmental sequence for the acquisition of the English *wh*-interrogation for L1 and L2.

On the other hand, I would think that it is also premature to conclude from this that the nativistic explanation is the only adequate one.

5.5 Language acquisition and language teaching methodologies

It makes sense to incur the costs of teaching and teaching methodologies only if their application results in something better than would be possible without them. This might happen if teaching would either alter the structure of the developmental processes or if it would speed up the development. As for L1 acquisition, it does not seem to be possible to deviate from the normal chronology in the acquisition of the linguistic structures, as the evidence from language pathology suggests. Retarded children seem to go through the same developmental sequences as normal children do, although with considerable differences in time, and this often in spite of the most intensive therapeutic treatment. Also, they do not seem to be able to reach the same degree of complexity in their development as normal children do (Lenneberg 1967 and references there). It seems that teaching methodologies — at least those that have been developed so far — can at best speed up the development for L1.

But what about L2 bilingualism under teaching conditions? Studies offering appropriate data are rare. Some inferences are possible from Natalicio & Natalicio 1971. They investigated the plural formation in the English of six to sixteen year old children from San Antonio, Texas. Half of the children spoke Spanish as L1 and English as L2; the other half were monolingual English. If regarded as a longitudinal study, both groups acquired the English plural variants in the sequence /-s/ and /-z/ before /-əz/. Here, also, the L2 children showed the same developmental sequence as one would expect for the L1 acquisition of English (Berko 1958; Anisfield & Tucker 1967; Cazden 1968).

However, it seems necessary to warn against premature conclusions. Many areas in the South-Western parts of the United States are bilingual English and Spanish. So is San Antonio, Texas. Natalicio & Natalicio 1971 did not make it clear whether or not they were dealing with naturalistic L2 speakers who, later on, received instruction in English or whether the children acquired English only through classroom instruction.

At this point the literature on foreign language teaching should be considered. This requires a separate study. However, as fas as I can make out, the issues hinted at above have so far not been given proper consideration when teaching programs were designed or when the effectiveness of such programs was evaluated. Nor have such considerations been noted in any theories on foreign language teaching (see, for example, the survey in Wienold 1973). The crucial question, then, is this: Do the insights developed so far lead us to conclude that L2 acquisition is, in principle, not possible on a behaviouristic basis? Does every type of language acquisition proceed according to some language acquisitional process which is different from conditioning? The issue can not be decided, due to lack of empirical evidence, because so far it has not been possible to give proper consideration to foreign language teaching because of lack of appropriate developmental studies from this area. At least for the sake of being able to devise appropriate experiments, it seems advisable to suggest two types of processes/mechanisms: one type which is different from conditioning, and which is weakened or obliterated as a function of increasing age; and a second type within which language learning is possible via conditioning. The latter one becomes more effective as a function of increasing age, with, possibly, further differentiation according to the structural areas to be learned. To be more precise, one would have to determine which structural areas become learnable via conditioning as a function of age. If formulated in this way, empirical verification or falsification is possible in the sense of § 0.

The importance of such issues for foreign language teaching is obvious. If it is to be successful the methodology must be designed to fit the linguistic structures to be learned. That is, whether they are learnable via conditioning or not. And it is just this which either contrastive analysis or the various techniques of error analysis fail to achieve. Any results arrived at within such frameworks, it seems, can only be used sensibly if they are seen in conjunction with the question of the learnability of the respective linguistic structures. If learnability in the sense as proposed here is not considered, as seems to be the case at the present state of the art, then, I think one simply has to admit that, at present, we do not know whether the students, in a foreign language class, learn a language because of, or in spite of, the teaching methodologies which are applied. Or — to put it differently, but equally provocatively — at present it is impossible to determine in detail what it is that language teaching methodologies achieve.

6 Perspectives

It seems that naturalistic L2 bilingualism is going to prove to be a field of great potential. Research in this area is urgently needed.

First of all, we need large scale empirical investigations providing detailed accounts of L2 case studies. The subjects should be grouped according to age and other variables. Migrant workers, their children, and others, offer many opportunities.

There is no lack of practical applications that might be derived from such research: speech therapy, foreign language teaching and developmental psychology should benefit most. Linguistics is offered great opportunities for studying coexisting systems in statu nascendi and to observe how they develop. It is by no means certain that the now available linguistic models and theories will adequately capture those facts.

Notes

* Revised Version of Arbeitspapiere zum Spracherwerb No. 1, Englisches Seminar der Universität Kiel, 1972. Reprinted and translated by permission from *Linguistische Berichte* 32 (1974), pp. 15-36

1 Such a project is currently in preparation at the English Department of Kiel University, Kiel, West Germany. We are working on English and German. Two languages were chosen in order to be able to check whether any peculiarities in the acquisition of one language are due to the acquisition of the other language.

2 Unless indicated otherwise, age is marked as to year, month, and day of contact. For example, 1;8 means at the age of 1 year and 8 months.

3 If one accepts the social stratification of speech it can be argued that, ultimately, every speaker is — L1 and/or L2 — multilingual, because every speaker commands several sociolects (Swain 1971). The above scheme is much less detailed. Future results on natural L2 acquisition will have to show to what extent it is useful to refine the notion of multilingualism in such sociolinguistic ways.

4 With many children, pivotal constructions are the first syntactic constructions that can be identified among **two-word** utterances. The lexicon of these children contains (a small number of) words with distributionally limited privileges of occurence. Other lexical items are not positionally restricted. Braine 1963 labelled the former type *pivot* (P), the latter sort *x-word* (X). Such pivotal constructions are remarkable because the sequence of P and X need not be the same as in the model. Cf. (1) in § 2.
It seems to me that the notion of pivot has been criticized in too global ways (e.g. Bloom 1970, 1971, Slobin 1970). New material appears to require a more differentiated view (Wode forthcoming). The original assessment very likely derived from the data collection in the evaluation procedures. Braine did not have great quantities of data. In other studies which came up with the same results the data were evaluated only selectively (e.g. Brown/Fraser 1963, Miller/Erwin 1964).

5 Handy surveys of the history and state of development of research on L1 acquisition include Leopold 1939-49 (a critical review on the whole literature until ca. 1940. Leopold shows that language acquisition as an object of inquiry was discovered remarkably late after psychologists and educationalists had long accepted it); Leopold 1959 (continues the survey until the end of the 1950's); Menyuk 1971 (reviews the state of the art from the point of view of generative-transformational grammar. Menyuk deals with the L1 acquisition of English and refers primarily to the literature written in English. The historical perspective is lacking); Slama-Cazacu 1972 (summarizes the research on child language in Europe since ca. 1920); Leopold 1952 (most detailed bibliography on child language, revised and expanded by Slobin 1972); Slobin 1973 (a useful survey of those languages about which reports on language acquisition are available). Useful short summaries from handbooks and monograph series include Ervin-Tripp 1966 and McNeill 1970b.

6 As for L1 acquisition, English is probably the best documented language today. Menyuk 1971 offers an abundance of references.

7 These three stages can be further differentiated e.g. based on the data by Bloom 1970. Cf. also McNeill 1966. For the purposes of this paper the division into three stages will do.

8 The literature on linguistic aspects of naturalistic L2 acquisition is extremely scarce. Ruke-Dravina 1967 reviews the literature until ap. 1966. Ruke-Dravina does not differentiate according to naturalistic conditions of acquisition versus school-room instruction. Unfortunately, the majority of studies offer only anecdotal material which was collected without the precision that is required for data that are to be interpreted linguistically. Multilingualism is discussed by Ruke-Dravina according to traditional and linguistically unrewarding points of view, such as whether early bilingualism is detrimental for the development of a child, the

time it takes a learner to learn a second language, the different uses that he makes of his languages, etc. Almost no indications are given about the developmental process of the acquisition of the linguistic structures.

Reports which are linguistically more revealing (although the majority of them are unsystematic and not detailed enough) include Burling 1959 (L1 English/L2 Garo); Pavlovitch 1920 (L1 Serbo-Croatian/L2 French); Malmberg 1945 (L1 Finnish/L2 Swedish); Natalicio/Natalicio 1971 (L1 Spanish/L2 English); Dato 1971 (L1 English/L2 Spanish); Christian 1971 (L1 Gujarati/L2 English); Ervin-Tripp 1973 (L1 English/L2 French).

More detailed data can be found in addition to Ravem 1968, 1969, 1970 (L1 Norwegian/L2 English); in Huang 1971 (L1 Taiwanese/L2 English).

[9] Apparently, an account in terms of word reduction in the sense of Brown/Fraser 1963 does not appear to be plausible for L2 acquisition either.

[10] For example, the pronunciation of Joseph Conrad is said to have remained so poor throughout his life that he was not asked to give public lectures (Scovel 1969). Reference could also be made to such contemporaries as former United States' Secretary of State Henry Kissinger (L1 German/L2 English).

[11] There have been some attempts to explain the particular phonetic difficulties involved in natural L2 acquisition by recourse to neuro-physiological theories. The process of lateralization is said to be completed around age 12, i.e. hemispheric dominance is firmly established (Lenneberg 1967). Scovel 1969 refers to this by explaining the phonetic difficulties as a lack of motor flexibility. In fact, phonetics is the area where speech is „translated" into sound. I do not know to what extent such theories are tenable from a neuro-physiological point of view. My personal experience, which I have not been able to check via controlled experimentation, leads me to assume that it is possible under naturalistic conditions to acquire a native-like L2 pronunciation after the age of sixteen. It seems, therefore, that even in this area sociocultural phenomena may function as an important variable.

FOCUS ON THE STUDENT: FOREIGN LANGUAGE TEACHING FROM THE LEARNER'S POINT OF VIEW*

Henning Wode

1 The Learner's Point of View

Current foreign language teaching as well as the research associated with it is beset with a number of serious problems. I'm not referring to some of the unpleasant consequences of recent educational reforms. Rather I'm thinking about the disappointments more directly related to teaching. Basically, this is the disappointment among many teachers about the linguistic and the communication theories suggested during the past decade or two. None of them has proved useful as a pedagogical grammar. I'm referring further to contrastive analysis and error analysis. Contrastive analyses of linguistic structures have so far not led to reliable error prognoses. The predictions did not come true in any sufficient measure and, consequently, they did not prove to be helpful to the teacher beyond what he already knew from his own practical experience. I'm further referring to technological innovations. Do we really know by now how all these technological devices are to be incorporated into the theory of language teaching in a way that is not trivial? For example, what is the exact place of the language laboratory within the total learning process?

One of the crucial reasons for this deplorable state of affairs seems to be that researchers on foreign language teaching have so far not been able to give proper consideration — methodologically — to the student and his learning behaviour as considered from the learner's point of view. Of course, research on foreign language teaching has been concerned with the teacher, with teaching methodologies and with technical equipment of various sorts; and, the student and his behaviour has, of course, also been considered. Only, it seems that the questions that have been asked let alone the results produced in response to such questions do not seem to be such that they fully solve the most important problems which the student poses. This still is the learning of linguistic structures, that is, the way in which linguistic structures are processed by human beings and how this knowledge is accumulated throughout the learning process.

Of course it is well known that the speed of learning may correlate with variables like IQ, motivation, learner type, empathy, and so forth. (The literature can be traced via Wienold 1973, Burschmidt & Götz 1974, Solmecke 1976). But none of these variables determines the linguistic structure of learner/student utterances (Wode 1974, 1977a). These variables simply do not explain why German students make word order errors like *I cannot the fog see* for *I cannot see the fog*, or why utterances like *that's no my comb* for *that's not my comb* cannot only be heard from German children who learn English.

Moreover, variables like IQ, motivation, etc., do not explain the way in which the development in the accumulation of — linguistic — knowledge proceeds, why, for example, certain errors appear early, whereas others appear late (Wode 1977a). Hints about L1 transfer, which are quite fashionable in this connection remain global circumscriptions of the phenomena but they do not explain them. Any adequate explanation has to start from the processes and regularities which are provided in, and by, the student. These regularities are still largely unknown. Unfortunately researchers on foreign language teaching have so far hardly made any attempts to detect them. It is in this sense that I think that foreign language teaching and the research associated with it have, to date, not focussed sufficiently on the learner.

It seems therefore that the deplorable situation pertaining to foreign language teaching research is due to methodological weaknesses in the sense that possibilities have to be devised which will allow us to determine the regularities according to which the foreign language is learned in the classroom on the part of the student. The alternatives are fairly clear. Either every student proceeds differently — but then the question is why basically the same errors recur with many (all?) students; or all human beings have the same (genetically endowed?) mechanisms in order to learn languages including foreign languages. The second alternative, it seems to me, can scarcely be doubted any more these days, even if details are not sufficiently known[1]. Human beings must have certain capacities in order to learn languages and in order to be able to be taught one in the classroom. Therefore it is of prime importance for foreign language teaching to determine the following questions: To what extent are the individual language acquisitional types, like first language acquisition, the acquisition of a foreign language, and so forth, governed by separate acquisitional mechanisms and regularities? To what extent do these acquisitional mechanisms/regularities apply to different acquisitional types and/or situations? What are the restrictions, if any?

Starting with considerations of this sort, the task is to devise possibilities for foreign language teaching to investigate empirically these naturally given learner capacities and their regularities. This is one of the goals which I have been pursuing together with a group of collaborators for some years in a series of interrelated research projects. We have traced the acquisition of selected structural areas (primarily interrogation, negation, inflections, phonology) across a number of acquisitional types. This has been done for two languages, English and German. Within this research, the most important acquisitional types are: the acquisition of the first language (L1), i.e. the mother tongue, and the acquisition of a second language (L2) at a point when the L1 has already been mastered completely or at least in part. For the latter type we strictly distinguish between naturalistic L2 acquisition, i.e. the acquisition of a second language under non-classroom conditions, as opposed to L2 acquisition in foreign language teaching, i.e. L2 acquisition under classroom conditions (FLT) (for details on the approach see Wode 1974, 1976a, 1977a, c; Felix 1977a, b, d, 1978b). So far we have collected data for L1 German, L1 English, naturalistic L2 German acquired by children with English as L1, naturalistic L2 English acquired by children with German as L1; classroom L2 English acquired by German sixth graders and naturalistic re-acquisition of L2 English by children with German as L1. At first, our central concern was naturalistic L2 acquisition. It is with respect to this acquisitional type that it had to be determined to what extent regularities from L1 acquisition are also available for the subsequent acquisition of a L2. As far as classroom L2 acquisition is concerned, the comparison with naturalistic L2 acquisition is likely to show to what extent learning regularities can be influenced by conscious manipulation in terms of teaching methodologies. If, in spite of the intervention of teachers, the same errors occur in the classroom as they do in naturalistic L2 acquisition, then it is reasonable to assume that these phenomena are due to the naturally given capacities and the language acquisitional regularities derived from them. They seem to apply despite the teaching procedures utilized. In other words: It is hoped that, in the long run, such comparisons will enable us to determine in a much more profound way the contributions due to language teaching procedures as opposed to those due to the student's natural capacities.

The detailed results of our work so far are available elsewhere (see Wode 1976a, 1977a, c, 1978a; Felix 1977b, 1978b, Wode et al. 1978). In this paper I would like to give a condensed overview and inquire into the relevance of such results for the problems of foreign language teaching and the research associated with it. The topics that pose themselves include, amongst others, whether FLT is something special as opposed to other language acquisitional types; error analysis (EA) and contrastive analysis (CA); interim languages; linguistic theories and pedagogical grammars; assessing achievement in foreign language teaching; learning theories and the acquisition of languages; the extent to which the teacher can determine the student's linguistic development; the applicability of technological equipment. Whether and to what extent investigations into naturalistic L2 acquisition can be a challenge for foreign language teaching can be illustrated most markedly, by, first, contrasting it with the developmental sequences of the non-classroom acquisitional types; and, second, by pointing out the main differences between the L1 and L2 types of acquisition.

2 Developmental Sequences and L1 Transfer in the Non-Classroom Acquisitional Types

Both L1 acquisition as well as naturalistic L2 acquisition proceed according to strictly ordered developmental sequences. These are chronologically ordered sequences of developmental stages. That is to say, children do not acquire their L1 or their L2 all at once. They learn the language step by step. This applies to individual structures as well as structural areas. That is to say, children do not acquire a structural system, such as negation, in such a way that they master the whole system all at once. Instead, they do it such that they filter out step by step individual structural properties, which are then reintegrated, again step by step, via the learner's interlanguage

system towards the target structure. In doing so, the children commit developmental errors. These errors are systematic in the sense that they do not appear in a
random way. Furthermore, they are type-specific because every acquisitional type
is characterized by some error types of its own. Lastly, these so-called errors are
determined by a specific stage of development, which means that they are integrated into the overall development. These errors are unavoidable in the sense that
language acquisition does not seem to be possible without their comission. The degree to which these errors are systematically integrated into the total development
is obvious from the nature of the developmental sequences. The succession of the
developmental stages in the naturalistic acquisitional types is so strictly ordered
that the resulting developmental sequences can be predicted. The crucial variables
which govern the rise of these sequences and the error types are not general cognition, intelligence, motivation, or the like, but cognitive correlates of the formal devices used in natural languages, like word order, free vs. bound forms, or suprasegmental vs. segmental marking.[2]

The various acquisitional types have different developmental sequences. For example, despite some parallels, the L1 developmental sequence is not necessarily like
the L2 one when the same language is acquired in both cases. There are systematic
differences as a function of the L1 acquired previously in the case of L2. In FLT,
this phenomenon is well known as interference. The most important point about
the evidence from naturalistic L2 acquisition is that this reliance on L1 is not random
but systematic. That is, before L2 children rely on their L1 knowledge, i.e. before
they produce interferences, specific linguistic prerequisites have to be met within
the L2 development of the child. In more general terms, the L2 structures which
the child has at his disposal in his L2 development must be similar in crucial ways
to those available to him from his L1 acquisition, before this L2 child relies on his
L1. If no such crucial similarity is met between the linguistic structures involved,
then there will be no reliance on L1. Reliance on L1 is an integral part of naturalistic L2 acquisition. Human beings cannot learn a second language in any other
way but by relying systematically on their L1. L1 transfer errors are developmentally obligatory in this sense.

3 FLT Problems Considered in the Light of Naturalistic L2 Acquisition

It is not yet quite clear what the exact implications deriving from these results are,
results which, after all, are not really surprising. But even so, some tentative explanations and new perspectives can be offered for some of the FLT problems enumer-
ated above.

3.1 Contrastive analysis (CA) and error analysis (EA)

The difficulty with the type of CA that is claimed to be relevant for FLT, is that
merely stating differences between L1 and L2 is simply not enough. These differ-

ences have to be interpreted language-acquisitionally. That is, when learning a L2 the child is faced with a confrontation of two structures, namely, the L1 and the L2 structures. The naturalistic data clearly show that the child solves such situations not by drawing randomly on the L1 or the L2 structure. Instead, he follows regularities which can be specified linguistically. For example, as pointed out above the L2 child relies on his L1 only under specific conditions. If these prerequisites are not met, the respective L2 structure is acquired without reliance on L1.

As an illustration, consider the L2 acquisition of the English retroflex /r/ [ɹ] by German children with an L1 uvular /r/ [R], and their acquisition of the English vowels. It is not the L1 [R] which is substituted in such situations, but /w/. /w/ is only later given up in favor of the target-like [ɹ]. Note that there is no reliance on L1. The acquisition of the English vowels is different. Consider /æ/ and /əʊ/. At first, they are replaces by the German vowels [ɛ] and [o]. In this case, there is L1 transfer. (For details on phonological acquisition cf. Wode 1977c, 1978a; for comparable problems relating to other structural areas see Wode 1976a, 1977a).

It seems to me that CA and EA will not be very useful for FLT unless such acquisitional regularities are given due consideration. After all, it is regularities of this sort which determine how the structural confrontation is resolved by the learner. These insights appear to offer great opportunities to develop more adequate error prognoses and methods for error corrections, which are those areas where CA and EA have so far failed most drastically (cf. Wode 1978e).

3.2 Interim languages, interim systems

Reference is made to Corder 1967, interlanguage (Selinker 1972), approximative systems (Nemser 1971) and similar concepts. The basic assumption is well confirmed by insights from the naturalistic types of acquisition. But it seems that two points should be given more consideration than in the past. On the one hand, these interim systems are not static in themselves, but they continue to develop. They have to be viewed as dynamic systems, lastly as developmental sequences. On the other hand, interim languages are a reflex of the languages involved. They determine the structure of these systems, namely, via those regularities according to which structural confrontations (in the sense of sec. 3.1) are resolved language-acquisitionally. Here, too, it is important to predict such solutions. It is no help for the teacher at all if interim systems are set up post hoc. He has to know what to expect so that he can organize his activities accordingly.

3.3 Pedagogical grammars and linguistic theories

Pedagogical grammars and linguistic theories are of little avail as long as those properties which learners first and foremost rely on when acquiring linguistic structures do not occur in such grammars/theories at all. Unfortunately, as far as I can see, no presently available linguistic theory meets these requirements. Consequently, no pedagocially useful grammars can be derived from them. Consider again the example of the L2 acquisition of [ɭ] (sec. 3.1). I am not aware of any phonetic/phonological theory which assigns a common feature to both [ɭ] and [w] that can be used to derive the fact that [ɭ] and [w] are more similar to each other than, for example, [ɭ] may be to [R]. Such features are required in order to explain why L2 children with an L1 [R] acquire the L2 [ɭ] via [w] and not via [R] (Wode 1977c). Similar examples can be cited for other structural areas (Wode 1976a, 1977a; Felix 1978b). All this seems to suggest that those pedagogical grammars and linguistic theories which are to be real in the learner's sense should be worked out from language-acquisitional data. The linguistic theories should be devised in accordance with such empirical facts.

3.4 Assessment and achievement tests

If the insight that there are ordered developmental sequences is also accepted for FLT, then it becomes difficult to defend the way in which grades are currently given. The simple binary scheme of correct vs. incorrect is no longer adequate. Errors indicating later developmental stages should be assessed higher than those indicating earlier stages of development. If this is not done, the student's advancement in terms of what he knows about the structure of the language is not given proper credit. The same applies to the problem of how to evaluate the student's overall achievement (Wode 1978d).

3.5 Learning and learning theories

The way in which language learning proceeds in the naturalistic acquisitional types differs drastically from what is implied by certain teaching techniques, for example, when rules are given from which utterances are to be produced. This formal type of learning is lacking in the naturalistic types of language acquisition. The general question, therefore, is whether learning a language is possible via different learning principles. The answer will very likely be no. For one thing, our data make me suspect that this type of rule learning does not necessarily lead to the type of competence required for everyday spontaneous communication. (See also Felix 1977e).

4 Conclusions: The Special Status of FLT?

The remaining issues raised in section 1 require rethinking in similar ways (for more details cf. Wode 1974, 1978e). However, all of this, in particular the empirical evidence (not only from our project)[3], leads me to conclude that there is no justification at all for the frequent claim that FLT is categorically different from the naturalistic types of acquisition (e.g. Lane 1962, Wienold 1973, Burgschmidt & Götz 1974, Littlewood 1974). Of course, naturalistic and classroom L2 acquisition are more similar to each other than either is to L1 acquisition. But it has already been shown that some acquisitional regularities apply to L1, naturalistic L2 acquisition, as well as FLT (Wode 1979; Felix 1977b). Consequently FLT cannot seriously be regarded as fully determined and controlled by the teacher and his methodology as long as it remains unclear what it is that is controlled and manipulated. Finally it seems to me that FLT and FLT research cannot be conducted any longer in isolation from the research on other acquisitonal types. There is no empirical justification for this. The usual arguments in favor of such a special status for FLT have to be reconsidered in the light of the evidence from all acquisitional types (for more details see Wode 1978e).

Notes

* Reprinted by permission from H. Hunfeld, ed., *Neue Perspektiven der Fremdsprachendidaktik — Eichstätter Kolloquium zum Fremdsprachenunterricht* 1977. Kronberg: Scriptor Verlag, 1977, pp. 17-23.

[1] The important point here is not the controversy between nativistic, behavioristic and cognitive hypotheses about the nature of language acquisition. The important point is the verification of these hypotheses via empirical evidence. From this point of view all three hypotheses are inadequate (Wode 1974).

[2] Some data and some attempts to predict such developmental sequences including data for verification can be found for L1 acquisition, e.g. in Wode 1977b; for L2 acquisition, e.g. in Felix 1976b, Wode 1976a, 1977c, 1978a. More references are given there.

[3] Research on naturalistic L2 acquisition has only recently come into being. Overviews are included in Wode 1974, Hatch 1978b, Felix 1977b.

Commentary

Subsequently, the various topics, in particular those of the first paper, were developed further, new issues were raised, and some topics have proved to be less interesting. The typology of acquisitional types was broadened. The universals issue was subsequently extended so that now the issue is whether there are universal language learning regularities in the sense that they apply in all language learning situations irrespective of the age of the speaker and regardless of which language is being learned. The relationship of language acquisition to cognition now appears to be such that human beings are biologically endowed with special cognitive abilities — here termed linguo-cognitive — which allow man to process speech data for the purpose of acquisition. The question of whether SR-theories adequately describe the facts of language acquisition seems very much decided. They do not, so that the term *learning* can now again be used without invoking SR-implications. The role of L1 transfer is still very much debated. That there are parallels between L1 and L2 acquisition is well recognized.

Applied issues, like age and the critical period hypothesis, lateralization, educational implications, etc. can now be considered with much more confidence than four or five years ago, because the amount of empirical data available around the world has become quite impressive. The views which were held about the role of age in conjunction with the critical period hypothesis during the 1960's and early 1970's must be drastically revised. The importance of insights from naturalistic L2 acquisition for foreign language teaching is now generally recognized, although it is less clear, at present, how to convert these results into useful teaching techniques.

Part II

LANGUAGE LEARNING AND COGNITION

Introduction

One of the dominating issues since the revival of interest in language acquisition during the 1960's and early 1970's was the relationship between language learning and general cognitive development. In particular, Piaget's theory about the cognitive development of children was frequently adopted as a starting point. One approach was to explain the child's linguistic development through his/her non-linguistic development, in particular through concept formation and the development of logical thinking. Numerous aspects about the development of the ability of the child to communicate verbally no doubt correlate very closely with the development of non-linguistic capacities and abilities. But, whichever way one looks at this, certain aspects remain which cannot be explained in terms of concept formation, or the development of logical thinking, notably the acquisition and development of the formal properties of linguistic devices. The point is fairly easy to establish with reference to, say, adult L2 learners. For example, if an L2 learner is late in using an interrogative pronoun designating ‚cause', like English *why*, then this cannot be explained as due to the lack of any concept of causality, if this L2 learner can be shown to have such a concept in his L1.

This section presents three papers which are intended to establish this point for L1 acquisition as well. The papers deal with interrogation, negation, and intonation. These structural areas were chosen for several reasons. Both the concepts and the formal devices to express negation or to ask questions in natural languages are fairly easy to identify. The paper on intonation was included because many people relate pitch contours, pauses, and stress differences, to various emotional categories. This paper is intended to show that even the acquisition of pitch patterns requires linguistic knowledge of a highly abstract formal kind. Consequently, even the child's learning of the intonation system of a given language cannot be explained by the rise of emotional categories.

FOUR EARLY STAGES IN THE DEVELOPMENT OF L1 NEGATION*

Henning Wode

Abstract

No reasonably successful theory of the acquisition of negation seems to have yet been proposed. Most studies describe *post hoc* what has taken place; but they fail to go on to suggest a theory that will predict what will take place. McNeill seems to be the only one to have explicitly aimed at a theory with at least a certain amount of predictive capacity, but his views leave much to be desired. This paper outlines an alternative proposal to cover four very early stages for the acquisition of negation systems in natural languages. It emphasizes the formal linguistic devices as the major variables that determine the various language-specific developmental sequences.

Introduction

The early literature on language acquisition contains several accounts of the acquisition of negation, e.g. Gheorgov 1908, Scupin & Scupin 1907, Stern & Stern 1907 and Grégoire 1937, 1947, but from the viewpoint of a theory's predictive capacity, their statements make no claims — or implications for such claims — that merit discussion here. Even more recent studies fail to make overt predictions. Klima & Bellugi 1966 and Bloom 1970 for instance, restrict themselves to describing the developmental sequences of those children they studied. It is unclear whether these researchers would be prepared to argue that their studies did, none the less, involve claims about predictions, namely those that are implied in the transformational-generative theory underlying their descriptive framework. In any event, it is difficult to see what such predictions might be based on, because both studies are limited to English, and pay no attention to the then available data from other languages. McNeill 1970a: 87ff. and elsewhere seems to be the only one to have aimed at a theory with any predictive capacity. He relies on Klima & Bellugi 1966, cites one example for Russian from Slobin's 1966 summary of Gvozdev 1949, mentions Grégoire 1937, and quotes his own work on Japanese (McNeill & McNeill 1968). He takes the acquisition and development of negation to begin with a *neg* element preposed to affirmative sentences: *neg* + S. This may alternate with S + *neg*. This schema is claimed to be „fixed, simple, and universal". Children do not have to acquire it. It is part of their innate knowledge about the structure of human language.

This view raises several unanswered questions, primarily:

(a) is McNeill's schema *neg* + S ~S + *neg* really the beginning of negation?
(b) are all utterances conforming to the above schema to be considered the same semantically and developmentally?
(c) what is universal about this schema?
(d) is there not evidence to suggest that these schemas are not innate?

To decide what the beginnings of negation are is largely a matter of definition. However, once the onset has been defined, this should not blind one to the possibility of developmental fore-runners. As for negation, before English children begin to produce utterances like those quoted by McNeill, e.g.

(1) more ... no
(2) no a boy bed
(3) not a teddy bear

they have surely produced negative one-word-utterances, namely *no*, as well as multi-word utterances of a specific semantic subtype, that I shall call (following Bloom 1970) *anaphoric:*

(4a) Adult: Do you want salt?
(4b) Child: No, sugar.

In (4b) the negative relationship does not hold between the two items in the utterance. Anaphoric negation differs from (1)-(3) in that in the latter the negative relationship does hold between *no/not* and the rest of the utterance. This type will here be called *non-anaphoric.* [1]

It is not at all clear that McNeill's examples are to be treated as developmentally the same. First, he does not differentiate semantically between anaphoric and non-anaphoric negation. Secondly, utterances involving *not*, as in (3), are either early unproductive stereotypes, or they belong to a much later stage. They certainly do not belong at the beginning. This will become more obvious from the cross-linguistic evidence of the next section. Thirdly, McNeill's claim about the universality of his schemas remains unrevealing as long as he does not make precise what is universal about them. Just because the data come from English? Even at the time of his writing there were studies providing data against which he could have checked his claims (e.g. Gheorgov 1908, Scupin & Scupin 1907, Ruke-Dravina 1963). He would, indeed, have found that children tend to use structures which conform to the positioning implied in his schemas. But these positional peculiarities are not the only thing to be noted. Why, for instance, should the children choose negatives like English *no*, German *nein*, Russian *njet*, Latvian *nē*, etc. to express non-anaphoric negation whereas the target language requires a different form, namely, *not ~ –n't; nicht, kein; ne; ne-, etc.?*

McNeill's claim about the universality of the position of *neg* is neither very informative, nor well supported by the available data. If his schemas mark the beginnings of negation, then they should apply to the two-word stage, which would mean that at that stage *neg* + S would be in free variation with S + *neg*. This, in turn, implies that word order, at least in negated utterances, would be free. However, those languages for which more than one child is on record do not support McNeill's claim. Again, more precision is needed here.

There are at least two interpretations of his claim.

(a) Both schemas vary freely with one and the same child. An instance of this, apart from the Harvard children McNeill is referring to, might be found with one of the Latvian children studied by Ruke-Dravina 1963. But then, this state of affairs did not persist very long with this child. Why?

(b) Both schemas may occur when children acquire the same language, but they need not co-occur with every child. I venture to guess that this is what McNeill has in mind. And in fact, this is not very much at odds with the available data. But why should children do this, if they are born with the same capacities for language? And why is it that most children prefer the schema $neg + S$?

Fourthly, I do not think that McNeill's schema $neg + S \sim S + neg$ should be thought of as being innate. The evidence to be reviewed in the next section suggests to me that the schemas are acquired. All the languages for which acquisition data are available have a construction $neg + S$ to express anaphoric negation, comparable to (4b). Children tend to produce such anaphoric negative utterances before they use the same word order to express non-anaphoric intentions. I therefore see no need at all to invoke innateness: the latter can be regarded as overgeneralizations of the former, and these, in turn, are picked up from the target language. To me the issue is, why do children start with anaphoric negative constructions rather than with others?

As for the later stages of the acquisition of negation, McNeill summarizes, and in part re-interprets, the Klima & Bellugi 1966 data. No predictions for other languages are offered.

McNeill's theory, in short, does not deal with a number of important issues, such as the choice of negative morphological items, the child semantics of negated utterances, and what is universal and innate about his schemas. His account provides hardly any predictive capacity beyond the most elementary and almost trivial insights relating to the position of *neg*. Above all, he fails to relate early development to other variables which could function as the determinants of the developmental course(s) that children take. The notion of innate linguistic knowledge itself has to be spelled out in much more detail before it can allow for the predictive capacity of a theory of language acquisition.

Some typological distinctions of negation systems

Regrettably, I have not been able to discover a typological study of the negation systems of natural languages. I shall, therefore, set down briefly some typological distinctions of my own. Only those languages for which there are data on the acquisition of negation will be included. Moreover, I shall note only those properties which seem to be reflected in the four early stages proposed below for children's developmental sequences.

Semantically, as we have seen, there is anaphoric vs. non-anaphoric negation:

(i)   *anaphoric negation:* the negative relationship does not hold between *neg* (morpheme or particle) and the rest of the utterance (sentence or phrase) with which *neg* occurs in construction, e.g. English *no* (4 *a-b*), German *nein:*

(5)   nein, Klaus
       „no, (I didn't meet Hans, I met) Klaus"

(ii)   *non-anaphoric negation:* the negative relationship holds between *neg* and some part or the whole of the sentence or phrase with which *neg* occurs in construction, e.g. English *not/-n't*, German *nicht:*

(6)   I don't want to go

(7)   ich will nicht hier bleiben
       „I don't want to stay here"

Formally, languages differ as to the types of formal devices used to express negation. Some differences are:

(iii)   *free vs. bound form,* e.g. English *no* vs. *-n't.*

(iv)   *position,* e.g. English *not/-n't* is placed after the first finite auxiliary, but not after finite full verbs; whereas in German *nicht* is positioned after the first finite verb, no matter whether that is a full verb or an auxiliary.

(v)   *various syntagmatic relationships,* such as the discontinous *neg*, e.g. French *ne ... pas* (if it can be assumed to still occur in colloquial French), Egyptian Arabic /*ma ... š*/ (Omar 1970).

(vi)   *number of occurences of neg* within one sentence or phrase: we may distinguish in particular:

(a)   multiple *neg,* e.g. in Latvian, for certain constituents to be negated they each have to be marked by *neg* irrespective of how often *neg* occurs in the sentence or phrase, e.g. (from Ruke-Dravina 1972):

(8)   neviens   nekā   nezina
       (nobody   nothing not-knows)   „nobody knows anything"

(b)   single *neg,* e.g. in German *neg* may occur only once in a sentence, barring a few marginal cases.

Languages differ as to what use is made of these and other formal devices as well as in the ways they are combined to form the various negation systems. Languages generally tend to show much more structural diversity of formal types for non-anaphoric negation than for anaphoric negation, this being at least the case with those languages for which we have acquisition data. For anaphoric negation, all the languages for which there are reliable acquisition data employ free morphemes or particles, like English *no*, German *nein*, Swedish *nej, nä*, French *non*, Latvian *nē,* Russian *njet,* etc. However, Sascha Felix of Kiel University tells me that at least some varieties of Chinese do not utilize anaphoric segmental negative particles. Instead, certain parts or the whole of the preceding utterance is repeated plus a negative marker. To my knowledge, acquisition data on this type of negation are not yet available.

Negation in Children's Speech

I shall chiefly rely on longitudinal data from Bulgarian (Gheorgov 1908), Latvian (Ruke-Dravina 1963), Russian (Gvozdev 1949), English (Klima & Bellugi 1966, Bloom 1970), German (unpublished data from my own ongoing project), and Swedish (Lange & Larsson 1973). The most detailed and, for a variety of reasons, the most illuminating data come from German. Therefore, I shall draw on the German data as my main evidence. The remaining material will be used for contrastive purposes.

The German data from the Kiel Project

The evidence comes from my son Lars, born in May 1969, and from my daughter Inga, born in May 1971. Inga seems to be the slower of the two, at least as far as the acquisition of syntax in the early stages of her development is concerned. What appear as simultaneous developments with Lars are in most cases well separated in time with Inga. I shall, therefore, primarily follow her. Moreover, it is comforting to be able to report that the development of the two is in other respects strikingly similar.

The data have been collected in a day-by-day routine in the form of written notes and tape-recordings. The latter are used as a corrective to the notes taken when no tape-recorder was in operation. I have never maintained a rigid data-collection procedure including fixed intervals, time limits of recording sessions, etc. It seems to me that such rigid procedures, as applied by other researchers in the past, have not produced data rich enough to give us really a detailed picture of a child's language development.

Developmental sequences in German. In citing examples from the two children, I shall not use conventional spelling, since the children's phonetics provide valuable clues as to the morphemic element that has probably served them as a model. The four major early stages in the developmental sequence for Inga can be summarized in the following way:

Stage I: one-word negation
    [nɛ ~ nɛɩ ~ naɩ ~ ne][2] nein ,,no"
The child's phonetics indicate that adult *nein* must have served as a model.

Stage II: two- or more-word negation involving [naɪ], etc.

Two types will be distinguished here: anaphoric and non-anaphoric negation. The former type develops before the latter.

Stage II a: anaphoric negation
  (9)   (1;7.3) Father (F) tries to keep his notes from Inga (I). I protests and in-
        sists on having them.
        I: [ˈna ˝ɪ] nein, ich „no, I"

(10)   (1;8.28) I rejects the fluid F tried to give her in favour of [mel], her term
        for milk and other varieties of drinkables.
        I: [ˈnai ˅mel] nein, Milch „no, milk"

Stage II b: non-anaphoric negation
  (11)   (1;11.2) F: Komm, ich mache dich sauber „come on, I'll clean you"
        I: [˅naɪ - δaɷba]³ nein sauber (machen) „ I don't want to be cleaned"

  (12)   (1;11.15) I keeps pounding her hand on a book. F imitates her and bangs
        much harder. I protests and wants F to stop.
        I: [˅naɪn - haɷn] nein hauen „ don't bang"

I have not discussed the intonational peculiarities, because there is no evidence from other languages to compare them with. Furthermore, I make no attempt here to work out semantic sub-types for II a-b. And, lastly, I have not listed vocatives in construction with [naɪ] etc. They belong to II a, but have specific intonational pecu- liarities that set them apart from non-vocative constructions (cf. Wode 1980b).

As for the models that may have been followed, type II a is in full accord with the adult model, both semantically and syntactically — at least if one considers spo- ken adult German. Type II b seems to combine the syntax and phonetics of II a with the semantics of adult intra-sentential negation, which in adult German is, in general, expressed through *nicht* and others, but not through *nein*. Type II b looks like over- generalization: new semantic intentions are first expressed through old machinery. (It should be remembered that type II a preceded II b developmentally.) The over- generalization is extended even to cases where the constituent following [naɪ] etc. is structured internally in fairly complex ways, reflecting grammatical relations of the adult model:

(13)   (2;0.7) I tries to shoot an arrow but she doesn't manage to pull the bow
        properly. F demonstrates the procedure, but I still doesn't manage. Even-
        tually, she gives up.
        I: [nɛ - θaf iç]

        nein schaffe ich „I can't manage it"

(14)   (2;1.18) I's older brother Heiko has been wearing the cap of a neighbour's
        boy. I charges into the house and reports:
        I: [ʔo naɪn haɪkʰo mytʰθə]
        oh, nein Heiko Mütze „oh, it isn't Heiko's cap"

All in all, however, there are relatively few instances of such complex constituents in construction with non-anaphoric [naɩ] etc.

There has been some dispute in the literature over type II *b* for English. Bloom 1970 found no evidence in her data that utterances like

(15)   no the sun shining

may be intended by children to mean „the sun is not shining". Bloom 1970 therefore claimed that utterances like (15) are all anaphoric. My findings from German as well as from other languages, however, suggest that non-anaphoric II *b* may even occur in such complex utterances as (15). It seems that (15) illustrates a genuine stage of development found across languages. There will be more evidence of this sort below, when other languages are considered.

Stage III: [nɩç ~ nɩ ~ nɛç] *nicht* and intra-sentential negation

This type gradually replaces II *b* syntactically and phonetically. In addition, the range of „negated" relations and constituents gradually expands. The details of this stage of development are not very clear, and they are too complex to be presented her in detail. Basically, what is involved is the children's handling of the position of *nicht* in relation to verbs and other constituents of the adult model. Roughly speaking, in main clauses and imperatives, adult German places *nicht* after the finite verb or after the imperative form of the verb, respectively. Infinitives and participles are placed after *nicht* and other constituents as the case may be:

(16*a*)   ich will nicht schlafen
(16*b*)   ich habe nicht geschlafen
(16*c*)   ich schlafe nicht
(16*d*)   schlaf nicht
(16*e*)   nicht schlafen

(The situation is actually even more complex than (16), since certain noun phrases, adverbs, and other elements, may be placed between the verb and *nicht*. Cf. Stickel 1970 for details.)

Lars started off by using a pivot[4] construction with [nɩç] etc. as the pivot and a preposed open-class here designated as O[nɩç] (17). Later, he admitted another constituent X before O[nɩç] and/or Y after [nɩç] as in 18-20):

(17)   (1;10.22) [naɩn vɩl ɩç]
        nein, ich will nicht   „no, I don't want to"
(18)   (1;11.2) [haɩko taᵊ nɩç]
        Heiko darf nicht   „Heiko is not allowed to"
(19)   (1;11.10) [naɩn hat nɩç ʔaʔa hɛnɩnk]
        nein, ich habe nicht Aa gemacht, Henning   „no, I haven't dirtied my pants, Henning"

(20)   (1;11.14) [hɛnι pʀaꞷ nι ʔꞷni]
Henning braucht nicht in die Uni   „Henning doesn't have to go to the University"

(O[nιç] contains only verbs that occur more often than not as finite verbs in adult German.) Shortly after, Lars began to develop additional structures involving [nιç], etc. and the constituents X and Y of (18-20):

(21)   (1;11.21) [haιko nιç]
Heiko nicht   „not Heiko"
(22)   (1;11.24) [pʰala nιç mιt]
Pallas (=a dog) nicht mit   „Pallas can't come along"
(23)   (2;0.10) [nιç tʰιç]
nicht auf den Tisch (klettern) „don't (climb on the) table"

There are a few minor developments, such as negated imperatives and infinitival constructions, which will not be discussed further here.

In summary, the major constructions involving [nιç] are:

(24a)   X   O[nιç] [nιç] Y
(24b)   X   [nιç]
(24c)   X   [nιç]   Y
(24d)   [nιç]   Y

There is considerable overlap between X and Y. Setting aside morphological details, X and Y present constituents of basic relations such as identy, location, direction, actor-action, etc.

The younger child, Inga, evidenced the same types of constructions as the boy. However, the chronology is not quite the same, nor did she separate the sets O[nιç] and Y of (24) as strictly as Lars did. Though Inga started off with utterances like (17-19), but not with (20), she subsequently seemed to disfavour this type. A great deal of evidence was produced for (24 b-d), whereas utterances involving O[nιç] as in (24 a) were noted only infrequently. Only later did she produce substantial evidence for structures like (20) or (24 a). It therefore seems best to leave stage III as described in (24 a-d) and to wait and see how other children fare in this area. As for the most likely model of stage III as summarized in (24), the phonetics of [nιç] point to adult *nicht.* What can be deduced about the semantics also seems to point in this direction. So does syntax, but only to some extent, because the children's utterances do not yet reflect certain positional peculiarities relating to the definite vs. indefinite noun phrases of adult German as illustrated in

(25)   unser Hund hat den Mann nicht gebissen
(26)   *unser Hund hat nicht den Mann gebissen

The sequence NP + def, like other types of constituents, is positioned between the finite verb and *nicht,* as in (25). (For details, cf. Stickel 1970). The children's utter-

40

ances at stage III do not yet reflect this subtlety of adult German. They place [nɪç] before Y as in (24 *a*) and (24 *c*) even if Y is represented by substantives or names. The mastery of these positional subleties takes some time to evolve and marks off stage IV. The major variables governing the details for stage IV cross-linguistically seem to be the positional peculiarities of the languages to be acquired. This topic requires a separate paper.

Developmental Sequences in Other Languages

Unfortunately, the available evidence from other languages is much smaller in quantity and much less detailed. Some data will be briefly summarized and to some extent re-analysed to bring out the various parallels to the German data. Roman numerals refer to the comparable developmental stages described for German. Hints on the situational setting, the semantics, and the most likely intentions of the children, will be given only when provided in the original studies.

Swedish. Lange & Larsson 1973 have described the development of a girl aged 1;8-2;1. The data were collected in 10 sessions (2 per month), each session lasting half an hour. Consequently, the data are not very extensive. No phonetic transcription, or intonational marking, is provided. Unfortunately, the material is broken down into 70-days spans, with each span analysed as a whole. All in all, the data-collection procedure as well as the evaluation of the material does not provide a very clear picture of the developmental sequence. Nevertheless, as far as it goes, the Swedish material is strikingly similar to the German data.

II *a*: anaphoric negation

Apparently, the child started off with anaphoric negation. Lange & Larsson say nothing about whether the child used stage I, one-word negation, before stage II, two-word negation. The negative element is spelt *nä, nej,* pronounced [nɛ ~ nɛj] (personal communication). In parentheses I add Lange & Larsson's numbering. Their E2, E3 etc. refer to the respective recording sessions.

(27) nä den
       „no, that/it" (E2, 430)
(28) nej mama
       „no, mother" (E2, 433)

Semantics and phonetics point to adult *nej, nä* as the model probably followed by the child. In adult Swedish, *nej* and *nä* are used only anaphorically. They are placed in utterance-initial position.

II *b*: non-anaphoric negation

The non-anaphorice type with *nej, nä* is attested through only one utterance:

(29) nei kossa
       „no moo-cow" (E2, 446)

III: intra-sentential negation and *inte*

Next in appearance is *inte,* first in the stereotype phrase *vill inte* „want not" as early as E$_5$. Subsequently, *inte* becomes productive. It is used exclusively in non-anaphoric negation with a variety of positional sub-types. A clear developmental sequence cannot be discerned. I have altered Lange & Larsson's grouping somewhat, in order to make the parallelism with the German and English data more obvious. Concerning the position of *inte,* there are at least six structural types in Lange & Larsson's data:

(30a) inte + $\left\{ \begin{array}{c} X \\ Y \end{array} \right\}$

(30b) X + inte + Y

(30c) (X) + V$_{fin}$ + inte + Y

(30d) X + går + inte + Y

(30e) V$_{imp}$ + inte + $\left\{ \begin{array}{c} X \\ Y \end{array} \right\}$

(30f) inte + X + Y

To give an idea about possible adult analogues, the examples to illustrate (30 *a-f*) will be subgrouped according to the comparable adult word-class of the child's X and Y:

(31) inte + Adj
      inte gul   „not yellow" (E$_6$, 225)

(32) inte + N
      inte juice   „not juice" (E$_7$, 219)

(33) inte + locative
      inte där   „not there" (E$_8$, 227)

(34) inte + V$_{inf}$ + X
      inte gömma barnet   „not hide the child" (E$_8$, 242)

(35) inte + V$_{participle}$
      inte gått sönder   „not gone broken" (E$_7$, 257)

(36) X + inte + Y

(36a) Embla inte ha täcket   „Embla not have quilt" (E$_8$, 245)

(36b) Embla inte naken   „Embla not naked" (E$_8$, 246)

(37) (X) + V$_{fin}$ + inte + Y

(37a) jag vill inte   „I want not" (E$_7$, 233)

(37b) vill inte rida   „will not ride" (E$_8$, 236)

(37c) vill inte tvätta håret   „want not wash the hair" (E$_8$, 241)

(37d) älg säger inte mu   „Elk says not moo" (E$_7$, 250)

(37e) det är inte apa   „that is not ape" (E$_9$, 253)

(38) V$_{imp}$ + inte + X
      gör inte det   „don't do that" (E$_9$, 256)

(39) inte + X + Y

(39a) inte mamma tvätta „not mother wash" (E$_8$, 231)

(39b) inte mamma hälpa Embla „not mother help Embla" (E$_9$, 232)

The data are too scanty to support far-reaching conclusions. However, the major stages in the development agree quite well with the German data. The girl starts with anaphoric negation; next comes non-anaphoric negation, expressed — perhaps only for a very brief span — through the devices of anaphoric negation. This stage is quickly superseded by the appearance of *inte*. Except for possibly (34) and (39), all sub-types reflect the adult target very closely. In particular, the situation as regards verbs is quite parallel to the German material. In adult Swedish and in adult German *inte/nicht* are placed after the finite verb, no matter whether auxiliary or full verb. Consequently, there are two verbal sub-types: the one with the verb/aux before *nicht/ inte* reflecting the position of the finite verb or the imperative, as in (37 *a-e*); the other with *nicht/inte* before the verb reflecting other non-finite verb-forms, as in (36 *a-b*). As for the Swedish types (32, 37*e*), the child uses *inte* instead of *ingen* „kein". This is comparable to German children's use of *nicht* (ein) instead of *kein*. It is diffi-cult to say whether (34) and (39) reflect adult usage. At least (39) would be unlikely among adults. It is possible, however, that utterances comparable to the child's (34) and (39) may be used by adults/parents in talking to children. One would have to examine what kind of structures Embla was exposed to. There are no comments on this point in Lange & Larsson.[5]

English. Data are available from Klima & Bellugi 1966 on three children and from Bloom 1970 on three other children. Both studies used the interval technique for data collecting. They both disregard phonetics, including intonation. Klima & Bellugi, furthermore, provide no information on the semantics and the children's intentions; Bloom, however, is careful to do so. Unfortunately, her intervals are so long (7 weeks) that no detailed developmental sequence can be established from her study, either, with any degree of certainty. However, the structural types that both studies des-cribe are just those which we would expect in view of the German data. Putting the evidence from both studies together, I venture to hypothesize the following develop-mental sequence. The examples are marked for source and child (B = Bloom 1970; K & B = Klima & Bellugi 1966).

I: one-word negation

Most frequently the morphological item is *no,* less frequently *no more* (B, Eric).

II *a*: anaphoric negation

   (40)   no, outside
            „no, I want to go outside" (B, Kathryn, p. 149)

II *b*: non-anaphoric negation

   (41)   no close
            „I can't close the box" (B, Kathryn, p. 149)

Just as with the German data on *nein,* there are only very few instances where *no* is used non-anaphorically in „whole sentences" in Bloom's data. She lists one example from Kathryn:

(42)   no Daddy hungry (p. 162)

However, no gloss is provided, and the utterance is unclear with regard to the child's intention. Bloom's evidence led her to conclude that utterances of the type *neg* + S are always anaphoric in child language. However, the cross-cultural evidence surveyed in this paper does suggest that *neg* + S may, in fact, be non-anaphoric. Klima & Bellugi have apparently found at least a few unambiguous instances of this sort for English; Bloom quotes (43) from their study:

(43)   no I see truck
        „I can't/don't see the truck" (B, p. 162)

Ròger Brown (personal communication) adds (15), which we repeat here:

(15)   no the sun shining

III: intra-sentential negation

(44)   Kathryn no like celery (B, Kathryn, p. 160)
(45)   Kathryn not quite through (B, Kathryn, p. 191)
(46)   I can't open it (B, Kahtryn, p. 195)

III is a mixed bag. It must be left to future investigations to determine whether and which developmental differences occur. Forms like *don't, can't, doesn't,* etc. are still monomorphemic negatives, as noted by both Bloom (p. 195) and Klima & Bellugi. They are morphologically re-interpreted as *aux* + *neg* at a later stage of development.

As for the most likely models, *no* of I-II *a* probably goes back to adult anaphoric *no*. Syntax, semantics (and phonetics?) all point in that direction. Child anaphoric *no* is generalized to II *b*, which has no adult analogue. This is so even if the majority of the examples are regarded as "subjectless predicates", as Bloom 1970: 148 ff. seems to think. However, if Bloom's view were correct, we would expect *not;* what we find, however, is *no*. For stage III, forms like *can't, doesn't* must go back to the respective *aux* + *neg*. There are no examples like **n't does*. That is, when these composite negatives do appear, they are apparently always reproduced by the children with *-n't* following the element corresponding to the adult *aux*. The children's *not* in III is probably based on adult *not*. It tends to appear in environments closely analogous to adult usage. But *no* as in (44) does not have a direct adult analogue; adult English would have *-n't* or *not*. There are no parallels from German. Maybe morphophonemic similarities between *n't, not* and *no* lead English children to do this. More likely, this problem is related to the status of *neg* as a bound vs. free or isolatable form. This issue will be discussed, including data from Latvian, in a separate paper (cf. Wode & Ruke-Dravina 1977).

Other sources. In our research group at Kiel we have also gone through Scupin & Scupin 1907, Ramge 1973, Stern & Stern 1907, Park 1970, Neugebauer 1914 and Grimm 1973 for German; Gheorgov 1908 for Bulgarian; Grégoire 1937, 1947 for French; Gvozdev 1949 for Russian; Kaper 1959, 1975 and Schaerlaekens 1973 for

Dutch; Bowerman 1973 for Finnish; McNeill & McNeill 1968 for Japanese; Omar 1970 for Egyptian Arabic; and Volterra 1972 and Antinucci & Volterra 1973 for Italian. I have also had oral reports from M. Smoczynska on ongoing work on Polish; and from S. Savić on Serbo-Croatian. I shall not summarize these studies in detail here because, except for a few minor differences, they all conform to the four major stages set up above. However, I do not attach too much import to this, either in terms of conformity or non-conformity. Except for Schaerlaekens 1973 these studies offer only fragmentary data (including Gvozdev 1949 in spite of Slobin's 1966 appraisal). Nevertheless, Stern & Stern 1907, Park 1970, Ruke-Dravina 1963 and Gheorgov 1908 have some data on stage II*b* with *neg* in final position. Thus, at least for some languages, *neg* may appear in that position. Unfortunately, it cannot as yet be determined whether this is peculiar to certain languages, to certain children, or to something else.

Cross-Linguistic Developmental Trends

In spite of the heterogeneity and considerable inconclusiveness of some of the data, the major developmental trends are clearly discernible as common to the material as a whole.

I: one-word negation

The children start with one-word negation. Morphemically, the negative elements are modelled on those of the adult language which can be used in isolation and which, amongst other things, express anaphoric negation.

II: two- or more-word negation

II *a*: anaphoric negation

Two- or more-word negation is at first anaphoric. The negative morpheme tends to be the same as for one-word negation, but it is occasionally different, as seems to be the case in Gvozdev's 1949 data (cf. Wode & Schmitz 1974). In any event *neg* is modelled after adult anaphoric negatives. To date, in those descriptions that are not too fragmentary or anecdotal in character, there is evidence that the negative element is placed in utterance-initial position.

II *b*: non-anaphoric negation

At first children overgeneralize the morpho-syntactic devices of II *a* to express non-anaphoric negation. In most studies the children placed *neg* utterance-initially. There are a few cases, however, where *neg* was in final position. Unfortunately, in some of these cases it is not clear whether these were truly non-anaphoric.

III: intra-sentential negation

The morpho-syntactic devices of II are abandoned in the case of non-anaphoric negation in favour of the non-anaphoric elements of the adult language. That is, children switch from *nein* to *nicht* in German, from *nä, nej* to *inte* in Swedish, from *njet* to *ne* in Russian. English children depart from this scheme in that *no* tends to be retained for some time against *not* or *n't*; it is striking that in this case the respective negatives are phonologically fairly similar. Alternatively, it may be possible that the English data somehow reflect the fact that adult *no* also occurs non-anaphorically as in *no house, no money,* etc. It is more likely, however, that this is dependent on whether the target *neg* is a bound or a free form (Wode & Ruke-Dravina 1977). The actual syntax of III is now clearly modelled on the respective adult language, with numerous language-dependent peculiarities. English children, for example, place *neg* between subject and verb (45-46). German and Swedish youngsters have two types: one with *neg* after the verb, the other with *neg* between subject and full verb. The first type reflects the position of *neg* after finite verbs including auxiliaries; the latter type relates to adult structures with *neg* in front of non-finite full verb forms. A detailed investigation of this stage requires a separate paper.

Obviously, the above account is far from complete. The number of languages and the total number of children studied provide only a quantitatively weak basis for conclusions along universalist lines. We need many more detailed studies, preferably on languages structurally different and more complex than the ones referred to above, e.g. French with its split negatives *ne ... pas, ne ... rien,* etc.; or Finnish (in spite of Bowerman 1973) with its inflected negative element; or languages without anaphoric negative morphemes. Moreover, this summary merely covers rather gross steps of the early development. Later developments such as the negative indefinites (German *kein, nichts,* etc.; English, *any, nothing,* and the like) have to be added. Bloom 1970, for example, has noted that identificational structures such as *this is candy* are at first negated by children as (47) and not as (48) as one might expect, since children at that age already have (49)

(47) no candy
(48) this no/not candy
(49) this candy

Details such as this need to be explained, and related to adequate cognitive studies as to what is involved in negativity, before any satisfying predictive theory of the acquisition of negation can be achieved.

Notes

* Reprinted by permission from *Journal of Child Language* 4 (1977)pp. 87-102.
For help, criticism and comments I am indebted to various people in our research group, notably Sascha Felix, Dietrich Lange, Dieter Furkmann, Christa Meyer, Theo Schmitz, Ocke Bohn and Detlef Ufert.

[1] I am assured by Roger Brown (personal communication) that at least some negated utterances like (1)-(3) were, in fact, non-anaphoric.
[2] The segmental transcription is I.P.A. and slightly narrower than standard phonemic. Intona-

tional markings follow familiar conventions (for details cf. Wode 1980b: `falling centre (falling nuclear pitch); ´rising centre (rising nuclear pitch); "extra-high centre (extra-high emphatic nuclear pitch); – post-contour (tail); ˈhigh pendant (high stretch before centre); ˌlow pendant (low strech before centre). Some examples below will not be provided with an intonational transcription. These instances usually come from the written notes. Sometimes I have missed the intonation and so could note only the segmental material.

3 Both Inga and Lars have a lisp with, at first, [θ, ð] substituting for [ʃ, ʒ, s, z], and, at a later stage, only for [s, z].

4 In spite of the well-known weaknesses I use the term *pivot* here as a convinient short label in the familiar sense.

5 Thanks are due to Christina Melin, Nordisches Seminar der Universität Kiel, for help with Swedish.

SOME STAGES IN THE ACQUISITION OF THE QUESTIONS BY MONOLINGUAL CHILDREN*

Henning Wode

This article summarizes data on the acquisition of questions from German, English, Latvian, Swedish, and other languages. More specifically, it deals with the production of questions by children. The aim behind this survey is to prepare the ground for developing a theory on the acquisition of questions by children in such a way that the developmental sequence can be predicted for any natural language. Of course, at the present state of affairs, researchers are still far from this goal. Therefore, though I shall present the outlines of a theory on the acquisition of questions, this survey constitutes an overview which seeks to establish, and to make amenable to future detailed investigations, those major issues which a full theory would ultimately have to account for with much more precision than is now possible.

The major issues are the developmental sequences (1) for the various formal questions (i.e., intonation questions vs. segmentally marked questions vs. word order questions), (2) for the interrogative syntax (e.g., inversion, word order of interrogative markers, etc.), and (3) for the various segmental interrogative markers: pronoun or other (e.g., locative vs. instrumental vs. temporal, etc.). I shall tentatively propose a developmental sequence for all three types.

Whereas many researchers these days prefer to look at child-language acquisition from the point of view of cognitive development, the evidence summarized in this article leads me to emphasize the role of the formal properties of the linguistic devices used in natural languages. It is these formal properties which, more than anything else, seem to determine the developmental sequence characteristic of a given language. Some such formal properties are: free versus bound form, position, suprasegmental versus segmental, and generality of rules and items.

1. Introduction

This article attempts to arrive at a theory about the acquisition of questions by monolingual children. Such a theory is, of course, bound to remain highly tentative at the present state of affairs. More specifically, this report summarizes developmental trends in children's production of questions, rather than in their ability to comprehend adult questions, child questions, or both. The work has grown out of a project on language acquisition presently under way at Kiel University in West Germany.

In my view, the main objective for a theory on the acquisition of questions should be that it correctly predict the developmental sequences found when children acquire the interrogative system of any language. At present, researchers are far from this goal, mainly for two reasons. First, there are not enough data from languages of sufficiently diverse structural types. Second, the available data are not rich enough as regards a number of issues crucial to any understanding of the acquisition of questions. The general aim of this article, therefore, is to prepare the ground for setting up such a theory. My more immediate aim is to present an overview which seeks to establish, and to make amenable to future detailed investigations, those issues which a full theory would ultimately have to account for with more precision than is now possible. I have been able to draw on studies of Bulgarian (Gheorgov 1908), Latvian (Ruke-Dravina 1963), German (my own studies; Stern & Stern 1907; and other studies), English (Klima & Bellugi 1966; Brown 1968; Miller 1973), Swedish (Lange & Larsson 1973), and Finnish (Bowerman 1973).

It seems to me that previous studies are too fragmentary in one way or another. Whereas older studies primarily examined the overall developmental sequence of the interrogative pronouns (for example, Stern & Stern 1907; Gheorgov 1908), the more recent study by Klima and Bellugi (1966) deals with syntacic problems like inversion, *do-* support, and so on. Both aspects are important but misleading in that they are not integrated into any overall developmental description. For one thing, though the acquisition of interrogative pronouns can be summarized into such a developmental sequence, this sequence, nevertheless, must be described in much more detail with reference to the morphosyntactic environments in which the pronouns appear. In German, for instance, *wo* 'where' is first aquired in constructions reflecting adult equational strings. However, *wer* 'who' first appears in utterances which reflect nonequational adult strings (i.e., full verbs or modal verbs); it occurs decidedly later in utterances apparantly modelled on equational adult structures — sometimes so late, indeed, that other interrogative pronouns have already been acquired.

Moreover, the evidence reviewed in this report strongly suggests the following: if we are to get at the cognition that underlies the acquisition of questions, we are well advised to relate cognitive concepts and linguistic semantics to the types of formal devices used in forming questions in natural languages. The way to accomplish this purpose is to compare the acquisition of questions in languages which employ different formal types of question structures. Thus, *yes/no* questions in English do not contain interrogative pronouns; Finnish marks them through an affix; Latvian has at least two options—*yes/no* questions may be marked by an interrogative particle placed at the beginning of the question or by +INTER(rogative) intonation without word order permutations or the particle. Studies of this sort will, I hope, allow us to differentiate between the various types of cognitive growth involved in, or associated with, language acquisition. Ultimately, it seems that we should set up a typology of linguistic devices according to their formal properties. Such a typology should be based on empirically observable evidence from child language rather than on the prescriptions of linguistic theories. This typology should account for a good deal of the difference in the developmental sequences of individual languages.

The whole subject matter is too complex to be treated in detail in one article without other studies to prepare the ground. To provide this groundwork I have already analysed my German data in detail. The results are summarized in section 3 below. They provide the focus for the rest of this article, which centers on an overall cross-cultural comparison of the acquisition of questions.

This article is organised as follows: section 2 presents a brief typology of speech questions; section 3 summarizes my own as well as previous investigators' data for German; section 4 contrasts this material with studies on other languages; section 5 points out the commonalities of the various data and suggests a general hypothesis for the acquisition of questions; and section 6 contains proposals for future research in this area.

2. Types of questions

To my knowledge, the only recent attempt at a survey of question types is the one by Greenberg (1966), which is, however, rather fragmentary. Moreover, acquisition data are available only for a limited number of languages, which, unfortunately, are not structurally diverse enough. Therefore, only a few distinctions are drawn below in such a way as to allow me to handle those languages for which acquisition data are available.

First, I wish to restrict the term *question* to *speech questions* (Q). Nonspeech questions (i.e., gestures and other sorts of demands) will not be treated here. Speech questions can be classified according to their formal devices or their semantics (i.e., in line with the information sought).

Formally, there are intonation questions, segmentally marked questions, and word order questions. *Intonation questions* (IQ) are those for which the only +INTER feature is the intonation (i.e., with no +INTER word order or segmental markers). Since the data to be reviewed below do not provide enough details about the respective +INTER intonations, I will only go so far as to note the absence or presence of +INTER intonations irrespective of their phonetic properties.

Segmentally marked questions (SQ) are those which contain a segmental morpheme or marker to signal +INTER. Languages vary as to type and number of such segmental interrogative markers. Some languages restrict them to questions about location, agency, and so on (e.g., English and German); other languages may also have segmental +INTER markers for *yes/no* questions (e.g., Bulgarian and Latvian).

SQ can be further subdivided according to the position and the type of the markers. *Pronominal questions* (Qpron) involve free-form markers, such as the interrogative pronouns of English and German. *Particle questions* (Qpart) involve bound-form markers (e.g., Finnish *-ko ~ -kö*). Both the +INTER pronouns and the particles can be placed in various positions in a sentence, depending on the language. However, since there are not sufficient data to determine the relative chronology of such positional subtypes, I shall, at present, not pursue this matter any further.

Word order questions (WOQ) are those which have a particular word order associated with them. In the languages to be discussed below which have +INTER word order, this order always takes the form of subject-verb inversions of various sorts.

These formal devices may co-occur in various ways in different languages.

Semantically, there are yes/no questions and information questions. *Yes/no questions* (YNQ) are those in which the information to be elicited is *yes/no* or some such equivalent; they ask for confirmation or denial. *Information questions* (INQ) seek more particular information: location, agency, time, and so on. The expected answer is not merely confirmatory or disconfirmatory.

Data are available concerning the acquisition of question types IQ, WOQ, Qpron, and Qpart.

3. Developmental sequences for German

3.1 Adult German. Adult German has INQ and YNQ. The former are SQ — to be exact, they are Qpron. The pronouns more often than not are placed initially; they may also take the position of the interrogated constituent without front-shifting, particularly in repeat questions. The YNQ are either IQ or WOQ, but there is no segmental marker for YNQ.

German has a complex system of inversion which also applies to -INTER structures. The +INTER inversion requires a shift of the subject after the finite verb irrespective of whether it is an auxiliary or a main verb. There is no *do*-support or the like.

3.2 Child German

3.2.1 The Kiel Project data. I have collected my data from my two monolingual children: Lars, born on May 22, 1969, and Inga, born on May 20, 1971. They are both acquiring German as their first language. The material was gathered in a longitudinal day-by-day routine involving both written notes taken spontaneously and tape recordings. I have followed no fixed time schedules or the like. My experience has been that such rigid schemes are inferior to flexible day-by-day routines. (For details on the data, the project, and some results that have come out of it, see Wode 1974, 1980b; Wode & Schmitz 1974.)

This report is based on a sampling of the written notes. I have not been able to evaluate all the tapes yet. Some, however, have been sampled to cross-check whether the notes were selective, which, in fact, they proved not to be.

In quoting examples, I rely chiefly on Inga because she is the better documented of the two. Moreover, she progressed much more slowly than her brother did. She therefore provides clearer data for inferences.

3.2.2 Developmental sequence for Lars and Inga.

Stage I. Holophrastic questions. With both children the first questions can be traced to the holophrastic (i.e., one-word) stage. There are two types ordered developmentally: IYNQ and SQ.

Ia. Holophrastic IYNQ. The first type of question was the one-word intonation question. Such questions were distinguished from nonquestions only by the intonation. For details on child +INTER intonation in German, see Wode 1980b). Some examples follow.

188[1]
December 6, 1972
1;6.17

1. I. is showing a wooden toy railroad track to F.[2] It is broken.

    I.: ꞌpɷ [3]
    "Kaputt?"
    ("Broken?")
    I. is satisfied with F.'s confirmation that it is, indeed, broken.

242
December 25, 1972
1;7.5

2. I. is waving a sheet of paper which she threatens to deposit anywhere. F. tries to tell her not to. I. then asks, "There?"

    I.: ꞌtá
    "Da (werfe ich es hin)."
    ("There [I'm going to deposit it].")

F.: "Nein."
("No.")
I. pointing to the wastebasket:
I.: 'ta
"Da?"
("There?")
F.: "Ja."
("Yes.")
I. puts the sheet into the waste-
basket.

246
December 26, 1972
1;7.6

3. During a walk, I. and F. are trailing
behind. The other members of the
family have moved on out of sight.
I. asks whether the others are gone.
I.: 'fɛ 'fɛ
"Weg? Weg?"
("Gone? Gone?")
F.: "Ja."
("Yes.")
I. calls M.:
I.: 'mami
"Mami."
("Mommy.")

I have found no evidence that such holophrastic IQ were intended other
than as YNQ.

Ib. Holophrastic SQ. Before questions of two or more words began to
appear, both children produced some holophrastic SQ (i.e., questions con-
sisting of a segmental-interrogative morpheme). Inga used [vo, fo] and
occasionally [vovo]. Lars used [vuθi] and [vo]. These questions are pronominal in type.

The children's intentions were stative location (i.e., not 'direction from'
or 'to'). Inga clearly modelled her forms on adult *wo* [vo]. Lars's forms
seem to reflect adult strings involving *wo ist*, which in the type of German
that the children were accustomed to hear tends to be pronounced like
[vos . . .]. In any case, the forms were monomorphemic for the children,
since there is no trace of such forms elsewhere in their speech at that tıme.

Stage II. Multiword questions. The development of stage I is carried
over to combinations of two or more words. For the SQ, the children will
have to acquire the interrogative pronouns and inversion. In addition to
IQ they will have to master WOQ.

IIa. Multiword IQ. The IQ state of Ia at first remains unchanged. There is still no interrogative word order. The only marker is the intonation. Semantico-intentionally there are two stages of development.

IIa$_1$. Multiword YNQ. At first two-word IQ are YNQ, as in examples 4 to 6.

371
April 14, 1973
1;10.24

4. F. is pushing I. in her perambulator. He runs fast and imitates the sound of a motor car. All along F. is jerking the perambulator forcefully. When F. stops, I. asks for more, which sends F. off on another gallop.

    I.: ′meᵊ ′tɛtɛt

      "Mehr tetet?"

      ("More tetet?")

The scene is repeated several times.

374
April 19, 1973
1;10.29

5. B. has just left in a car to spend the night with friends.

I. inquires:

    I.: ˈaɷto ′vɛk

      "Ist das Auto weg?"

      ("Is the car gone?")

382
April 24, 1973
1;11.4

6. Breakfast. I. pushes her boiled egg toward M., wanting her to break it.

    I.: ˋaɪa ˏʔaɷfə

      "(Machst du das Ei auf?"

      ("Will you break the egg?")

IIa$_2$. Multiword IIN Q. Subsequently, there are some instances in which the children's intentions are clearly of the sort which in adult German would be expressed through SQ (i.e., through an interrogative pronoun).

1583
February 17, 1974
2;8.28

7. I. is pointing to a white car outside the grocer's.

    I.: ˈhɛnɪk tiða ˋʔaɷto ˏkʰöᵊt

      "Henning, (wem) gehört dieses Auto?"

      ("Henning, whom does this car belong to?")

    F.: "Ich weiß nicht."

      ("I don't know.")

54

I. begins to suggest names of possible possessors herself:

I.: ˀᵓoda ˅kʰɑιl

"Oder (=entweder) Keil (=Name des Kaufmanns)."

("Either Keil [name of the grocer].")

F.: "Ja?"

("Yes?")

I.: ˀᵓoda ˅buχlokˁ

"Oder Buchloh (=F.'s Kollege in der Universität)."

("Or Buchloh [name of F.'s colleague at the university].")

In example 7 the child herself gives the answer, and it certainly is not *yes/ no.*

1590
February 19, 1974
2;8.30

8. F. has just paid a visit to the neighbour next door. I. meets him at the front door.

I.: ˈhɛnιŋ tu ˅veθ

"Henning, (wo bist) du gewesen?"

("Henning, where have you been?")

1612
February 25, 1974
2;9.5

9. Morning. F. is reading the paper with I. on his lap. I. points to a picture of a helicopter in the paper.

I.: ˈtiða ˈhaιθt

"(Wie) heißt dies?"

("What's this called?")

F. does not react at all. So I. tries again:

I.: ˈhɛnιŋ tiða ˈhaιθ

"Henning, (wie) heißt dies?"

("Henning, what's it called?")

F.: "Hubschrauber."

("Helicopter.")

I. turns away completely contented.

Note that the word order in examples 7 to 9 still does not reflect adult +INTER word order (i.e. inversion). Note further, however, that the interrogated constituent (i.e., the one on which the information is sought) is missing in such utterances.

Type IIa$_2$ is later supplanted by appropriate SQ. There are difficulties, however, which I cannot resolve here. First, it is not clear yet whether the point when IQ are replaced by SQ can be specified—let alone predicted—in any precise way, or whether this has to be ascribed to the idiosyncrasies of children.

Second, it is not clear whether the range of overgeneralizations can be specified. In other words, are all types of intentions which are expressed through SQ in the respective adult language liable to be rendered via IIa$_2$, or will children overgeneralize only with respect to certain intentions? My German data point to the latter possibility. What, then, are the determinants? It is not known yet.

(For a related problem [i.e., overgeneralized usages of child interrogative pronouns], see the treatment of nonstative location involving *wo* below.)

Third, where are type IIa$_2$ utterances to be placed in the overall developmental sequence? Some of these pronounless questions occur when the children have already acquired some +INTER pronouns but lack others. It is for these and their semantico-intentional properties that children revert to forms previously used such as type IIa$_2$. Recall, for instance, example 7. The pronoun *wem* tends to be acquired very late.

Before these problems can be resolved, more detailed data on the intentions involved in children's questions are needed.

IIb. *Multiword SQ: wo + N/NP.* For quite a while the only SQ to occur with either child are questions reflecting adult *wo*. Semantico-intentionally, there are two subtypes:

IIb$_1$. *Stative location: wo + N/NP.*

934
September 20, 1973
2;4.0

10.　F. and I. are driving around in search of L.
　　　I.: 'vo‿la°θi ‚hɛnɪŋ
　　　"Wo (ist) Larsi, Henning?"
　　　("Where [is] Larsi, Henning?")

1053
October 9, 1973
2;4.19

11.　Outside the grocer's. M. has sneaked away to go inside. F. is pushing I. in her perambulator trying to divert her, so that she should not decide to follow M. I., on noticing M.'s disappearance:

I.: ˈhɛnɪŋ vo ˇmama
"Henning, wo (ist) Mama?"
("Henning, where [is] Mom?")

F. pretends not to have understood.

F.: "Was?"
("What?")

I.: ˈvo ˈmama
"Wo (ist) Mama?"
("Where [is] Mom?")

F.: "Bei Keil."
("At Keil's [=name of the grocer]").

I.: is quite satisfied with this reply.

1069
October 11, 1973
2;4.21

12. F. has tried to coax I. away from a spot where she was not to go. He has pointed out a pond to her. To get her attention he had suggested that there were fish in it. But it turns out that there are none.

I.: vo fɪθə
"Wo (sind die) Fische?"
("Where [are] the fish?")

F.: "Was?"
("What?")

I.: vo fɪθə
"Wo (sind die) Fische?"
("Where [are] the fish?")

The interrogative was [vo] with Inga, and monomorphemic [voθa ∼ voða], later ousted by monomorphemic [voθ] with Lars. The interrogative pronouns were placed in initial position, barring vocatives. The items following the interrogative, and in construction with it, all reflect adult N or NP, again barring vocatives. As for possible adult models, it strikes me that they must be provided by strings like example 13:

13. wo + *sein* + N/NP

IIb$_2$. *Nonstative location involving wo.* Before the influx of additional interrogative pronouns, I have noted utterances much like examples 10 to 12, but which clearly are not intended to refer to stative location. I have found clear evidence for the intentions 'where from' (exs. 14 and 15) and 'where to' (exs. 16 to 18) with Inga.

1066
October 10, 1973
2;4.20

14. During a ride B. is chewing a piece of gum. I. turns to M. It seems that I. wants a piece, too.

I.: mama vo pɛᵉki kʰaɷpi

"Mama, wo(her) hat Birgit (das) Kaugummi?/Woher ist Birgits Kaugummi?"

("Mom, where is Birgit's gum from? [i.e., where did Birgit get it from?]")

1100
October 15, 1973
2;4.25

15. L. has been bought a view master (a little machine through which slides can be viewed). Back home I. notices what L. has. She turns to F. and, pointing to L., she complains:

I.: ˈhɛnɪŋ vo laᵉθi ˅tiðəθ

"Henning, wo(her hat) Larsi dies?/Wo hat er dies gekriegt?"

("Henning, where did Larsi get this?")

F.: "In der Stadt."

("In town.")

I.: ʔɒn˅iç ˡʔɒn˅iç

"Und ich? Und ich?"

("And I? And I?")

1087
October 13, 1973
2;4.23

16. On a walk through the woods. M., walking in front, has disappeared. I. inquires after her several times.

I.: ˈvo ˅mama

"Wo (ist) Mama?/Wo (ist) Mama (hin)?"

("Where [is] Mom?/ Where [has] Mom [gone to]?")

F.: "Was?"

("What?")

I.: ˈvo 'mama

"Wo (ist) Mama?/Wo (ist) Mama (hin)?"

("Where [is] Mom?/ Where [has] Mom [gone to]?")

1349
December 26, 1973
2;7.6

17. I. is pushing a chair toward the table next to M., who has already taken her seat.

I.: ˡtiða tul ˈˀaɔχ

"Dieser Stuhl (soll) auch (an den Tisch)."

("This chair [should be at the table], too.")

I. continues to manoeuvre the chair.

I.: ˡmama vo tiða ˇtul

"Mama, wohin (soll) dieser Stuhl?"

("Mom, where [should] this chair [go]?")

1950
June 6, 1974
3;0.17

18. F. and L. are setting out to buy a pocket knife for L. I. runs after them.

I.: ˡhɛnɪŋ vo ˈkeθ tu ˈhɛnɪŋ

"Henning, wo(hin) gehst du, Henning?"

"Henning, where are you going, Henning?)

Of course, the intention ‚where from' is less subject to situational ambiguity than the type ‚where to' (see ex. 16). However, there are also such unambiguous instances of ‚where to' as those in examples 17 and 18. Moreover, at the time when Inga began to show evidence of ‚where to' intentions, she produced a few questions which did, in fact, contain [vohɪn ~ vo...hɪn], which clearly reflect adult *wohin* ~ *wo . . . hin*. She discarded this type, though, and reverted for a long time to type IIb$_2$ to express 'direction to', as in examples 16 to 18.

Notice that with type IIb$_2$ the constituents following *wo* no longer reflect adult N or NP structures (seees p. ex. 15). Never has [laˤ θi tiðəθ] been an NP with either child. It is therefore not clear how the children arrive at type IIb$_2$ structures. They may overgeneralize from IIb$_1$ as far as *wo* is concerned. But this interpretation is amiss for the constituent in the construction with *wo* in IIb$_2$. In IIb$_1$ they reflect adult N or NP. In IIb$_2$ there are also sentential relationships which seem to reflect adult structures like subject–object and the like.

Moreover, there is a more general problem that relates to overgeneralized usages of +INTER pronouns and which, in some ways, is similar to the overgeneralized IINQ of type IIa. Which overgeneralizations occur? Can the range of overgeneralizations be specified so that, ultimately, those liable to turn up can be predicted? In other words, which pronoun will be overgeneralized to cover which intention(s)? For instance, child *wo* is attested in the sense of 'where, where to, where from', but never for adult *wie* 'how', *wer* 'who', and so on. Likewise, child *wer* 'who' occurs for adult *wer*, as well as in place of adult *wie*, namely, in connection with the verb *heissen* 'to be called' when children ask for a person's identity. In adult German one would say *wie heisst er*? "What's he called?" Children probably overgeneralize largely on a semantic basis. After all, *wie* in the example just given inquires not about modality but about identity—and that is what *wer* is generally used for in German. It seems likely that children pick the most general item for a specific cognitive-semantic category, overgeneralize it, and later restrict it in accord with the adult standards along lines suggested schematically in figure 1. A downward reading through the branchings gives the overgeneralizations which are liable to occur: *was* may be used instead of *wer*, but not vice versa; likewise, *wo* may be used for *wohin* or for *woher*, but *wohin* and *woher* will

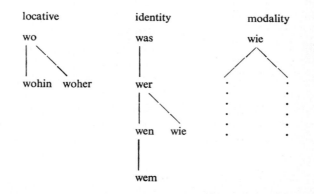

Figure 1. Branching diagrams for some overgeneralizations of interrogative pronouns in child German. (Read downward only. Any step—downward—from one node to the next or to others below marks a potential type of overgeneralization.)

not substitute for each other. A separate in-depth study of this topic is being prepared using the German data of our Kiel project. (Greenhalgh 1976).

Stage III. Incorporation of verbs into SQ. The next major stage in the development of SQ is marked by the acquisition of verbs. The details differ for both children. I suspect, however, that these differences reflect different stages in the development of the VP, rather than in SQ-formation proper. All in all, there are three types, depending on the position of the verb: verbs following *wo*, verbs in final position, and finite verbs with adult-like positioning.

IIIa. Incorporation of ist/sein. The first verbs to appear are reflexes of the adult *sein*-paradigm, notably adult *ist*. The verb is placed second after *wo*. No other verbs occur in SQ at this stage (cf. exs. 19 to 21).

1459
January 17, 1974
2;7.28

19. I. is to go and play outside. F. explains to her that he is going to find her doll's perambulator. I. agrees that this is what should be done.

I.: ˈja ˈvo‿ʔɩθa
"Ja, wo ist (sie)?"
("Yes, where is [it]?"

1474
January 20, 1974
2;8.0

20. I. is looking for M. all over the house.

I.: ᵛmama ˈvo ˈpɩθ ˈtu/ˈvo ˈpɩθ‿tu
"Mama, wo bist du? Wo bist du?"
("Mom, where are you? Where are you?")

1501
February 3, 1974
2;8.14

21. Breakfast. I. is having cereal in a cup. She wants milk with it and gets it. The milk makes the cereal float on top so that I. cannot see the milk underneath. I. is annoyed and complains strongly to M.

I.: ˈvo ʔɩθə ˄mɩlç
"Wo ist (die) Milch?"
("Where is the milk?")

The forms [ʔɩθa, pɩθ, ʔɩθə] are all monomorphemic at this stage of development. The children's intentions are clearly stative location. Type IIIa is recorded for both Lars and Inga.

IIIb. Verbs in final position. After type IIIa Inga produced a fair share of *wo*-questions with verbs in final position (cf. exs. 22 to 24).

1478
February 21, 1974
2;8.1

22. Breakfast. I. inquires about her cousin Björn, who paid us a visit the day before. Björn lives in Ratzeburg, a fact well known to I.

I.: ˈhɛnɩŋ vo ˈjø°ni ˈvon
"Henning, wo wohnt Björn?"
("Henning, where does Björn live?")

F.: "In Ratzeburg."
("In Ratzeburg.")
I.: 'ne ^kʰil
"Nein, (in) Kiel."
("No, [in] Kiel.")
It is not quite clear whether I. in fact intended [von] for 'wohnt'.

1516
February 5, 1974
2;8.16

23. Supper. The children take different seats than they normally do. I. gets furious.

I.: ˈvo ˈˀiç ðɪtʰθə
"Wo (soll) ich sitzen?
Wo sitze ich?"
("Where do I sit?")

1551
February 10, 1974
2;8.21

24. I. is searching for her cap, which she had taken off shortly before. She is annoyed.

I.: ˈvo maɪnə ˈmytʰθə‿kaŋ
"Wo (ist) meine Mütze (hin) gegangen (=ge‐kommen)?"
("Where [has] my cap gone?")

Lars very rarely used utterances like those in examples 22 to 24.

Some of the type IIIb utterances might be interpreted as reflecting and intending adult complex VP, with the auxiliary in second place and the main verb shifted to the end. This cannot be the full explanation, however. Adult German would not require an auxiliary in example 22; it would be optional in example 23, although in the colloquial German that the children were accustomed to hearing, the auxiliary *sollen* or some equivalent was rarely used. Only example 24 would obligatorily require an auxiliary, namely, *ist* or *war*.

The end-placed verb forms seem to reflect forms of adult full verbs like *haben*, *gegangen*, *wohnen*, *sitzen*, and *gehen*. However, there is an isolated instance or two in which Inga's and Lars's questions involving forms of *sein* had [pɪn] 'bin' (*am*) end-placed. This occurred around the time when type IIIb came into use (cf. ex. 25 from Inga).

1615
February 25, 1974
2;9.5

25. We are looking at photographs. The first ones did not show I.

I.: vo ˀiç pɪn
"Wo bin ich?"
("Where am I?")

The next pictures still do not show
I. She complains again.
> I.: ˈvo ˈˀiç_pɪn
> "Wo bin ich?"
> ("Where am I?")

IIIc. Adult-like positioning of finite verbs. Type IIIc marks the adult-like positioning of adult finite verbs, whether they be *sein,* auxiliary, or main verb (cf. exs. 26 to 28).

1711/12
March 30, 1974
2;10.10

26. Lunch. I. finds two forks next to her plate. She holds one up and sings out.
> I.: ˈvɛ° kʰö°t i ˇkɑpɛl
> "Wem   gehört   die Gabel?"
> ("Whom does the fork belong to?")
F. explains that he does not know.
I. tries again.
> I.: ˈvɛ° ˈpɑɷχ_ti
> "Wer braucht sie?"
> ("Who needs it?")

1731
April 9, 1974
2;10.19

27. I. walks into F.'s study.
> I.: ˈhɛnɪŋk hɑθ tu θokoˇlɑdə/
> "Henning, hast du Scho-kolade?"
> ("Henning, do you have [a piece of] choc-olate?")
F. does not react at all.
I. tries again.
> I.: ˈvɑθ hɑθ tu ˇtɛn/
> "Was hast du denn?"
> ("What else have you got?")
Again F. does not react.
> I.: ˈvɑθ hɑθ tu ˈtɛn ˌhɛnɪŋk
> "Was hast du denn, Hen-ning?"
> ("What else have you got, Henning?")
Though the situation was not quite clear when I. said what she did in

example 27, I thought that she intended *was* as the object and not in
the sense of 'what is the matter
with you'.

1742
April 10, 1974
2;10.20

28. I. is watching B. construct something out of blocks.
    I.: ˡma vaθ maχ ˅pɛki
       "Mama, was macht Bir-
       git?"
       ("Mom, what is Birgit
       doing/building?")

Additional remarks on Type III. Whereas Inga fully produced all three
types—IIIa, b, and c—well differentiated in the developmental sequence as a
function of time, Lars provided substantial evidence only for types IIIa and
IIIc. I have noted very few examples of type IIIb. His types IIIa and IIIc were
developmentally ordered, however, as indicated above. I suspect that these
differences relate to the respective differences in the state of development of
the VP of the two children, when SQ formation set in.

Inga went through a lengthy stage in which all verbs were end-placed
in -INTER utterances (cf. exs. 29 to 31).

1370
December 29, 1973
2;7.9

29. Lunch. I. has finished her glass of
fruit juice. She places her glass in
front of the bottle, requesting more.
    I.: ˡᵖiç nɪç ˋmeᵉ‿hɑptˆ
       "Ich habe nichts mehr."
       ("I don't have any-
       thing left.")

1391
January 3, 1974
2;7.14

30. The family hamster, called Nagi,
has died unexpectedly.
    I.: ˡnɑgi ˋtʰot‿ʔιθ
       "Nagi ist tot."
       ("Nagi is dead.")

1512
February 5, 1974
2;8.16

31. F. has just returned from the university.
    I. (to F.): ˡhɛnιŋ tu ˄ʔuni‿vɑ
       "Henning, du warst (in
       der) Universität."
       ("Henning, you were
       [at the] university.")

Lars also produced some utterances like examples 29 to 31, but they were never numerous. I suspect that he passed through this stage of his VP-development rather quickly and that he was essentially past it when type IIIb should have become productive. Hence, he apparently went on to type IIIc.

Another point of interest concerns the relationship between the interrogative pronouns and types IIIa, b, and c. With both children type IIIa evolved around the locative *wo* long before any other interrogative pronoun was acquired. Similarly, type IIIb, though only fully attested in Inga's speech, first appeared with *wo*. Type IIIc, however, was first recorded from both children in a question formed with *wer* 'who' (cf. ex. 26 from Inga and ex. 32 from Lars.)

780
July 9, 1971
2;1.19

32. Lars is demonstrating his gymnastic abilities by swinging his legs around. He addresses his amused child audience.

L.: ˡvɛə ˈkʰan‿taθ
"Wer kann das?"
("Who can [do] this?")

It is not clear, however, whether examples 26 and 32 attest to truly productive patterns at that time. The issue of their productivity is taken up under types IVb and IVc. Here I will go only so far as to suggest that at least type IIIc need not arise via *wo*. This is probably so because of the semantics of these phenomena and, very likely, because of certain cognitive aspects relating to this problem. The details are not known.

Lastly, it is quite clear from my data that the children treat the interrogative pronouns as a set when they acquire them. Thus, once the placement of the verbs has been mastered at stage IIIc, all subsequent interrogative pronouns are used in full accord with the basic process of this stage. I have found no examples with nonadult-like verb placement in SQ involving interrogative pronouns acquired subsequent to stage IIIc.

I have not touched on the rise of adult-like verb placement in WOQ (i.e., +INTER inversion). In adult German, this placement is closely linked to other -INTER types of inversion. This requires a detailed study of its own, which has not yet been completed. My impression so far is that +INTER inversion occurs first with pronounless questions (i.e., WOQ).

Stage IV. Developmental sequence of interrogative pronouns. The overall developmental sequence for the interrogative pronouns is not the same for both children if the pronouns are lined up one after the other. Nor is it the same cross-culturally, as will be seen in section 4. There, however, it appears that there is a developmental sequence if it is arranged as a function of the formal question types. Moreover, there are conspicuous developments which are internal to the development of the individual pronouns. I shall therefore summarize some of them individually and then compile their overall developmental sequence for the early stages of development.

IVa. wo. The first interrogative pronoun to be acquired by either child was *wo.* (For details, recall stages Ib and IIb.) Semantically, *wo* at first signals stative location. But, as indicated above, there were some overgeneralizations with the intentions of "where to" and "where from". It may be that the "where from" type is prior to the "where to" type. The evidence for this assumption, however, is weak. Furthermore, there was clear evidence only from Inga.

IVb. was. It is not clear from the speech of either Inga or Lars whether *was* or *wer* was used productively first, in spite of the fact that there are some instances of *wer* before *was.*

In adult German there are, apart from numerous stereotypes, four major uses of *was*:

33a. Inanimate subject to main verbs:
"Was liegt dort?" "Ein Apfel."
("What lies [i.e., is] there?" "An apple.")

33b. Inanimate object to main verbs:
"Was siehtst du?" "Einen Apfel."
("What do you see?" "An apple.")

33c. Verbal action:
"Was machst du?" "(Ich) Bau(e)."
("What are you doing?" "[I am] Building [something].")

33d. Identification in equational constructions:
"Was ist das?" "Ein Apfel."
("What is this?" "An apple.")

The use exemplified under 33a was attested conspicuously later than the other three uses (cf., in Inga's speech, exs. 34 to 36).

1750
April 11, 1974
2;10.21

34. Supper. The family is discussing the big event of the day: a visit to the zoo. For a little while I. was being asked what she liked best about it, what she had seen, and so on. Now

she reverses the procedure and puts the questions herself.

I.: ˡmami vaθ ˋnɔχ ˍviᵊ ˊðet
"Mami, was (haben) wir noch gesehen?"
("Mommy, what else did we see?")

1762
April 13, 1974
2;10.23

35. F. is running about the room in search of the cord for his microphone.

I.: ˡhɛnɪŋk vaθ ˋðuχ ˌθu
"Henning, was suchst du?"
("Henning, what are you looking for?")

1746
April 11, 1974
2;10.21

36. At the zoo. We had just seen a type of nondomesticated horse. Moving on to the next exhibit, I. is again confronted with horses, though of a different type.

I.: mami ʔɒn vaθ ʔɪθ tɛθ
"Mami, und was ist das?"
("Mommy, and what is this?")

M. does not react.

I.: mami ʔɒn vaθ ʔɪθ tɛθ
"Mami, und was ist das?"
("Mommy, and what is this?")

At first, the morphological variability exemplified in 33d is limited to the children's equivalent for adult *das*. It takes a little while before adult nouns proper commute with *das*. (For the subject-type in 33a, cf. ex. 37 from Inga).

1795
April 29, 1974
1;11.9

37. Bedtime. I. and F. are playing with the tape recorder. There is a sudden humming when F. sets the recorder to rewind.

I.: ˡhɛnɪk vaθ ˋɪŋ ˊtɔᵊt
"Henning, was singt dort?"
("Henning, what is singing there?")

I.'s exact intention was not quite clear.

With Lars the verbal subject-type exemplified in 33a first occurred after *wer* was in productive use.

Overgeneralizations were noted: *was* instead of adult *wonach* (as required by adult *sehen* and *gucken*) and instead of adult *woher* or *von wem* (as required by *kommen*).

IVc. wer. For the purpose of this article, I distinguish two types of constructions in adult German:

> 38a. Equational:
> "Wer ist das?" "Andi."
> ("Who is this?" "Andy.")

> 38b. Nonequational:
> "Wer kann das?" "Andi."
> ("Who can do this?" "Andy.")

With both children subtype 38a occurred decidedly later than subtype 38b. Note example 39, which is the first instance of *wer* from Inga. This example is an isolated one. The real onset of productivity occurs with example 26.

1634
March 3, 1974
2;8.11

39. F. is preparing the car to go on holiday. I. walks up to F. and points to the front seat.

> I.: ˈveə ˇtɪnə
> "Wer (soll da) drinnen (sitzen)?"
> ("Who is to sit there?)"

For the equational subtype 38a, see example 40 from Inga.

1876
May 21, 1974
3;0.1

40. I. looks into the paper while M. is reading it.

> I.: ˈvɛºθ ˈkʰlaɪna/ ˈtu
> "Wer ist kleiner? Du?"
> ("Who is smaller? You?")

> F.: "Was sagst du, Muschi?"
> ("What did you say, Muschi?")

> I.: ˈvɛº θ ˈkʰlaina
> "Wer ist kleiner?"
> ("Who is smaller?")

Overgeneralizations included *wer* instead of adult *von wem* (*kaufen* 'buy'), and, quite frequently, *wem* (*gehören* 'belong to') or *wie* (*heissen* 'be called').

IVd. wie. Both children acquired *wie* 'how' after *wer/was.*

Adult German has two major uses for this construction:

> 41a. Attributive:
> "Wie alt bist du?" "Zehn."
> ("How old are you?" "Ten.")

> 41b. Nonattributive:
> "Wie heißt du?" "Lars."
> ("How are you called [=What's your name]?" "Lars.")
> "Wie geht das?" "So."
> ("How does it work?" "Like this.")

Both children used subtype 41a productively before subtype 41b (see exs. 42 and 43 from Ingas' speech).

2093
July 18, 1974
3;1.26

42. M. is having a long telephone conversation.
F. (to I.): "Frag Mama mal, wie lange sie noch telefonieren will."
("Ask Mom how long she's going to stay on the telephone.")
I. walks up to M.
I.: mama vi laŋə vιθ tu tɛn teləfiᵊn
"Mama, wie lange willst du denn telefonieren?"
(Mom, how long do you want to stay on the telephone?")

1786
April 24, 1974
2;11.4

43. I. has climbed to the top of a climbing pole.
I.: ˈmami/ˈvi kʰəm iç ʁɑnta
"Mami, wie komm ich runter?"
("Mommy, how do I get down?")

I have noticed one type of overgeneralization: both children use *wie* for adult *wieviel* (*kosten*). There are further developments relating to the various uses of *wie* in connection with different verbs, like *Wie heißt du* "What's your name?" and *Wie groß bist du* "How tall are you?"

IVe. Other interrogative pronouns. There are three highlights in the development of the remaining pronouns. First, they are not used by the two children productively in the same one-after-the-other order. Second, the development of individual pronouns is quite close to adult usage, except for that of *wen* and *wem*. Before *wem* was used productively, the children employed *wen* instead. Third, Inga used the nonattributive *welch* before the attributive one. With Lars the sequence was reversed.

The overall sequence is included in tables 1 and 2 without further comment. For the purposes of this article, I restrict myself to giving only some of the initial stages.

In table 2, *warum* 'why' has not been listed at all. In the spontaneous notes on Lars's speech, I have a few instances which precede the appearance of *wann* 'when'. They are suspect, however, in that I cannot decide whether they are stereotypes or truly productive. The tapes which I have cross-checked were not conclusive either.

3.2.3 Other studies. Except for two points, neither the older diary-type studies on the acquisition of German[4] nor the more recent one by Grimm (1973) provide any evidence that Lars and Inga went through developmental sequences which are not characteristic of the acquisition of German. It must be mentioned, though, that the studies just cited are highly fragmentary and fraught with methodological weaknesses.

One exception concerns the position of interrogative pronouns in type IIb and the other, the rise of inversion in pronounless questions which are semantically equivalent to adult SQ. Stern & Stern 1907, p. 213, cite examples 44 and 45 for their daughter Hilde:

1;9
44. 'Apfe wo.'
    "Where (is the) apple?"

45. 'Natz (=Schere) wo?'
    "Where (are the) scissors?"

There are no data enabling one to decide whether these examples are variants of structures with *wo* in initial position. Hilde's brother seems to have used his form for *wo* in initial position. But Stern and Stern list very few examples for either child. In view of the comparative evidence from other languages (see sec. 4), I think it not at all unlikely that both positional types should occur in German at stage IIb.

TABLE 1. OVERALL DEVELOPMENTAL SEQUENCE OF INTERROGATIVE PRONOUNS.
INGA: GERMAN

Date	Child Form	Child Intention	Adult Form	Productivity
December 16, 1972 1; 6.22	vo	Stative Location	wo	Full
October 15, 1973 2; 4.20	vo	Direction from source		Probably full
November 12, 1973 2; 5.22	vohın~ vo...hin	Direction to	wohin wo...hin	None
February 17, 1974 2; 8.28	vaθ	Identification	was	Weak
March 3, 1974 2; 9.11	vɛ°	Identification	wer	Unclear
March 30, 1974 2; 10.10	vɛ°	Identification Nonequational	wer	Probably full
Approximately April 1, 1974 2; 10.12	vo	Direction to		Full
April 9, 1974 2; 10.20	vaθ	Identification	was	Full
April 13, 1974 2; 10.24	vi	Modification	wie	Full
April 13, 1974 2; 10.24	vɛıçə	Choice Nonattributive	welch	Full
April 14, 1974 2; 10.25	viяom	Not clear	warum	Full
April 24, 1974 2; 11.4	van	Time	wann	Full

TABLE 2. OVERALL DEVELOPMENTAL SEQUENCE OF INTERROGATIVE PRONOUNS.
LARS: GERMAN

Date	Child Form	Child Intention	Adult Form	Productivity
March 11, 1971 1; 9.17	vo ~ vuθ ~ voθa ~ voða	Stative location	wo	Full
July 9, 1971 2; 1.19	vɛ°	Identification	wer	Unclear
July 15, 1971 2; 1.25	vaθ	Identification	was	Full
July 21, 1971 2; 1.30	vɛ°	Identification Nonequational		Full
September 10, 1971 2; 3.19	vi	Modification Attributive	wie	Full
October 1, 1971 2; 4.9		Nonattributive		Full
October 11, 1971 2; 4.19	vɛ°	Identification Equational	wer	Full
October 16, 1971 2; 4.24	van	Time	wann	Full

The second point concerns the early use of IQ or pronounless WOQ as INQ. Stern and Stern report the following examples for their daughter Hilde (1907, p. 30 and p. 191):

1;6		46.	das hier "(Was ist) das hier?" ("What is this here?")
1;6		47.	das is "(Weißt du, was) das ist?" ("Do you know what this is?")
1;6		48.	is'n das "(Was) ist denn das?" ("What is this, then?")
1;6		49.	das? das? "(Was ist) das?" ("What is this?")
1;6.15		50.	is'n das hier [no gloss]
1;8		51.	is'n da "(Wer) ist denn da?" ("Who is there, then?")

Examples 46 to 51 are all INQ. Examples 46, 47, and 49 are purely IQ, however, while examples 48, 50, and 51 show reflexes of adult inversion. They differ from adult INQ, though, in that they do not contain an interrogative pronoun. Utterances like example 48 are also reported by Stern & Stern 1907 for Lindner's daughter at the age of 1;8 years, and utterances like example 51 for Neugebauer's son at the age of 1;7 and for the Sterns' son at the same age (p. 191). Additional evidence can be found in Scupin/Scupin 1907, 1910.

The difficulty with all these data is that no intonation is given, that the productivity cannot be fully assessed, and that the range of intentions cannot be determined. Above all, however, it is not clear whether such utterances were in use before or after SQ.

With the Stern's son, wo-questions appeared at 1;4 years of age (1907, p. 88). Thus, they apparently antedate utterances like those in examples 46 through 51. The same seems to hold for the Scupins' son. Moreover, with both Bubi Scupin and the Sterns' son, the use of pronounless WOQ to signal INQ preceded its use as YNQ.

As for the intentional range of such WOQ used as INQ, the Scupins report that Bubi used them to signal locative 'wo', verbal action 'was', verbal object 'was', equational-identificational 'was', and identificational (probably agential) 'wer'. There are some parallels to this range from Swedish (see sec. 4.3). Nevertheless, since such early uses of WOQ as INQ are not attested in my data above, I prefer not to pursue this issue further. Future research on German should investigate this matter more fully.

4 Developmental sequences for other languages

4.1 Bulgarian

4.1.1 Adult Bulgarian. Bulgarian has SQ and iQ. The IQ are YNQ, and the SQ may be Qpron or Qpart. The Qpart involves -li, which can be attached to a variety of constituents. Also, Qpart are YNQ. Some of the + INTER pronouns are inflected for gender, number, and case.[5]

4.1.2 Child Bulgarian. For the developmental sequences in child Bulgarian. I rely on Gheorgov 1908. He has described certain aspects of the speech development of his two sons, dealing primarily with their speech production rather than with their comprehension. Gheorgov seems to have followed the day-by-day diary type of longitudinal study. The data for the development of his two sons is quite similar to my data from German. Unfortunately, however, he does not treat the holophrastic stage; his study begins at may stage II.

Gheorgov's data can be used for inferences about IQ, Qpart, early locative questions, and the developmental sequence of +INTER pronouns. In quoting him, I shall leave his transcriptions unchanged, since it is not clear to me exactly what they indicate. His German glosses are translated into English.

Stage II. Multiword questions.

IIa. IQ. Among types IIa and IIb, Gheorgov gives instances comparable to type IIa_1: IYNQ and IIb_1: SQ "stative location". With his second child (ch. II) the first instance of type IIa_1 precedes type IIb_1:

633
1;8.24

52. The child is pointing towards water.
     ch. II: da i kâm
       "I want water."
     father: vodáta e fa
       "The water is beh (=bad)."
     ch. II. dáta fa
       "Water beh?" (1908, p. 342)

The child uttered the question in example 52 with an indisputable interrogative intonation *(mit deutlichem Frageton)*.

With the first child (ch. 1) the first record of a type IIb SQ in Gheorgov's report antedates the first instance of type IIa. It is better not to make too much of this, however, since Gheorgov offers no data on stage I for these children. Moreover, he does not deal with the problem of the relative priority of IYNQ, SQ, and so on.

Nevertheless, some points are worth keeping in mind. First, before the children acquired -*li*, the segmental marker for YNQ, their YNQ were all IQ. I cannot tell whether they also had a special interrogative word order since Gheorgov is silent on this point. I take his remarks on page 410 and elsewhere to imply that the intonation is the only marker for this type of question. Second, he does not mention overgeneralizations of type IIa$_2$, nor does he deal with this issue at all.

IIb.

IIb$_1$. With each child the first instances in Gheorgov's report on SQ are all type IIb$_1$ stative location. Ch. I's form is given as *kamo* ~ *kam*. Gheorgov suggests that it reflects adult *kamo*, the more colloquial form to express stative location in adult Bulgarian. Ch. II used *de*, which reflects the less colloquial adult *de*.

Both children used two variants positionally. Thus, *kamo/de* could be placed initially or finally. Among the examples offered by Gheorgov, though, the two variants occur only with two-word combinations. There are no instances with type III. I cannot tell whether this is accidental or whether it is developmentally significant since he does not deal explicitly with this point. (See exs. 53 and 54 from ch. I and exs. 55 and 56 from ch. II.) Note that with ch. I prepositioning antedates postpositioning; with ch. II the sequence is reversed.

680 1;10.10	53.	kámo bíto (=kibrita) "Where (are) the matches."
827 2;3.6	54.	čaškata kam (=kámo) "The (little) glass, where (is it)?"
675 1;10.5	55.	lado de "Where (is) Vlado?"
694 1;10.24	56.	de dínat (=edinijat) "Where (is) the one?" (1908, pp. 311, 312, 410, 422)

There is a special problem with utterances like examples 57 and 58 from ch. I and examples 59 and 60 from ch. II, all of which conform superficially fully with adult Bulgarian.

861 2;4.9	57.	kámo go "Where (is) she?"
	58.	kámo sâ "Where are they?"

705	59.	de si
1;11.5		"Where are you (*sg.*)?"
758 and 770	60.	de go
2;0.28		"Where is he?" (1908, pp. 312, 410, 422)

The problem here is to determine the status of *go, sa,* and *si.* In adult Bulgarian *go* is the pronoun indicating the third-person singular masculine. Examples 57 and 60 therefore probably relate to my German type IIb. The forms *sâ* and *si,* however, are verbs in adult Bulgarian. There they indicate different numbers and different persons. Much as in Latin, person need not be indicated through a special free form, as is minimally required, for instance, in German or English. The difficulty is to determine whether the Bulgarian children used such forms as N on account of the adult inflection for person and number or as verbs, disregarding the N-indicating inflection, or whether they used these forms as verbs plus inflection. I leave the point unsettled, because Gheorgov does not discuss it and because I cannot work it out from his limited data. Consequently, I cannot decide whether examples 58 and 59 belong to type IIb or to type IIIa.

IIb₂. Type IIb$_2$ is attested only in ch. II for ‚where to’:

715	61.	de cédnam (= kadé da sedna)
1;11.15		"Where am I to sit down?"
749	62.	de túlite páloto (= kâdé šte túrite)
2;0.19		"Where will you put the coat?"
769	63.	de si idél (= kâdé si chódil)
2;1.9		"Where did you go to?"
808	64.	de fâli go (= kâdé go chvârli)
2;2.17		"Where did you throw it?" (1908, p. 410)

These examples were recorded after the first instances of type IIIa. Nevertheless, they seem to be clear instances of overgeneralization. Moreover, when *kâdé,* which in adult Bulgarian can mean both 'where' and 'where to', eventually appears with ch. I, the only two examples that Gheorgov offers have *kâdé* in the sense of stative location:

859	65.	kadé e Vládo (= kâdé e Vlado)
2;4.7		"Where is Vlado?"
913	66.	ti pak kadé (= kâdé)
2;6.0		béše, na lábota (= rábota)
		"Where have you been again, "at work?" (p. 410)

No evidence for type IIb$_2$ is given for ch. I. Instead, he seems to have used *kâdé* in the sense of 'where to' at a comparable stage of his development:

740   67.   kámo kuča (=kljúča)
2;0.10   kâdé déna (=se déna)
                              "Where (is) the key, where did it go?"

745   68.   kâdé dénal kutíjka
2;0.15   (=kâdé se dénala kutijkata)
                              "Where has the key been taken/moved to?" (1908, p. 312)

The difficulty with examples 61 to 68, however, is in deciding whether they exemplify truly productive stages of development. Gheorgov's data are too fragmentary, and he does not provide much assistance in his discussion either.

Stage III. Incorporation of verbs. As for types IIIa, IIIb, and IIIc, there is only one point about which I feel quite confident: it appears from Gheorgov's data on ch. II that for type III it is the Bulgarian equivalent of German *sein* which is the first verb to be used productively in SQ. Moreover, just as with my German data, it is the stative location of type IIIa in which *e* first appears in SQ. With ch. I the evidence is not clear, because I cannot determine the proper onset of productivity of the various types (see ex. 69 from ch. II).

706   69.   de e kóškata (=kokóškata)
1;11.6   "Where is the hen?" (1908, p. 410)

Stage IV. Developmental sequence of interrogative pronouns. The data are presented for the two children separately in tables 3 and 4. An examination of these tables shows that the overall picture for the developmental sequence of all interrogative pronouns remains unclear, because Gheorgov's data are too fragmentary in many ways. The productivity cannot be assessed in many cases. Some pronouns are not listed, and the number of utterances cited by Gheorgov is low. Nevertheless, a few more general points parallel to the German data clearly emerge.

Whatever the ultimate explanation for the developmental sequence of the interrogative pronouns, one cannot expect to find it in the same superficial one-after-the-other order of appearance. This strengthens the insights derived from my German data. Moreover, the particle *-li* does not appear at the same time in the one-after-the-other developmental sequence of the two boys. There is a close parallel to the internal development of

German *was*. Type 35a (i.e., inanimate subject for main verb) is apparently later than other uses. Unfortunately, because of lack of data, I cannot ascertain the situation for *koj*.

According to Gheorgov, with ch. II *što* 'what' and *ko- ~ kakvó* ousted each other consecutively: *ko* was first modelled on adult *kakvo*; then *ko*

TABLE 3. DEVELOPMENTAL SEQUENCE OF INTERROGATIVE PRONOUNS.
CHILD I: BULGARIAN (Compiled from Gheorgov 1908)

Date in Days	Child Form	Child Intention	Adult Form	Productivity
680	kámo ~ kam	'where'	kamo	Full
733	koj	'who'	koj	None
		id.		
740	kâdé	'where to'	kâdé	Unclear
741	li	'confirmation'	li	Full
769	kakó	'what'	kakvo	Probably full
		id-eq.		
772	kolko	'how many/ how much'	kolko	Unclear
773	što	'what'	što	Probably full
		id-eq.		
777	kakó	'what' obj./verb. action	kakvo	Unclear, perhaps full
805	kakáv	'what kind'	kaʰâv	Unclear, perhaps full
953	što ~ zašto	'why'	zašto	Full
960	koja	'which' attr.	koj-a	Weak

TABLE 4. DEVELOPMENTAL SEQUENCE OF INTERROGATIVE PRONOUNS.
CHILD II: BULGARIAN (Compiled from Gheorgov 1908)

Date in Days	Child Form	Child Intention	Adult Form	Productivity
675	de	'where'	de	Full
703	što	'why'	zašto	Weak, perhaps none
708	ko	unclear 'what' or 'who'	kakvo	Weak
715	de	'where to'	de	Unclear
731	što	'what' object	što	
		id-eq.		Full
742				Full
742	što	'why'	zašto	Full
764	koj	'who'	koj	None
864	li	'confirmation'	li	Full
859	kadé	'where to'	kâdé	Unclear
898	kakvó	'what'	kakvó	Full

was supplanted by *što* modelled on adult *što*; then it, in turn, was supplanted by *kakvó*. However, it is not clear whether this process affected all of the subtypes. Moreover, there are no parallels from ch. I.

4.2 Latvian

4.2.1 Adult Latvian. Latvian is instructive, first, because there is neither a WOQ nor an +INTER word order in any type of question; second, because YNQ can be marked in three ways: by the particle *vai-*, by intonation alone, or by both; and third, because all SQ are Qpron.[6]

4.2.2 Child Latvian. Data for child Latvian are available from Ruke-Dravina 1963. She has done a day-by-day longitudinal study on the speech development of her son Dainis (*DD*) and her daughter Sarma (*SD*) from the very onset of speech. As for question formation, the data are primarily useful for the problem of an overall developmental sequence of the individual interrogative pronouns, for pronounless child questions semantico-intentionally equivalent to SQ in adult Latvian, and for the rise of YNQ as IQ and as SQ. Ruke-Dravina's data are summarized in table 5.

There are some limitations to the data presented in this table. My impression is that Ruke-Dravina collected her data primarily from the viewpoint of conformity of child utterances to adult speech. Thus, she states that the first *kāpēc* questions, as well as the *kad*-questions, were odd in that the children were obviously referring to situations in which adults would not ask why or when:

2;0.28   70. DD's suspenders have become loose. He turns to Ruke-Dravina.
DD: kāpḗc i vajâ
"Why is it/are they loose?"
(1963, p. 71)

Ruke-Dravina suggests that DD is really trying to say "fasten them up again."

71. kad debesis beîȝâs?
4;6.0   "When does the sky end?"
(1963, p. 125)

Unfortunately, Ruke-Dravina provides no analysis of these child intentions. Surely they are not peculiar to Latvian. Child language is full of them. But we sadly lack a systematic study. Furthermore, there is no discussion of, nor data to illustrate, overgeneralizations. I have found only one instance in Ruke-Dravina's data:

3;4.22   72. ku ¹mẹmmẹ iĕtu
"Where will Mama (=you) go?" (1963, p. 120)

TABLE 5. DEVELOPMENTAL SEQUENCE OF INTERROGATIVE PRONOUNS AND THE PARTICLE VAI-. TWO CHILDREN (DD AND SD): LATVIAN (Compiled from Ruke-Dravina 1963)

Section	Child Intention	Child Form and Onset of Productivity		Adult Form
		DD	SD	
§ 176/318	'where'	Ø 2;0.15 ku 2;0.30	Ø not mentioned ku 2;11.17	kur
§ 185	'whom', 'whose'	Ø not mentioned kàm 2;1.9	Ø not mentioned Ø not mentioned	kam (dative of kas)
§ 177/317/360	'what/ who'	Ø 2;0.20 kas 2;4.5	Ø 2;7.28 ka 3;0.16	kas
§ 195/203	'how'	Ø 2;2.27 kâ not given	Ø not mentioned kâ 3;7.29	kâ
§ 178/363	'why'	Ø not mentioned kapēc 2;22.1	Ø not mentioned kapêt' 3;9.7	kāpēc
§ 216/364	'when'	Ø not mentioned kad 2;8.18	Ø not mentioned kad at least 4;6	kad
§ 214/215/319 362	'yes/no'	Ø before 2;6 vaî missed	Ø 2;11.7 vaî 3;8.5	vaı

Notes: Ø: pronounless subtype.
   missed: the subtype was found, but the onset of productivity was missed by Ruke-Dravina.
   not given: the subtype was found, but onset of productivity was not mentioned.

In example 72, *ku* was used in the directional sense of 'where (to)'. The intention 'where from' is not mentioned.

Developmental sequence of interrogative pronouns. As for the overall developmental sequence of the interrogative pronouns, Ruke-Dravina does not provide the sort of analysis which was found to be illuminating for German and Bulgarian. Nevertheless, I am surprised to note how closely DD and SD parallel each other (see table 5). Thus, they both start out with *ku*, probably modelled on *kur*. Most of the examples given by Ruke-Dravina refer to stative location. This accords well with the data on German and Bulgarian.

   Next DD uses *kam*, probably reflecting adult *kam*, which is the inflected dative of *kas*. In the two examples that Ruke-Dravina gives (p. 72), DD asked for the possessor; *kam* is then followed by *kas*, reflecting adult *kas*. For SD *kam* is not mentioned. She has *kas* next after *ku~kur*. Just like the German and Bulgarian children, DD and SD acquire a pronoun which identifies something—object, action, possessor, or the like—after the locative pronoun.

   There remains a difficulty with DD, however. He used *kāpēc* before *kas*. But then he used *kam* before *kāpēc*. Perhaps *kam* took the place of *kas* with regard to semantico-intention. I cannot tell, because Ruke-Dravina neither discusses the issue nor does she give enough examples so that one can determine the full range of usage for DD's *kam*.

Next is *kâ*. With DD the situation is clear. With SD we do not have the onset of productivity. Also, there is some lack of clarity as regards *kâ* 'how' and *cikuos* 'which/what time'.

Caution is advisable in any event. Latvian *kâ*, like German *wie*, may be used to ask for the name of a person (wie heißt du?), the measure of things (wie viel[e]), degree of attributes (wie heiß), and so on. Without further detailed investigations as to the developmental sequence, if any, of these subtypes, one can only say at present that some *kâ*-uses or intentions are acquired after the identificational type. This is in agreement with the German data but only partly with the Bulgarian material. As seen earlier, with child I there were some instances of *kolko* 'how many/much' after the identificational type, barring *-li* for the moment. Yet the degree of productivity of *kolko* was unclear. For child II Gheorgov is silent about the 'how' equivalent(s).

The *kāpēc*-questions are produced next, followed by *kad*-questions. As discussed above, both question types tend to be odd when measured against what adults consider to be adequate questions about cause and time. This applies particularly when cause questions or time questions, or both, appear relatively early in the development of a child. One is tempted to suggest that at least the questions employing whatever in the adult language is the temporal pronoun may be related to the peculiar time-space relationship which Clark 1971 found in the acquisition of the English prepositions *before* and *after*.

The segmental marker for yes/no questions, *vai-*, is the last interrogative marker to be used by either child. This is so despite the fact that the homophonous conjunction *vai* had already been acquired.

It is difficult to generalize on this matter. The Bulgarian *-li* was employed by child I after the locative pronoun and by child II after the locative, the identificational, and the causal pronoun. It is pointless to make any detailed suggestions as long as we do not have more comparative data. There are too many variables involved. The position of adult *vai-* and adult *-li* is different: *vai-* is preposed and *-li* is postposed. In section 5, I shall tentatively suggest that the confirmatory category is late indeed but relative to the specific—formal—question type.

IQ and SQ. In table 5, I have also listed the onset of IQ in terms of chil intentions. The semantic range, just as in Swedish (see sec. 4.32), is much wider than that in my German data. However, not every SQ is matched semantically by an IQ. For some types there is no mention at all—whether intentionally or not, I cannot tell. For *vai-* it is clear that the type was productive, but the onset of productivity is not given.

Barring those instances in which Ruke-Dravina does not provide any information, the Ø-types, (i.e., the IQ-variants) precede the SQ-variants. Moreover, except for *vai-~Ø-vai-*, the relative chronology among the IQ variants mirrors that for the respective SQ.

The only exceptions to the above formulation are the two *vai*-types. For SD, Ruke-Dravina states that the Ø-variant occurred since 2;11.7 years of age; with DD, before 2;6 years of age. I am not sure whether this implies that YNQ as either IQ or SQ first occurred after INQ of either the SQ (locative) or the IQ (locative) type.

DD's first questions were IQ (locative). He used to say [e] with a "questioning tone" (*fragendem Ton*) when asking for a location (*Ortsfragen*). For SD, there are no data on this point.

4.3 Swedish

4.3.1 Adult Swedish. In adult Swedish YNQ are either IQ or WOQ. INQ are Qpron with subject-verb inversion.

4.3.2 Child Swedish. Lange & Larsson 1973 have studied the speech development of a girl named Embla. The data were collected in thirty-minute interviews once every two weeks.

The data are fragmentary, and the types of utterances obtained in the various sessions are biased by the fact that the activities during each session were not varied much. Furthermore, the report ends when Embla was 2;1 years of age. The number of questions obtained was so small that such topics as productivity and developmental sequences cannot be tackled in any profound way.

Lange's and Larsson's study is interesting, however, because with pronounless questions they found a fairly wide range of semantic intentions which in adult Swedish are signalled through SQ. Moreover, most of these pronounless questions had reflexes of adult inversion.

The first question was *heja*. Lange and Larsson are at a loss to determine the adult model: *heja* does not exist as a question term in adult Swedish. But Robert Hvitfeldt (personal communication) suggests to me that the children's model may have been *hej*, which functions as an attention-getter. In any event, Embla used *heja* most often to ask 'what is this/that'. Lange and Larsson do not say what else it was intended to mean.

Subsequently, Lange and Larsson have registered only three SQ:

451	73.	var är dörr (E2)[7]
		"Where is (the) door?"
206	74.	vad är det (E7, E9, and E10)
		"What is it/that?"
214	75.	/heja/ vad gjorde missen? (E10)
		"Heja/ what did the pussy cat (do)?"

Questions without an interrogative pronoun are more numerous. Semantically, there are YNQ, and INQ. For either semantic type the child had verb and subject inverted, if there was a verb. If there was no verb, then there was no inversion. Uninverted verbless utterances are cited in examples 76 to 78.

200   76.   stora nallen (E7)
                             "(Is this) the big teddy bear?/(Is)
                             the teddy bear big?"

208   77.   och det (E8, 2 ex.; E96, 4 ex.)
                             "And (what is) that?"

218   78.   andra ögat (E7)
                             "(Where is) the other eye?"

Inverted questions follow (note the semantic range of these questions).

202   79.   är det dörren (E7)
                             "Is that the door?"

205   80.   kan den blunda den? (E10)
                             "Can it shut its eyes?"

207   81.   är det (E8)
                             "(What) is it/that?"

                       82.   heter det (E9, 1 ex.; E10, 7 ex.)
                             "(What) is it/that called?"

215   83.   gjorde barnet (E8)
                             "(What) did the child (do)?"

217   84.   sa Ragnhild nu, mama (E10).
                             "(What) did Ragnhild say now,
                             mother?"

It seems advisable not to attempt to establish any relative priority of types in view of the limitations of Lange's and Larsson's data. What their study convincingly shows is that children may use pronounless structures to express what in the adult language would require a segmental marker. In particular, the semantic range of this phenomenon is quite large in their material. Instances given here include the types YN (exs. 79 and 80), identificational-equational (ex. 81), identificational (naming) involving *heter* (ex. 82), verbal action (ex. 83), and object to main verb (ex. 84). This is a much wider range than I have found in my German data. But Ruke-Dravina 1963 has reported comparable facts about Latvian (see sec. 4.2.2).

Moreover, all of these (Swedish) pronounless questions have inversion. There is no substantial parallel to this feature from the other languages discussed in this article, except for the few German instances (see sec. 3.2).

4.4 English

4.4.1 Adult English. In adult English YNQ are IQ or WOQ. There are no SYNQ. The INQ are SQ; the SQ are Qpron with subject-verb inversion.

4.4.2 Child English. Data for child English are available from the projects at Harvard and at Berkeley. My chief source for the three Harvard children is Klima & Bellugi 1966. More or less the same data are also discussed by Brown 1968 and McNeill 1970a. For the Berkeley children I rely on Miller's short summary on five children (1973).

The data on the Harvard children were collected at regular intervals. No child intentions, no semantics, are available to me. The data for the children are pooled so that individual differences, if any, cannot be identified. No developmental sequence for the interrogative pronouns has been published. Klima and Bellugi-Klima, as well as both Brown and McNeill, are primarily interested in transformations and related problems. Hence, their data are illuminating only for some aspects of my stages II and III.

Basically the same data-collecting procedures were adopted for the Berkeley children. For these children, too, no semantics are available to me. Moreover, the published information on the acquisition of questions with these children is extremely fragmentary. However, the overall picture which emerges, if the data from the two projects are taken together, is much as I would expect because of what has been reported for other languages.

Neither project provides data on the holophrastic stage. They set in at my stage II. For this stage Miller reports that with all five children (non-inverted) IQ preceded (inverted) WOQ. He mentions only YNQ. Moreover, SQ without inversion were in use before WOQ. In the Harvard and Berkeley data which have come to my attention, these SQ were Qpron with preposed +INTER pronouns. Brown was surprised not to find them postposed (1968).

Unfortunately, the developmental sequence of SQ over IQ or vice versa cannot be ascertained because of lack of data on the holophrastic stage. As for the developmental sequence for the acquisition of the interrogative pronouns, Miller reports that questions with *where* and *what* were in productive use long before any other interrogative pronouns were used.

In order to clarify and illustrate the points above, I shall discuss some of the child utterances provided by Klima and Bellugi-Klima. They distinguish three periods (their examples follow).

Period 1   85. Fraser water?
                      86. I ride train?
                      87. No ear?
                      88. Ball go?
                      89. Who that?

90. Why?
91. What'(s) that?
92. What cowboy doing?
93. Where Ann pencil?
94. Where horse go?

Period 2   95. See my doggie?
96. That black too?
97. Mom pinch finger?
98. This can't write a flower?
99. Where my mitten?
100. Where me sleep?
101. What soldier marching?
102. Why you wake me up?
103. Why not he eat?

Period 3   104. Oh, did I caught it?
105. Will you help me?
106. Can I have a piece of paper?
107. Can't you work this thing?
108. Where small trailer he should pull?
109. What he can ride in?
110. Why Kitty can't stand up?
111. How he can be a doctor?

Period 1 contains YNQ and Qpron. The YNQ are all type IIa IQ without inversion (see exs. 85 to 88). The Qpron of period 1 are either type IIb or early type III. The status of the verbs as in examples 92 to 94 is not clear. Klima and Bellugi-Klima suspect that the relationship between the verb and the interrogative pronoun is not yet that of grammatical object or adverb. In the absence of further details, these utterances cannot be interpreted properly.

Period 2 shows the influex of verbs. The YNQ are still IQ without inversion (see exs. 95 to 98). They are type IIa. The Qpron are now definitely type III with more or less—I suspect—appropriate grammatical relationships between verb and interrogative pronoun. But with these Qpron, too, there is no inversion yet. As far as the position of the various constituents after the interrogative pronoun is concerned, this stage seems to be peculiar to English. Developmentally, such utterances probably relate to the German type IIIb as a stage preceding proper adult-like usage.

The YNQ of period 3 (see exs. 104 to 107) now have adult-like inversion. The Qpron, however, do not (see exs. 108 to 111). Though Klima and Bellugi-Klima do not treat the development subsequent to period 3, I take it that the next major stage will be the rise of adult-like inversion in Qpron.

Unfortunately, apart from the points noted above, many issues remain in the dark: What is the developmental sequence with the verbs that appear in SQ? Or with the verbs and N/NP that appear in inversion? Are there any overgeneralizations in either Qpron or IQ? Are there instances in which main verbs are inverted? Or where the dummy *do* is present in non-inverted utterances, as in example 112? (I made up ex. 112 by analogy and in contrast with ex. 113, which was actually recorded.)

112. *What you did doed?
113. What did you doed?

Nevertheless, in summary, it seems that the development of YNQ is much as one would expect on the basis of the German data. The development of SQ suggests that the peculiarities of verb placement depend on the structure of English. Unfortunately, it cannot be decided what determines this development until the problems hinted at above have been investigated more fully.

4.5 Finnish

4.5.1 Adult Finnish. The data on the acquisition of adult Finnish are crucial for this article because adult Finnish is unique among those languages for which acquisition data are available to me, in the following respect. According to Bowerman, it has neither IQ nor any +INTER intonation associated with any question type. All questions, whether YNQ or INQ, are SQ. The INQ are formed by preposing interrogative morphemes to the rest of a sentence. These interrogative pronouns are inflected for a considerable number of categories. The YNQ are formed by attaching the interrogative particle *-ko ~ -kö* to the verb and placing the whole word in sentence-initial position. For special emphasis the particle can also be attached to other words. This word is then placed sentence-initially. There is no special +INTER word order apart from the above (Bowerman 1973, pp. 105 and 235 f.).

4.5.2 Child Finnish. I know of only two studies on the acquisition of Finnish. I have already cited the one by Bowerman, who has recorded two children: a boy (Seppo) and a girl (Rina). Data collection began at 1;10.15 and 2;0 years of age, respectively. In general, Bowerman made thirty-minute tape recordings once a week for eight months with Seppo and for some two years with Rina. The children came from different families which at that time were living near Boston, where their fathers were doing graduate work. It is not known to what extent their Finnish was influenced by the English that they occasionally heard (p. 16). The second study is an unfinished one by Argoff which is quoted in passing by Slobin 1970.

Neither study has—so far at least—reported on the holophrastic stages Ia and Ib. Moreover, the published material (i.e. Bowerman) offers very little on the acquisition of questions: it is limited to other aspects of early syntax. Regrettably, therefore, there are no data on the developmental sequence of the interrogative markers, in particular on *-ko~-kö*. Bowerman mentions two facts, however, which are highly relevant to this article. During the early part of her work, neither Seppo nor Rina asked YNQ, and they did not use IQ either (p. 110). Slobin reports the same findings for the Argoff data (personal communication). Moreover, the first questions that I can find in Bowerman's data for both Seppo and Rina are SQ; more precisely, they are locative. Rina used only two questions. They seem to reflect adult equational structures with a predicate N; apparently, they are stative location.

114.　missä kynä
　　　　"Where pen?"

115.　missä keksi
　　　　"Where cracker?" (App. M (12),
　　　　p. 279)

For Seppo there are eleven questions. They are all locative, though I cannot tell whether all of them are stative location. The majority reflect adult equational structures with a predicate N, as in examples 116 and 117.

116.　missä loikka
　　　　"Where Volkswagen?"

117.　missä kassi?
　　　　"Where bag?" (App. I (14), p. 265)

Three of Seppo's questions, however, contain adult verbs like those in examples 118 and 119.

118.　missä vetää
　　　　"Where pulls?"

119.　missä ui
　　　　"Where swims?"

Seppo also used one question in which *missä* was placed finally:

120.　auto missä
　　　　"Car where?" (App. K (1), p. 268)

Bowerman suggests that example 120 is probably a "mistake", but she does not explain why she thinks so. In fact, there is comparable evidence from

German (see sec. 3.2) and from Bulgarian (see sec. 4.12) that children may place interrogative pronouns either in front or at the end of a construction.

Though the Finnish data are quite limited, they are nonetheless highly illuminating. Apparently, children will acquire IQ as their first type of question only when the adult language also has this type, as is the case for German, English, Latvian, and Swedish. If these conditions are not met, the children's first questions seem to be those that reflect interrogative pronouns which in the adult language are themselves free forms (i.e., independent words, like Finn *missä*, G *wo*, Bulg *de~kamo*, E *where*, etc.). There is also the possibility that adult word order may be involved as an explanation. Bulg *-li* and Finn *-ko~-kö* are noninitial. G *wo*, E *where*, and so on, are initial most of the time. But so is Latvian *vai-*, which is nevertheless acquired after other interrogatives. The Finnish material, fragmentary and limited as it is, clearly shows that the peculiar developmental sequence in the acquisition of questions cannot be explained by exclusive reference to cognitive maturation in terms of concept formation. There are overriding restrictions imposed by the formal structure of the language to be acquired.

5 A generalized developmental sequence for the acquisition of questions

The data reviewed in sections 3 and 4 strongly suggest that any attempt to devise a general hypothesis about the developmental sequence of the acquisition of questions has to be based first and foremost on the formal properties of the linguistic devices which are used in, or provided by, the language to be acquired. First, there is the situation exemplified by Finnish. Here YNQ are acquired neither first nor early, and they are not signalled by IQ in the adult language. The situation is different in Bulgarian, German, English, and so on, where IQ signal YNQ.

Second, YNQ were acquired late in Latvian, although the interrogative particle *vai-* is front-positioned in adult Latvian, just like the +INTER pronouns. On the other hand, Bulg *-li*, far from being acquired at the same time in the two children's overall superficial developmental sequence of segmental interrogative markers, was nevertheless not acquired as late as Latvian *vai-*. It will be difficult to explain all this by simply referring to (cognitive) concept formation. Consequently, I shall start from the linguistic structure proper—more specifically, from a typology of such structures.

5.1 Stage I. Holophrastic questions. Those reports which include the holophrastic period trace the beginning of question formation to this period. There are different developmental sequences depending on the formal devices employed in the language to be acquired. One common denominator for this stage, however, is that children first use items in their questions which in the adult model are free forms (i.e. words). Inflectional marking (i.e. using bound forms) becomes productive decidedly later.

Ia. IQ. In languages which have IQ, the first child-questions are IQ. As for the semantics of these first IQ, Ruke-Dravina's article is the only source known to me in which, semantically, the first IQ were not YNQ. In her study location questions developed first (see sec. 4.22). In all the adult languages reviewed above, IQ are YNQ. Hence, one cannot really raise the issue of priority of semantic subtypes within IQ since the adult language offers nothing to choose between.

Subsequently, there may be some nonadult-like instances of what might turn out to be overgeneralizations (i.e. IQ which are semantically locative, identificational, or other). We do not have enough data yet to go into this matter very deeply; that is, we cannot yet determine the semantic range of such overgeneralizations. Nor can we specify the time of onset: whether some or all may be holophrastic, or whether some do not occur prior to the two-word stage. Above all, it is not yet clear how such overgeneralizations link up with the subsequent development of other question types (e.g. locative SQ). In languages which do not have IQ (or interrogative intonation?), children do not develop IQ. Instead, here the first questions to appear are SQ, as summarized in the paragraphs which follow.

Ib. SQ. We have data on two types of SQ: (1) Qpart, as attested by Bulgarian *-li* and Finnish *-ko ∼ -kö*, and (2) Qpron, as attested by the interrogative pronouns of German, Latvian, English, and so on. The data in sections 3. and 4. suggest that the second type is acquired first—or, more precisely, that, if holophrastic SQ occur, they are modelled on the adult interrogative pronouns. No child is on record who has used Qpart productively at stage I (see, e.g., the evidence from Finnish and Bulgarian).

It is not clear at present what is the crucial property to cause the priority of Qpron over Qpart. For evidence consider Latvian *vai-* as against Finn *-ko ∼ -kö* in conjunction with Bulg *-li*. Note, first, that *-li, -ko ∼ -kö*, and *vai-* signal YNQ. Second, *-li, ko ∼ -kö*, and *vai-* are particles. Third, *vai-* is preposed, like the Latvian interrogative pronouns, whereas *-li* and *-ko ∼ -kö* are postposed. It is not clear from the presently available data whether the crucial property is position or free versus bound form, though one would opt for the latter explanation on other grounds. It is quite evident, however, that semantics is not crucial here. Although Latvian *vai-* was acquired late by both Latvian children, *-li* was mastered relatively early in Bulgarian. Both *vai-* and *-li* are—at least to some extent—optional in the adult languages, and all four children used IQ before SQ to signal YNQ.

Semantically, the first Ib Qpron are those marking stative location. I have no clear instances on record of overgeneralizations for stage I. Overgeneralizations, however, do occur, at least from the two-word stage on.

Before I proceed to multiword questions, I shall discuss the developmental sequence for segmental interrogative markers.

5.2 Developmental sequence for segmental interrogative markers. It strikes me that, if there is to be a developmental sequence for segmental interrogative markers, then this sequence is likely to be specific to the various formal question types as set out in this article and that, consequently, it makes no sense to set up an overall developmental sequence across different question types (see the crucial data for YNQ at the beginning of sec. 5). The only formal question type for which the issue of developmental ordering of items can be raised is Qpron. With IQ and Qpart the adult languages for which acquisition data are available provide nothing for children to choose between.

It seems that the interrogative pronouns are acquired in such a way that a more general item in the adult paradigm is mastered first and that there is not necessarily a cross-relationship to other paradigms in the subsequent developments emanating from these general items. Among the languages reviewed above, Latvian is the most illuminating on this issue. There are relatively few interrogative pronouns with relatively few categories marked overtly. For instance, *kas* has both personal and nonpersonal reference. In contrast, German and English have the personal *wer* and *who*, respectively, as against the nonpersonal *was* and *what*. Likewise, *kur* in Latvian is locative in both the directional and the nondirectional sense. German and Bulgarian have nondirectional *wo, de~kamo*, and *kâdé*, as against directional *wohin, woher*, and *kâdé*, respectively.

Very tentatively, I suggest the sequence given below.

I. Location. G *wo*, E *where*, Latvian *kur*, Bulg *de~kamo*, and Finn *missä*.

  A. Stative:
    At first location is stative.

  B. Directional:
    Subsequently, location may be differentiated directionally as 'where to, where from'. These may first be expressed through the item used for stative location, either via overgeneralization, if the language has separate directional items (cf. Inga's questions in sec. 3.22 and child II of Gheorgov in sec. 4.12), or through the appropriate item (cf. child I of Gheorgov, who used *kâdé*, and the occasional use of *wohin* by Inga).

II. Identification. G *was, wer*; E *what, who;* Bulg *kakvo, što;* and Latvian *kas, kam*.

  A. Nonpersonal.
    The first items tend not to be differentiated according to whether they are personal or nonpersonal, even if the adult language has this distinction. The forms which are first used productively tend to be

modelled on the adult form not limited to the personal (e.g., **G** *was*, **E** *what*, and Bulg *što, kakvo*). But, as we have seen, there were early, though probably unproductive, instances of the personal item in both German and English.

We have no conclusive data on the developmental sequence for case-inflected interrogative pronouns. In Latvian, *kam* preceded *kas* in DD's speech. Unfortunately, I cannot ascertain the productivity of this usage.

B. Personal.

The item with personal reference tends to come into productive use later (e.g., **G** *wer*, **E** *who*, and Bulg *koj*). The Bulgarian data suggest that numerous other items may be acquired before the personal pronoun appears.

III. Modality. **G** *wie* and Latvian *kâ*.

The term *modality* is used here in a very vague sense on purpose. What these items seem to have in common is the fact that they indicate the modality of an action (how is it done?), the degree-modality of an attribute (how hot?), and the like. In any event, the data from German and Latvian prompt me to capture these *how*-pronouns under one heading. Because of lack of data, I refrain from subgrouping them further.

IV. Causality. **G** *warum*, Latvian *kāpēc*, and Bulg *zašto*.

It remains to clarify the peculiar semantics of these questions which, when used early, tend not to be proper cause questions according to adult standards.

V. Time. **G** *wann* and Latvian *kad*.

Here, too, the early instances tend not to be proper time questions. The details are still unclear.

I suspect that a more detailed and a more refined version than the above reflects the cognitive, in particular the conceptual, growth which interacts with the various formal interrogative devices of the language to be acquired in order to produce the developmental sequence of interrogative pronouns. Moreover, I venture to predict that, if we had acquisition data from a language in which other formal question types—IQ, Qpart, or other—are not limited to just one semantic category (like the YNQ of Latvian, English, and Finnish), we would probably find the same developmental sequence of items as outlined for the +INTER pronouns above. In any event, the fact that in all the data examined in sections 3 and 4 YNQ were early when signalled through IQ seems to me to be due not to some general cognitive primacy of the confirmatory category but to the fact that these adult languages signal only one semantic category via IQ, namely, confirmation.

5.3 Stage II. Multiword questions. The development of multiword questions is specific to the types described in section 5.1 and elsewhere in this article. In general, the task for the child is to integrate the type-I questions with the other parts of his growing syntax and to carry on with their development. Primarily, this involves the positioning of the segmental interrogative markers in SQ and the acquisition of appropriate interrogative word order. Furthermore, Qpart may arise. But, unfortunately, no data at all are available to shed light on their development, in particular on how Qpart is integrated within the rest of the developing syntax.

IIa. IQ. Multiword IQ at first do not reflect adult interrogative word order if it differs from the noninterrogative one. The languages to consider include English, German, and Swedish. The child data on English and German support my view. The Swedish data are unclear. Yet, since the material is quantitatively weak, Swedish has to be set aside.

Interrogative word-order permutations such as subject-verb inversion in German and English appear markedly later. Here again, however, we should recall that the Swedish data were peculiar. Moreover, interrogative permutations appear first with those question types which are not SQ in the speech of the children and in the adult language.

Semantically, there may be some overgeneralizations, though neither their ful semantic range nor their point of onset can at present be determined. Above all, it is not even clear to me what should be the domain for these overgeneralizations; that is, it is hard to determine to what extent such IQ are overgeneralizations of the child's own previous structures, as seemed to be the case in the German data in section 3.22, or of some adult structure, as might apply to the Swedish material in section 4.3 and the German data in section 3.23, all of which were puzzling because of the reflexes of adult inversion.

IIb. SQ. Not all children who acquire a language which has interrogative pronouns primarily in initial position produce multiword SQ with the interrogative pronoun in initial position. The two German children dealt with in section 3.22 placed the interrogative exclusively in front position. However, other studies on the acquisiton of German have also recorded the type with an end-positioned interrogative, as mentioned in section 3.23. Likewise, the English data for the Harvard and the Berkeley children attest only the type with fronted interrogative. With the two Bulgarian children both types were in free variation. The evidence, though, was limited to the two-word stage and to the locatives *de* and *kamo*. Furthermore, it seems that the two Latvian children only had the fronted type. Note that, at least in adult German, English, and Bulgarian, the interrogative pronouns may occur initially and noninitially.

Whatever the ultimate explanation, two facts are quite clear. I know of no child for whom we have a good amount of evidence who used only the type with end-positioned interrogative. Moreover, this type has so far been found only for early IIb. Thus, for the German child analysed in section 3.2.3, only two *wo*-questions are given in the source.

The later development of Qpron closely interlocks with the growth of sentence structure as reflected in the developmental sequences of the individual languages. As such, it is not peculiar to the acquisition of questions. The whys and hows are not understood at present, and they are doomed to remain obscure until we get detailed studies of this structural area for a variety of languages. The data on German and English make me assume that we can expect to find more or less the same stages of development in the structure of Qpron as we do for noninterrogative sentences.

If comparable word-order permutations are involved in Qpron and WOQ in the adult language, then these permutations appear in Qpron after WOQ has been acquired. For this statement I rely primarily on the English data (see sec. 4.4). The situation in German is more complex. It has yet to be analysed in a wider context giving adequate consideration to the whole phenomenon of inversion which in German is not limited to questions and which applies to a much wider array of structural areas than it does in English. I return to this issue in section 5.4 in connection with the acquisition of WOQ.

IIc. Qpart. There are not enough data to place Qpart reliably within the developmental sequence(s) which I am trying to establish. The Finnish and Bulgarian data lead me to assume that Qpart are used later than IQ or Qpron. And I venture to add that Qpart does not appear at the holophrastic stage, although I have no data for this claim. But, for all we know about the acquisition of bound forms, it would be a great surprise if we did, indeed, find that Qpart can be used productively at the holophrastic stage.

5.4 Stage IIIc. WOQ and + Inter word order. In languages that have WOQ, like English and German, these are acquired after IQ of type IIa or Qpron of type IIb. Clear evidence comes from English and German. The Swedish data of section 4.3, though, may require a revision of this assertion.

There are no data at all to determine how Qpart fare in this respect. If comparable word order permutations also occur in Qpron, then these appear in Qpron later than in WOQ. Again my evidence is English and German. The English data are clear, and my German data point in the same direction. But I have not yet been able to analyse the whole phenomenon of inversion. Grégoire's data for French support this conclusion (1947, pp. 211–215).

On the whole, the details of this stage of development seem to differ drastically, depending on the language to be acquired. Consider, for example, stages IIIa through IIId of German (see sec. 3.22), the development of subject-verb inversion in English (see sec. 4.42), and early inversion in Swedish (see sec. 4.32). It is possible, however, that these details are not specific to the acquisition of questions—as, I think, some of the German evidence indicates.

6 Conclusion

This study and the generalized hypothesis disregard or fail to explain many details, such as the peculiar detailed developmental sequence found with the individual interrogative pronouns, as in German (see tables 1 and 2); the acquisition and development of indirect questions (i.e., sentence embedding); details about overgeneralizations; the growth of inflection with + INTER pronouns; and the comprehension of questions. I hope, however, that this review will provide issues, topics, and a direction for further research. This research should, much more than is currently done, probe into the formal properties of linguistic structures liable to cause children to acquire a language in the way in which they do. The emphasis on cognition and related matters, particularly on concept formation, which seems to prevail in present-day research strikes me as one-sided. Both cognitive maturation and the formal structure of a language, along with other variables, interact to produce the peculiar developmental sequences observable when children acquire a language. Moreover, if it can indeed be assumed, as psychologists seem to suggest these days, that children's cognitive growth is much the same across different cultural settings, then cognition cannot function as the point of departure for the prediction of developmental sequences. These could not differ between different languages. The predictive capacity of a language-acquisition theory has to be based on the *linguistic* structures of human languages.

Notes

* Reprinted by permission from W. von Raffler-Engel, ed., *Child Language, 1975,* Special issue of *Word* 27, pp. 261–310. – This is the revised version of my "Some Stages in the Acquisition of Questions by Monolingual Children. Part I: German," Arbeitspapiere zum Spracherwerb Nr. 6, Englisches Seminar der Universität Kiel, 1974, and "Some Stages in the Acquisition of Questions by Monolingual Children. Part II: Bulgarian, Latvian, Swedish, English, Finnish, and other Languages," Arbeitspapiere zum Spracherwerb Nr. 7, Englisches Seminar der Universität Kiel, 1974. These were distributed in limited numbers as mimeographed working papers. The review of the data was completed in October, 1974.

I am thankful for help and criticism to a number of individuals in our group, notably to Sascha Felix, Dietrich Lange, Dieter Furkmann, Christa Meyer, Theo Schmitz, and Robert Hvitfeldt.

[1] The figures on the left serve project internal data retrieval purposes. The lower figures give the month, day, and year of occurrence.

[2] For my German data I use the following abbreviations: I.: Inga; L.: Lars; F. Father (in the speech of I. and L. mostly referred to by his first name, *Henning*); M.: Mother; B.: Birgit, older sister to I. and L.; and H.: Heiko, older brother to I. and L.

[3] The intonation for my own German data (i. e., for Inga and Lars) is represented as and/ follows: ˈhigh pendant, ˌlow pendant, ˋfalling center, ˊrising center, – post-contour, pause. For details see Wode 1980b. Some examples below will not be provided with an intonational transcription. These instances are taken from the written notes. Sometimes, for obvious reasons, the intonation was missed and only the segmental material could be noted.

[4] See, for example, Lindner 1898; Neugebauer 1914, 1915; Tögel 1905; Scupin & Scupin 1907, 1910; Preyer 1882; and Ament 1899. See also the survey in Stern/Stern 1907, pp. 191 f. and 212–217.

[5] I am indebted to Dr. Zotschew of the Institut für Weltwirtschaft of Kiel University for his help with the Bulgarian material.

[6] I am indebted to my colleague Erich Hofmann for his help with the Latvian material.

[7] *E2, E3,* etc., refer to the respective recording sessions with Embla.

GRAMMATICAL INTONATION IN CHILD LANGUAGE*

Henning Wode

Purpose

The acquisition and development of grammatical intonation is probably one of the most neglected areas in present-day research on language acquisition. As far as I can see, reliable data are practically nonexistent. The main reason for this deplorable state of affairs seems to be that researchers on child language have so far failed to apply or develop models rich enough to cope fully with all of the complexities of suprasegmental analysis. Consequently, it is quite likely that we have in the past not been posing the proper questions.

In this paper, I explore and demonstrate some of the more basic potentialities inherent in an approach to the analysis and understanding of intonation that attempts to relate pitch, stress, and pause to linguistic structures such as morphosyntax, question-answer, and the like. My cover term for this is *grammatical intonation.* My claim is that a child has to master these various relationships if he is to master the intonation system of a language like English or German.

The approach is not described in full here (for details cf. Wode 1966, 1968, 1972a, 1972b). Below, I merely illustrate some of its major features and principles in order to be able to illuminate the nature of the child's task if viewed within the framework of grammatical intonation. Since the principles seem to be equally applicable to a variety of languages, such as English, German, French, and possibly others, I had hoped to be able to include a review of additional cross-cultural evidence and some general conclusions based on it. However, appropriate data, even from a language as widely studied as English, are so scarce that no serious attempt to generalize can at present be undertaken. Consequently, the major part of this paper presents the highlights of the first stages in the acquisition of intonation by Lars, a monolingual German boy.

The Nature of the Task: Grammatical Intonation

Although numerous studies, recent and less recent, deal with intonation in child language in one way or another, the term tends to be applied to such a variety of different phenomena — utterance boundaries, interrogation, and paralinguistic features (annoyance, emphasis), to name just a few (cf. Crystal 1973, for a survey) — that the term intonation has become too vague to be linguistically helpful. Moreover, many studies, it seems to me, have overlooked a very important point in any intonational analysis with respect to both fully fledged adult languages and language acquisition. The point concerns the type of relationship that may exist between the phonetic features proper and the various linguistic categories that are associated with them. Does one intonation or one intonational feature always imply the same distinction — for example, interrogation? Furthermore, does one intonation combine freely with any item in the linguistic system? My answer to both questions is no. In fact the complex interplay between intonation and morphosyntax also involves, it seems to me, such deep-rooted principles as structure dependence, so often discussed with reference to syntax (for instance, Chomsky 1965).

Intonation and Meaning

It seems to me that intonation research in the past — and not only with respect to English and German — has been primarily concerned with classifying, identifying, and labeling the intonation of particular utterances. With few exceptions (cf., for instance, Halliday 1967, but for some criticism cf. Wode 1969), no attempts have been made to generalize on these findings in order to predict which „meaning" will result if such and such an intonation is combined with such and such a segmental carrier phrase. For instance, compare examples (1a) and (1b):

(1) a ᵎMeet my asˋsistant_Mr. Peabody[1]
    b ᵎMeet my assistant Mr. ˋPeabody

If the phrase *Mr. Peabody* is regarded as a vocative, the intonation of (1a) carries no striking implications. In contrast, the intonation of (1b) highlights the vocative, perhaps as an admonition or the like. If, however, the phrase *Mr. Peabody* is interpreted as being an apposition to the preceding NP *my assistant,* then the highlighting effect is reversed: (1a) now highlights *my assistant,* and (1b) represents the straightforward intonation with no particular implications.

Thus, in English as well as in other languages, the particular meaningful implications attributed to intonation cannot be regarded as invariably inherent in the particular intonation per se. Rather, they arise from a complex interplay between the segmental carrier phrase and the intonation proper. It is therefore important to indicate briefly the range of restrictions that may hold between certain types of segmental carrier phrases and various intonational features.

Intonation and Morphosyntax

Restrictions between stress and morphosyntax of various sorts are familiar from many handbooks, in particular as they relate to word stress. However, the stressing of words in longer utterances, say, sentences, has been studied less extensively (Wode 1966). Comparable pitch restrictions have, to my knowledge, not been studied at length at all. I have no doubt that such restrictions do, in fact, exist. Compare, for instance, curses and vocatives in the English and in German examples (2) and (3):

(2) a ˋGeorge ᵎclear ˋout
    b ᶦGeorge ᵎclear ˋout
    c ˋHell ᵎclear ˋout
    d *ᶦHell ᵎclear ˋout

(3) a ˋLarsi ˈhau ˋab (Larsi, clear out)
      b ˊLarsi ˈhau ˋab (Larsi, clear out)
      c ˋVerdammt ˈhau ˋab (damn it, clear out)
      d *ˊVerdammt ˈhau ˋab (damn it, clear out)

Although utterance-initial vocatives in English and in German may be spoken with a falling intonation as in (2a) and (3a) or a rising one as in (2b) and (3b), curses in the same position cannot have the rising pitch, irrespective of whether they are to be interrogated or not. Examples (2d) and (3d) are ungrammatical. Furthermore, the rising pitch in examples (2b) and (3b) does not imply interrogation, as it might do if produced in the utterance-final position of certain constructions.[2]

It is clear, then, that there are structure-dependent limitations in the occurrence of the various intonational features — including pitch — with respect to the morphosyntactic properties of a given string. Every construction can be regarded as having a particular set of intonations that can be associated with it. Furthermore, to illustrate that examples (2) and (3) are by no means marginal cases, I add example (4), which contains a carrier phrase with quite a different morphosyntactic structure:

(4)   He has raised various economic religious and constitutional issues

Whereas example (4) can be intoned with a slight rise in pitch on *economic* and *religious,* no such a rise is possible on *various.* This holds true irrespective of the attitudinal or emotional intention that one may wish to convey.

Examples (1) through (4) illustrate distributional restrictions between morphosyntax and such smaller constituents as vocatives, curses, appositions, or adjectival modifiers. Other restrictions extend well beyond individual sentences to include, for instance, questions and answers to such sentences as those in examples (5) and

(6):

(5) a Who settled in Princeton in 16-something?
      b The PILGRIMS settled in Princeton in 16-something.
(6) a When did the pilgrims settle in Princeton?
      b The pilgrims settled in Princeton in 16-SOMETHING.

The strings (5b/6b) require the intonation center (capital letters) on *pilgrims* in answer to example (5a), as in example (5b), but on *something* in answer to example (6a), as in example (6b). Example (6b) as a reply to example (5a) would be ungrammatical, just as would example (5b) as a reply to example (6a).

In summary, then, it seems obvious to me that even the analysis of the emotional aspects of intonation cannot be carried out successfully unless grammatical aspects of intonation are taken into consideration. The next section summarizes some of the devices that have been found useful to cope with these problems.

Descriptive Devices

The particular intonation „meanings" illustrated by examples (1a, b) can be regarded as due to a shift of the respective intonational features from unmarked or neutral to marked or emphatic position. Elsewhere I have tried to show for English (Wode 1966, 1972a, 1972b) and German (Wode 1968) that the neutral intonation can be generated for any string or text by reference to its morphosyntactic structure. More specifically, I have suggested that the neutral intonation can be appropriately specified, if intonation is treated in terms of hierarchically organized constructions — much as in syntax (Wode 1972a). To simplify matters somewhat, an intonation minimally requires an intonation *center*, optionally a *pendant* (i.e. any segmental stretch preceding the center), and, also optionally, a *postcontour* either embodied within the pendant or following the center (Table 1).[3]

Table 1.   The basic intonation construction of English, illustrating the constituents pendant, center, and postcontour (adapted from Wode, 1972a)

Example	Pendant	Center	Postcontour
(1a)	'Meet my as-	ˋsistant	Mr. Peabody
(1b)	'Meet my assistant Mr.	ˋPeabody	

Emphatic intonations can be treated as shifts of various intonational constituents from neutral to non-neutral position. English vocatives may serve as a (simple) illustration. Under neutral conditions, they have postcontour (tail) intonation if placed non-initially in an utterance; they do not if placed utterance-initially. Compare example (1a) above with example (1c) below:

(1c)   'Mr.ˋPeabody 'meet my asˋsistant.

If the center is shifted to no-initial vocatives, the particular highlighting effects pointed out with respect to example (1b) in the section on *intonation and meaning*, may result.

The Child's Task

Within the framework suggested above, the child's task will be to master the intonational construction(s), to acquire their co-occurrence with morphosyntax, including the area beyond the individual sentence, and to acquire the regularities governing neutral and emphatic shades of meaning.

In the remainder of this paper my main focus is on the acquisition of the intonational construction(s) and the relationship of some intonational constituents with morphosyntax, rather than with the number of pitch levels, tones, tunes, stresses, pauses, and so on. That is, I primarily report on how the intonational constituents center, pendant, and postcontour evolved in the speech of Lars. My starting point is the point when the child begins to produce recognizable morphosyntactic carrier phrases, however rudimentary, i.e., when one-word utterances first appear. I have nothing to say on „intonation at the prelinguistic stage" of development.

The Data

The data come from a detailed longitudinal study of my son Lars, born in May, 1969, as the third of four children. He has been observed daily since he began to speak, and I have tape recordings as well as notes taken spontaneously at the scene of action. These notes include the child's productions, phonetic transcriptions, and his (most likely) intention. I am interested in all aspects of his linguistic development, intonation being only one of them. Ultimately, my aim is to develop an integrated theory that characterizes man's capacity for language acquisition. It is assumed that only man can acquire (human) languages, and that this capacity is not limited to L1 acquisition. Man can learn, forget, and relearn languages under a large variety of circumstances. Consequently, his capacity for language acquisition can only be characterized if the various types of language acquisition are brought within the scope of one integrated theory that describes both the commonalities and the differences, if any, between the various acquisitional types, including classroom teaching. (For details on these issues, see Wode 1974.)[4]

The Development of Grammatical Intonation

The key notion is the familiar concept of developmental sequence. It is assumed that learners pass through an ordered set of developmental stages on their way toward mastering a language or a given target structure. Each stage is marked by not necessarily target-like developmental structures peculiar to that stage. The sequence of these stages is the developmental sequence. Children may vary as to the amount of time it takes them to pass from one stage to the next, but the order of these stages is fixed relative to each other. Also, there may be some individual variations between learners, but such individual variation is not infinite, i.e., it occurs within predictable ranges (for details see Wode 1978b).

Stage I: – The holophrastic stage: The acquisition of the intonation center

During the holophrastic stage, the child produced texts where each different lexical item formed a separate intonation (tone group) with a pause of varying duration after each intonation. There seemed to be no organization across intonation boundaries that indicated any kind of structuring usually described in terms of linguistic structures. As for the intonation, there was some structuring, although it was confined to the domain of the individual intonation. I here discuss briefly the intonation center, the discrete two-term system ± inter(rogative), and the semi-gradient system of ± neutral.

The intonation center: Throughout the purely holophrastic stage the intonation center was formed by the individual lexical items. This was true for monosyllabic as well as for multisyllabic items. Under neutral conditions, the latter were stressed initially. For special emphasis (or playful amusement) other stresses could be added on non-initial syllables, or, alternatively, the stress could be shifted to non-initial syllables.

The development of stress contrasts is not pursued any further. Here I focus on pitch because numerous other intonational properties are acquired before the stress system is expanded. I distinguish the discrete opposition ± inter(rogative) and the gradient contrast of ± neutral.

Discreteness: ± inter: Investigators have frequently noted that children may have a binary system of rising (+ inter) versus falling (− inter) pitch at, or even before, the holophrastic stage, however difficult it may be to describe precisely just what distinctions the child may be signaling when he uses a rising intonation.

With the child under observation here it is not quite clear whether the two-term system arose with both terms simultaneously or whether the falling pitch developmentally preceded the rising one. However, his older brother clearly had the binary system before he had acquired any contrasting segmental lexical items at all,[5] whereas his younger sister had a marked time lag during the holophrastic stage before she was ever heard to produce a rising pitch in any utterance.

For this paper it is assumed that the two terms arose simultaneously with this child. Although the system is termed ± inter, the label is not meant to imply that the child was asking questions in the adult sense of the term. I am quite sure that what he was signaling was probably a real difference for him, although equivalents to adult queries cover only part of the information he may have been trying to convey or elicit.

The system ± inter operates at the intonation center. The actual auditory feature associated with ± inter is the direction of the pitch movement, with + inter requiring an up-glide and − inter a down-glide.

However, the child also produced emphatic level intonations implying insistance (or obstinacy) where it was difficult to choose between up and down. This is an instance of the gradient system ± neutral.

Gradiency: ± neutral   This is the area where most ink has been spilt by previous researchers (see Crystal 1973, for a survey), but where, unfortunately, little precision has been achieved. I am afraid I cannot do any better. I am sure that, to signal his intentions, Lars used a variety of suprasegmental parameters like pitch height, abruptness of pitch change, loudness, drawling, and others. However, I find it impossible to establish any clear-cut, let alone one-to-one, relationships between the observable phonetic features and the child's most likely intentions. It seems that adequate categories for the classification of this wealth of vocalization have yet to be developed. Therefore, instead of adding more data that remain at present unanalyzable, I merely note that this child was certainly capable of implying shades of meaning that were not part of the lexical meaning of a word by altering, among other things, his intonation. The distinction of ± neutral is introduced to account for this ability. In the following I am not concerned with − neutral, i.e., emphatic intonations.

Stage II − Holophrastic repetitions: The acquisition of the pendant

Before passing on to two-word utterances proper, another type of utterance must be considered, for which the term *holophrastic repetition* is suggested. To date, holophrastic repetitions do not seem to have received any attention in the literature.

While still at the genuinely holophrastic stage, children are known to optionally repeat a lexical item within one intonation, as in example (7):

(7)   Mama Mama Mama (calling for Mom)
         Decke Decke Decke (blanket)
         Apfel   Apfel   Apfel (apple)

Utterances like these are intonationally and semantically important. With the child under investigation here, the repeated items had the same referent throughout the utterances, i.e., the same Mom, the same blanket, and the same apple. At this stage, such utterances never referred to, say, different blankets, even if these were spread out in full view of the child. Optionally, strings like those in example (7) could be uttered as one intonation. Their status as ± inter was determined by the final token of the string. Thus the intonation center was located on the final token, and all of the preceding tokens formed the pendant. From the data on this child it appears that repetition strings are acquired subsequent to one-token holophrastic utterances and their intonational peculiarities.

Pitch restrictions and morphosyntax: Recall from examples (3c) and (3d) that, in German, initial curses are ungrammatical if spoken with a rise. Apparently, the child attended to this distinction already from the holophrastic stages − roughly since the age of 1:6-7 (1 year; 6-7 months, 0 days). Admonitions like *Mann* [man] or *Mensch* [mɛnθ][6] (both semantically interjectional admonitions) were never heard with a rising pitch.

Stage III − The two-word stage: Vocatives and postcontours

In passing from the holophrastic stages to two- or more-word utterances, this child did not follow the course one would expect on the basis of the findings by Braine 1963, Brown & Fraser 1963, and Miller & Ervin 1964 for English, as well as those summarized by Slobin 1970 for other languages. That is, this child did not directly go on to produce pivots like those of Braine. Rather, before doing so, he began, *inter alia,* to systematically use postcontour intonations. These seem to be acquired by age 1;10. They appeared roughly at the same time with vocatives as well as under certain contextual conditions that are rather difficult to specify, but that, on the whole, seem to be quite parallel to those of adult German. The latter type are not treated here. I briefly discuss the vocatives.

The child differentiated the vocatives in much the same way as in adult German: In utterance-initial position, vocatives either form independent intonations or they are part of the pendant; in other positions they form postcontours, optionally cut off by a pause. Some examples are shown in Table 2, with postcontours marked by a lowered dash (.).

As is obvious from Table 2, vocatives can be pre- or postposed. Word order is random in this instance. Yet, pre- or postposition is marked by intonation. The actual pitch features used by the child in uttering vocatives are: with preposed vocatives ¦ (level), ˋ(falling), ˊ(rising), or ˇ (falling-rising); with postposed vocatives the postcontours are level or they continue in the same direction as the pitch on the center. I have marked all these variants as _.

As for the developmental sequence, with preposed vocatives the falling-rising pitch is rare at 1;10. It is used freely only later; with postposed vocatives, rising ones are rare and probably unproductive at 1;10. The latter must be distinguished from the low rise following a fall and indicating + inter. This usage is acquired still later. Thus the developmental sequence is: with preposed vocatives, level, rising, and falling pitch precede falling-rising; with postposed vocatives, level pitch or pitch continuing a preceding fall precede pitch continuing a rise; this pitch, in turn, precedes the fall followed by a rise to indicate + inter.

Summary: Developmental Sequence

The developmental sequence of the three major intonational constituents corresponds to the generality of the categories in the adult model as defined by their hierarchical status: center before pendant, and postcontour last.

In addition, the child has grasped several basic insights relating to the intonation system of adult German. First, he has grasped the principle of correlating morphosyntax with intonation. If this view is not accepted with respect to stage I, it should surely be accepted at the age represented by example (c) of Table 2. Second, the child's productions evidence the principle that there are syntagmatic relationships between intonational constituents. Consider, for instance, the status of the various pitch features associated with postcontours as conditioned by the pitch of the center. Third, there is the structure-dependent principle that not all intonations are equally permissible with all morphosyntactic carrier phrases. Recall the status of curses, as mentioned briefly in the section on intonation and meaning, above.

Table 2. Examples of differentiation of vocatives by Lars

Example	Age	Child's utterance	Adult utterance	English translation
(a)	1;9,27	ˈHenning ˋkletter	Henning, ich klettere	Henning, I am climbing
(b)	1;9,29	ˊHeiko ˋarbeiten	Heiko, Henning arbeitet	Heiko, Henning is working
(c)	1;9,30	ˊrein‿Mama ˋMilch	Die Milch soll hier rein, Mama	The milk is to go in here, Mom
(d)	1;10,8	ˋgroß‿Henning	Das ist groß Henning	This is big, Henning
(e)	1;10,8	ˋschwimmt‿Henning ˋschwimmt	Das Schiff schwimmt, Henning, es schwimmt	The ship is moving, Henning, it moves
(f)	1;10,8	ˈˋbeißt ˋbeißt‿Henning ˋbeißt	Der Luftballon beißt, Henning, er beißt	The balloon will bite, Henning, it will bite
(g)	1;10,22	ˋne‿Mama ˋrunter‿Mama	Nein, Mama, ich will runter, Mama	No, Mom, I want to get down, Mom

Thus it seems that the basic properties of the intonation system are already acquired during the holophrastic and the early two-word stages. In the development to come, the child will expand his production capacity by increasing the complexity of the structuring in accordance with the basic insights stated above. This development is not described here. Suffice it to give a few illustrative examples, as summarized in Table 3. After the acquisition of postcontours, the child develops other constructions of various sorts. All of them have their own intonational peculiarities. In particular, they differ in the position of the intonational constituents (see Table 3). Without going into details here, utterances like those in Table 3 demonstrate that, in his subsequent development, the child extends his use of pendant, center, and postcontour productively to other constructions.

Cross-Cultural Evidence

Previous summaries (Weir 1966; Crystal 1973) have deplored the state of affairs of present-day research on suprasegmentals. They have noted the anecdotal character of many observations, and the preoccupation with the very early, in many cases even the prelinguistic, stage of development. I would like to add that most studies are concerned with the emotional aspects of suprasegmental features. Works that present systematic data on the acquisition of grammatical intonation (including pitch, stress, pause, and juncture), are very few in number, and the ones that I have been able to find all deal with English.

Age groups from 4;0 upwards have been covered by Hornby & Hass 1970, Hornby 1971, and Atkinson-King 1973. Hornby & Hass and Hornby are interested in the topic-comment distinction, with intonation as one of several linguistic means available in English to signal this distinction. Their work presents some evidence that children at 4;0 handle postcontours and centers in accordance with the adult model to signal topic and comment.

Atkinson-King 1973 (with a valuable review of the literature) has investigated stress contrasts in compounds versus noncompounds, chiefly of the *bláckbird* versus *bláck bírd* type. Younger age groups apparently have attracted only incidental comments in such reports as Weir 1962, Braine 1963, Miller & Ervin 1964, and others. Most of these observations relate to postcontours.

Braine 1963 has noted suprasegmentally differentiated terminal vocatives in the speech of one of the three children he studied. Similarly, Carlson & Anisfield 1969 have observed an instance where a 2-year-old child added a vocative intoned as a postcontour to an utterance begun by another interlocutor.

Weir (1962, p. 113), reports that her son, at about age 2;6 used examples (8a) and (8b) in close sequence:

(8) a 'big two 'trucks
    b 'three trucks

Table 3. Some utterance types and their intonation

Example	Age	Intonational constituents[a]	Child's utterance	English translation
(a1)	1;10,22	'P 'X / 'mein 'Stuhl	mein Stuhl	my chair
(a2)	1;10,17	'mein 'Sin	meine Medizin	my drugs
(b1)	1;10,28	'X 'P / 'mag _nicht	das mag ich nicht	I don't like it
(b2)	2;0,1	'schmeckt _nicht	das schmeckt nicht	it doesn't taste well
(b3)	2;0,1	Larsi 'hat_nicht Aa Henning	Larsi(=ich) hat nicht Aa gemacht, Henning	Larsi(=I) haven't dirtied my pants. Henning
(c1)		'X / 'Heiko 'Blume	Heikos Blume	Heiko's flower
(c2)		'Heiko 'teilen	Ich teile mit Heiko	I'll let Heiko have his share
(c3)		'Heiko 'müde	Heiko ist müde	Heiko is tired

[a] P = pivot like that of Braine; X = open class like that of Braine (see Braine, 1963).

Atkinson-King (1973, p. 13) cites similar evidence from Brown 1973. Little Eve, at approximately 1;10, „went around a circle of people, pointing to each person's nose and saying":

(9)   'that ʾPapa ͵nose
        'that ʾMama ͵nose
        'that ʾEve ͵nose

Miller & Ervin 1964 thought that they could analyze an "accentual system" in the speech of one of their subjects and claimed that they could differentiate intonationally a locative construction from adjectival and possessive constructions. However, the conclusions are not borne out by the data Miller and Ervin present.

Conclusion

Three major points emerge: any conclusions of a more general nature, let alone along universalist lines, are premature. At present, we need detailed empirical but linguistically sober longitudinal studies on the acquisition of the intonation of various languages. In attempting such studies, researchers will have to develop models for the analysis of intonation that are much more powerful than those presently available. The acquisition of intonation cannot adequately be described simply as the mastery of features like pitch levels, pauses, and so on. Instead, it involves more abstract categories (or facts described by linguists in terms of such categories) like center, pendant, postcontour, structure dependencies between intonation, and various other levels of structure. The status of such categories, both in the adult model and in the children's unfolding linguistic system, is much more complex than one might suspect in light of the preoccupation with the emotional aspects of intonation so often encountered in previous studies.

106

Notes

* Reprinted by permission from L.R. Waugh and C.H. van Schooneveld, eds., *The Melody of Language*, Baltimore: University Park Press, 1980, pp. 331-345.

¹ The transcription in this article use the following marks:
 ` Falling pitch.
 ´ Rising pitch.
 ⋮ High or low, more or less level pitch preceding ` or ´.
 _ Postcontour (i.e. tail intonation) following ` or ´ and starting at approximately the height of the endpoint of preceding ` or ´. (The transcription is refined and discussed more fully in "The Data," below.)
 * Ungrammaticality.

² Of course, one could redefine the term interrogation to include (2b) and (3b), perhaps as ,,incompleteness." This, however, makes the term vague, hence less useful.

³ The terms center and pendant are taken from Hockett 1958; the term postcontour is from Pike 1945. The above is a simplified description. It neglects hierarchical structuring in sequences of intonation (cf. Wode 1972a).

⁴ This report is a revised version of Arbeitspapiere zum Spracherwerb No. 2, Universität Kiel, 1974. Since then the project has developed further. We now have data on L1 English, naturalistic (i.e untutored) L2 English acquired by children with German as L1, naturalistic L2 German/L1 English, relearning of L2 English/L1 German, L2 English taught to German students, and pidgins of various sorts. The acquisitional types are compared for differences and parallels. The main results so far are: there are certain regularities that recur in all types of language acquisition; and other peculiarities are restricted to specific types. Learning a language requires a learning theory of its own. No type of language acquisition can be described in terms of behavioristic conditioning, nor in terms of a Piagetian type of approach based on conceptual or logical development. That is, just as the regularities in children's development of, say, gait cannot be explained by the development of visual perception, so the acquisition of the formal properties used in natural languages, such as word order or inflectional marking, cannot be explained by, say, the development of cognitive concepts or logical thinking. The ability to acquire such formal properties is specics-specific, and very likely biologically inborn, with *homo sapiens*. Just as it takes a goose to be imprinted, it takes a human brain to handle the formal properties of linguistic devices. The actual neuropsychological mechanisms seem to function on a categorical basis. (For summaries and further references see Wode 1976a, 1977c, d, 1978b, c, 1979).

⁵ He had a stereotyped dummy element [hagŋ] that, apparently, served no other purpose than to provide a segmental carrier for the rise versus fall of pitch. It seemed that he employed the up-glide as an attention-getting device, when, for instance, he wanted to join in the (adult) activities around him. The down-glide was heard only when no such desire was apparent, i.e., when, for instance, he was fully involved in his own activity and wanted no interference from outside. Cf. similarly Raffler-Engel 1964.

⁶ This utterance is modeled on German *Mensch* [mɛnʃ], literally meaning ,,human being." Colloquially it is very frequently used as an interjection roughly equivalent to *heck* or the like. Lars had a lisp at that time so that he substitutes [θ] for the target [ʃ].

Commentary

The joint impact of these three papers, it seems to me, is that learning a natural language requires specific linguo-cognitive abilities which are species-specific and very likely innate. These capacities are called linguo-cognitive because they seem to be especially geared to the handling of the formal properties of the linguistic devices used in natural languages. This topic is explicated in subsequent papers. It will be argued that these linguo-cognitive capacities can be thought of as a processing system that enables human beings to process speech data for the purpose of acquisition. This means that what is innate are not linguistic structures per se, as suggested by some researchers working within a generative-transformational framework (for example McNeill 1966, 1970a, but rather man seems genetically invested with a processing system which allows him to develop linguistic structures. The main task for future research will be to determine in detail the nature and the functioning of this linguo-cognitive processing system.

The three papers of part II illustrate developmental sequences, i.e. the chronological ordering so obvious in L1 children's speech development. This aspect has fascinated modern observers since the beginning of such research around the turn of this century. (The nature of developmental sequences is the center of interest in the papers of part III.) However, as we moved on in our research in Kiel to inspect other acquisitional types, less and less importance was attached to chronological ordering. The focus of interest has shifted to the developmental structures themselves, i.e. to the errors, as illustrated by the papers in parts IV through VI.

In the paper on L1 negation, I argued that the developmental type *neg X ~X neg* is probably not innate but acquired. I do not hold this view any longer. In later papers, in particular as in part V on universals, I take the view that *neg X ~X neg* results from an innate universal strategy.

Part III

THE NATURE OF LANGUAGE DEVELOPMENT

Introduction

This part contains two papers which examine the nature of the progression, if any, that a learner may go through, and some methodological issues on how to study such developments. The background is Jakobson's classic study on L1 phonological development. Jakobson's suggestion was that L1 children acquire the phonological system of a language in a specific chronological order. They pass through a predictable series of developmental stages. This progress can be predicted given the structure of the phonological system of the target language. The empirical details of this theory have been questioned by numerous articles (for example, Raffler-Engel 1970). Also, many aspects of how children acquire sound systems are not covered by Jakobson's theory at all (Ferguson & Garnica 1975). These empirical shortcomings notwithstanding, however, Jakobson's basic insights still stand, namely, that a language is not acquired all at once, but rather in a specific series of developmental stages. The papers of part II clearly show that these insights are not limited to segmental phonology.

By now, numerous studies are available which show that naturalistic L2 acquisition is also subject to ordered developmental sequences (for example, Huang 1971, Wode 1976a, 1977c, Felix 1978b, Ufert 1980). These L2 sequences may differ from the respective L1 sequences. Examples of such L2 sequences can be found in various papers of this volume (negation: paper no. 9; inflections: paper no. 6; phonology: paper no. 10).

The two papers reprinted in part III are concerned with methodological problems in conjunction with the nature of developmental sequences. The first study starts with a brief description of the general nature of developmental sequences and then evaluates critically the morpheme order approach as developed by Cazden 1968 and Brown 1973 and as used extensively in numerous studies produced in the USA, for example, Dulay & Burt 1972, 1973, 1974a. The result is that the morpheme order approach is ill-suited to describe language learning, because those language acquisitional regularities which occur before the learner reaches target-like mastery are not taken into account. The second paper is extremely important from the methodological point of view because it raises an issue which has not been discussed in the past at all. Experimentally elicited data are compared to material collected in natural spontaneous situations. This issue is important because most of the morpheme order studies as well as others employed experimental elicititation techniques to collect data. This data was taken as bona fide evidence for the developmental progress.

By contrasting experimentally elicited data with spontaneous material from the same subjects it is possible to show that the data are not isomorphic at all. A true understanding of the nature of language acquisition and language development can, therefore, only be arrived at if both experimental and spontaneous data are considered together. Relying only on one or the other of the two data types provides a lopsided view. This implies that a considerable amount of past research has to be redone.

DEVELOPMENTAL SEQUENCE: AN ALTERNATIVE APPROACH TO MORPHEME ORDER*

H. Wode, J. Bahns, H. Bedey & W. Frank

This paper is a critical evaluation of the morpheme order approach and it is intended to complement recent criticism raised by Rosansky 1976a-b and Andersen 1977. They emphasize methodological shortcomings that derive from data collection procedures and from the application of statistics in studies by Dulay & Burt 1974 a-b. It seems that Rosansky and Andersen, though questioning the extrinsic methodology, do not challenge the notion of morpheme order itself as an adequate approach to describe language acquisition. We think the criticism should be extended to the notion itself, irrespective of the methodological problems. Data on the naturalistic, untutored acquisition of the English plural inflections by four German children will be presented to illustrate that the morpheme order approach cannot capture numerous acquisitional regularities. Attention is drawn to the notion of developmental sequences as an alternative approach.

On the Notions of Morpheme Order and Developmental Sequence

The notion of morpheme order (or „order of acquisition" as it was first called) has grown out of the Harvard project (Cazden 1968, Brown 1973). It refers to the relative chronology of target-like mastery of several distinct structural items. Brown has used this notion to establish the order in which grammatical morphemes such as inflections and prepositions are acquired. Target-like mastery is defined by establishing the percentage of target-like usage in those environments where the target obligatorily requires the item. The critical point of acquisition can be set arbitrarily, preferably around 90 % of target-like usage. This approach has been widely adopted for recent L2 studies (for instance, Dulay & Burt 1974a-b, Hakuta 1974, Larsen-Freeman 1975, Bailey et al. 1974). Some researchers have found the morpheme order for second language (L2) acquisition to parallel closely that of first language (L1) acquisition (Dulay & Burt 1974a-b); others found it to differ (Hakuta 1974). The critical re-appraisals by Rosansky (1976a, b) and Andersen (1977) suggest that methodological problems concerning data collection procedures and statistical evaluation make these results difficult to interpret. We agree. Moreover, we want to point out additional weaknesses. Chief among them is the fact that the morpheme order approach misses what makes language acquisition attractive for, and subject to, developmental investigations, namely, to discover how language is processed by the child for the purpose of acquisition. This processing is reflected in the way that children decompose complex structural patterns and then rebuild them step by step until they finally reach target-like mastery. Therefore, pre-targetlike regularities must be regarded as an essential part of the total process of acquiring a language. Consequently, we need a concept broad enough to incorporate these facts.

The notion of developmental sequence is intended to do just that. It refers to the developmental stages that a child passes through on his way toward target-like mastery of a structure or an element of the target language. These stages are ordered chronologically. Children may vary as to the actual time it takes them to pass from one stage to the next, but the order of these stages is invariant. Some stages are obligatory with every child, others are optional in that children may vary as to which route to take. As they move from stage to stage there may be some overlap such that utterances of the prior stage co-occur with those of the subsequent stage. Moreover, if a new rule, or part of it, is acquired, not all items within the child's command to which this rule pertains in the target language will at once be incorporated into the child's version of this rule. Some items are affected later. Felix 1977c has shown that the same developmental process may be repeated for individual items with considerable differences in time.

The notion of developmental sequence is familiar from L1 research (for instance, Jakobson 1941, Leopold 1939-49, Klima & Bellugi 1966, Slobin 1973, Wode 1976c, 1977b). It has also been used for the analysis of various structural areas in L2 acquisition (Huang 1971, Milon 1974, Schumann 1975a, Wode 1976a, 1977c). The L2 acquisition of inflections, we think, can also profitably be studied within such a framework.

The Data

The project has been described in more detail in Wode 1976a, 1977c. Briefly, the data to be reported here come from Wode's four children: Heiko, born 1966, Birgit born 1967, Lars born 1969, Inga born 1971. Their L1 is German. In 1975, at ages 3;11 (three years, eleven months; (Inga), 4;11 (Lars), 6;11 (Birgit), 8;11 (Heiko), they acquired English naturalistically, (without classroom foreign language teaching) during a 6 month field trip to Trinity Center, California.

There are three types of data: tape recordings of experimental sessions; tape recordings of spontaneous talk; and hand written notes taken spontaneously at the scene of action. The latter include the child's utterance, phonetic transcriptions, situational comments, and the child's (most likely) intention.

For the purpose of this paper the spontaneous data will be kept separate from the experimental data, because, for reasons not clearly understood at present, the insights derived from these two types of L2 data are not strictly isomorphic (see Rosansky 1976b).

Singular vs. Plural with Nouns in Trinity Center English and German

The local variety spoken at Trinity Center will be called Trinity Center (TC) English. There are some phonological peculiarities. But the plural inflection does not differ from the standard pattern familiar along the west coast and the western parts of the United States.

The main differences between TC English and German relate to the morphophonemics and to the productivity of the inflectional variants.

A number of non-productive patterns aside, English has one dominantly productive tri-partite rule according to which stems ending in /(d)ʒ (t)ʃ s z / take /-əz/, those ending in a distinctively voiceless consonant take /-s/, and the remaining, including stems in /m n ŋ r l/ or a vowel, take /-z/.

German has at least eight fairly productive patterns: Umlaut (Mutter: Mütter „mother"); -e /-ə/, (Tisch: Tische „table"); -e /-ə/ plus Umlaut (Kuh: Kühe „cow"); -er /-a ~ -ɛᵊ/ (Kleid: Kleider „dress"); -er /-a ~ ɛᵊ/ plus Umlaut (Wald: Wälder „forest"); -(e)n /-ən ~ n ~ -ɛn/ (Kette: Ketten „chain"); -s /-s/ (Auto: Autos „car"); and Ø (Mädchen: Mädchen „girl"). There are further execptions and the membership of a given noun within these inflectional classes cannot be given by general rule. It has to be learnt as part of the lexical item. (For details see Grebe 1973).

The L2 Acquisition of the Trinity Center Plural

It is important to distinguish sharply between form and function in order to be able to determine whether a form containing a reflex of the target plural is used to signal plural, singular, or both.

Spontaneous evidence. The discussion will be resticted to the productive plural /-s ~ -z ~ -əz/. Only the most advanced child, i.e. the one aged 8;11 got to the point where, towards the end of our stay, he consistently used at least a few irregular plurals in target-like form. From all four children there were throughout our sojourn forms like *feets, trouts, mouses* used as plurals.

Stage I: One form for both singular or plural intention

In the beginning the children have but one form for each noun, for instance, *house, bike, ball, guys.* They are used with both singular and/or plural intention. From the point of view of adult grammar such early forms may look singular as in *ball,* or plural as in *guys,* that is, such forms may contain morphological reflexes of the target inflections. But from the point of view of the child's grammar these forms have no inflection yet. The child picks one form and uses it indiscriminately.

The children did not show the same preferences. There are quite a few items for which the first form is uniform with all four children, for instance, *fish, guys.* With other nouns the situation differed.

Stage II: Two forms for each noun reflecting target singular and plural

Forms reflecting the singular are used with both singular and/or plural intentions; the forms with plural target reflexes are restricted to plural intention.

The crucial points of this stage are as follows: there is not random use of forms to signal singular and/or plural intentions; and there is not arbitrary selection of one form over the other; but there is a structured choice reflecting the structure of the targets. That is, the children do not simply continue to use the early forms for singular or plural in accord with what it is a reflex of. Rather, the children employ the form that reflects the target singular, or the one they mistakenly take to be the target singular reflex, to signal plural and singular intentions. It is the reflex of the target plural proper, or what the children mistake it to be, that is restricted to plural intention, irrespective of whether this form was acquired first or second. Crucial cases include *eggs, bikes,* from Lars, *minutes* from Heiko. The more recently acquired forms are *egg, minute, bike.* It is these latter that are used to signal singular and plural intentions.

Stage III: Forms with plural target reflexes restricted to plural intention; forms with singular target reflexes restricted to singular intention.

Stages I-III mark the acquisition of the principle of plural formation. Tied into these stages is the sequence in which the allomorphs /-s, -z, -əz/ are acquired. The first to be used productively starting, roughly, at stage II above, is [-s], next is [-əs]; [-z] and [-əz] are last. There are two difficulties here. One relates to stems that require /-z/ in the target; the other concerns the status of such early plural's as *basses, fishes.*

For a good while the children devoice final consonant clusters. They pluralize nouns that require /-z/ in the target before they pluralize those requiring /-əz/. Due to the general devoicing rule both /-z/ and /-əz/ are rendered [-s] and [-əs], respectively. (For details on the children's L2 phonological acquisition cf. Wode 1978a, 1977c). Superficially, [-əs] may be used before [-z]. However, the principle whereby certain stems require /-z/ ([-s] due to the general devoicing rule) is mastered before the rule covering stems that require /-əz/. In the experiments it is clear that /-z/ precedes /-əz/.

A few forms like *fishes, basses,* though later in occurrence than either *fish* or *bass*, are, nonetheless, recorded and used consistently as plurals fairly early. They appear to be premature plurals. For one thing, they occur before the children begin to form such plurals with other nouns in greater number. Besides, forms like *fishes, basses* were also used by some of the local children as old as 6-10 years of age.

Experimental evidence. The experimental data are primarily enlightening for the sequence of the allomorphs. There were two alternatives for eliciting plurals. The first was to ask the child in German, whether he knew the English for X. If he did, he was asked in German how he would say two X's, or three X's, and the like. If the child did not know the English for X, it was given to him as a singular. The child was then asked to form the plural as above.

Nouns like *cattle* had to be handled differently. The German plural equivalent is *Rinder,* the singular *Rind.* Note that in German *Rind* is inflected, but in English *cattle* is not. So the child was told that he probably knew that *cattle* meant *Rinder.* Then he was asked how he would say *ein Rind* „one (head of) cattle" and *zwei Rinder* two (head of) cattle".

The inflectional experiments were basically of the Berko (1958) type, except for the use of pictures. Furthermore, nonsense words were deliberately avoided to keep the children from reporting such items back to their playmates and to be told that there were no such queer words. We do think, however, that the use of real words unknown to the children serves equally well, except that one can never be quite sure just how unknown they are.

Table 1 summarizes the data for two children from the experimental sessions conducted at 3;4 and 5;14. Target-like performance is indicated by *tl*; $\emptyset$ denotes uninflected forms. At the time of these experiments, the children had reached different stages in their L2 developments. However, the additional evidence from intermediate sessions as well as the data from the remaining two children conform to the general outlines apparent from Table 1. Furthermore, the development of all four children in these experiments is highly uniform. The error types in the last column are typical in that these types occurred with all four children.

TABLE 1

Plural inflections from two children, Heiko and Lars, elicited in two experiments at 3;4 and 5;14, respectively (tl = target-like; $\emptyset$ = uninflected form).

stems requiring	Heiko time of experiment		Lars time of experiment		typical errors
	3;4	5;14	3;4	5;14	
1. /-s/	tl	tl	mostly tl some $\emptyset$	tl	two cat
2. /-z/	mostly tl a few -s once $\emptyset$	tl	some tl a few -s some $\emptyset$	mostly tl a few $\emptyset$	two dog-s two dog
3. /-əz/	once tl mostly $\emptyset$ a few -z, -s	tl	$\emptyset$	mostly tl a few $\emptyset$ once -z	two crutch, hose two ditch-s, judge-z
4. -$\emptyset$	tl	once tl mostly -s, -z	tl	some tl some -s, -z, -əz	two sheep-s, feet-s, cattle-z, goos-əz
stems ending in					
5. /-ə ∼ -ər/	some tl some $\emptyset$	tl	$\emptyset$	tl	two catcher
6. /-θ/	some tl some $\emptyset$	tl	$\emptyset$	some tl some $\emptyset$	two moth

In agreement with the spontaneous data the first allomorph to be acquired is /-s/. The children most confidently employ it where required by the target, except after stems in /-θ/. It seems that at first they hesitate to use [-s] where not permitted by L2, that is after stems requiring /-z, -əz/, Ø, or suppletions of various sorts. It is in particular the unfamiliar items presented in the singular that the children at first do not inflect at all in the experiments. This strategy leads to target-like forms whenever singular and plural are homophonous, as, for instance, with *deer, fish, trout, salmon, cattle,* and *sheep.* Such surface forms do not imply that the child has acquired the target plural rule. These Ø-plurals are not based on any precise rule at all, but they are the negative result of the rule governing /-s/.

In the experimental data it is quite clear that /-əz/ is acquired after /-z/, namely from such errors where [-s] or [-z] are used instead of /-əz/ as in *judge-z, ditch-s,* etc.

Some Shortcomings of the Morpheme Order Approach

Several details about the developmental sequence for the L2 plural have been omitted. Also, only the acquisition of one inflectional paradigm has been described. However, according to our data, the L2 acquisition of other inflectional paradigms, like the genitive and third person singular present conforms well to the general outlines found for the plural. Thus, the Ø-strategy recurs; the sequence for the allomorphs has [-s] first and [-əs ~-əz] last for both the genitive and for third person singular present. It seems, therefore, that the above data provide an empirically well founded basis for an evaluation of the two approaches, morpheme order vs. developmental sequence. We shall note five points.

Morpheme order and language acquisition as a developmental process. Of course, the morpheme order approach does not deny the fact that language acquisition is a developmental process. However, by focussing on the relative chronology of target-like mastery of several items, this approach necessarily misses all developments leading toward and preceding the final state of achievement. To be sure, the relative chronology of the allomorphs /-s~z~əz/ can be captured with the help of the morpheme order approach. But, for instance, the fact that stems requiring /-z, -əz/ are at first also inflected by adding [-s] is beyond the scope of the morpheme order approach. The latter can therefore be said to lack depth and to disguise a fair amount of acquisitional developments.

Morpheme order and avoidance phenomena. The morpheme order approach cannot capture certain cases where an item manifests target-like use in only part of the total range of its target environments and where the remaining environments do not occur at all. What will the conclusions have to be in terms of morpheme order — total target-like mastery? To answer yes would be just as misleading as to answer no. Our tools have to be more sophisticated. And to show that this is no mere theoretical quibble we shall briefly report one such case from the children's L2 acquisition of the English genitive.

In English both names and common nouns can appear in the genitival construction N + gen + N (*Johnny's dog, the boss' car*). In the children's L1 (German) only names can be preposed to the head nouns as in English (*Heikos Angel,* ,,Heiko's fishing pole''); or elliptical as *das ist Heikos,* ,,that's Heiko's''. Common nouns are placed after the head (*das Ohr der Katze,* the ear of the cat''), but not **der Katze Ohr* ,,the cat's ear''.

There are plenty of ellicptical instances in the spontaneous data, like *this is Johnny's.* Similarly, such elliptical genitives as well as the non-elliptical instances like *this is Johnny's pole* were easy to elicit in large numbers. But for a long time there was no way of getting strings with common nouns in place of names. And there are at first no such utterances in the spontaneous data, either. To credit the children with target-like mastery up to criterion, as we think one would have to in terms of the morpheme order approach, would be thoroughly misrepresenting that stage of their development. The developmentally fascinating aspects during these stages would be to investigate how the children managed to avoid such N + gen (+N) structures. They invariably opted for the *of*-alternative, which they produced target-like from fairly early on. The reason for this course of development, we think, is clear. The children are influenced by the peculiar distribution of names vs. common nouns in their L1 German.

Morpheme order, cross-sections, statistical evaluation, and stereotypes. This point concerns morpheme order inasmuch as it has in the past been closely linked with cross-sectional data collection and statistical evaluation. Premature forms like, for instance, *guys,* may superficially be target-like and they would probably have to be scored as such. The same applies to early forms like *feet, sheep, fish, cattle,* used as plurals. The fact that they look target-like is not due to the acquisition of the $\emptyset$-plural, but due to the $\emptyset$-strategy described above. The developmental status of such forms, that is, whether they are stereotypes, monomorphemic, plurals based on the child's plural rule, or due to some avoidance strategy, can only be decided by placing such items within the developmental sequence. Establishing mean values will obliterate this fact.

Morpheme order, and acquisitional strategies and principles. The orderliness and the systematicity so obvious from the data above confirm what can be concluded from studies about the L2 acquisition of other structural areas besides inflections, namely, that these surface regularities must be due to more deeply seated that principles (Wode 1977a, c, 1979). If we are ever to discover them we will have to go beyond surface orders of morphemes and look in great detail at developmental sequences, that is, at how not only L2 children first decompose target structures and then re-build them step by step (Wode 1976d). It is here that we can observe these principles and strategies at work. Recall, for instance, the use of $\emptyset$ in Table 1, or note the systematicity in the children's reliance on L1 (see below). The morpheme order approach will disguise such strategies.

Reliance on L1 (German). Whereas the points raised above hold for L1 and other acquisitional types as well, the present point is restricted to L2 acquisition. Consider the late incorporation of stems ending in $/-\theta/$ into the $/-s/$ rule, and the late incorporation of stems ending in $/-\vartheta\sim-\vartheta^r/$ into the $/-z/$ rule. We can see no reason within the structure of Trinity Center English why the children should treat such stems the way they do. We suspect that their L1 German shows through here. For the children the L2 $/-\theta/$ relates to their L1 $/s/$ (Wode 1978a). There are no long consonants in German. Hence L2 stems cannot be pluralized until the child has established a different status for his L2 $/\theta/$. Similarly, German Stems in $/-\varepsilon^\vartheta\sim-a/$ often take the $\emptyset$-plural, for instance, *Keller: Keller* „basement(s)", *Fahrer: Fahrer* „driver(s)", and *Werfer: Werfer* „pitcher(s)". More often than not German $/-\varepsilon^\vartheta\sim-a/$ is a deverbal nominal affix. We suspect that this L1 morphological rule causes the children to treat nouns like *pitcher, teacher, hammer* different from other nouns.

The earlier account on the four children's acquisition of the TC inflections in Wode 1976a was limited to the spontaneous data. The addition of the experimental material above reinforces the earlier conclusion that reliance on L1 is an integral part of the L2 acquisition of inflections. Moreover, the experimental evidence suggests that reliance on L1 may also affect structural subareas such as the inflection of stems requiring $/-\vartheta z/$ via the $/-s, -z/$ rule, that previously seemed unaffected (Wode 1976a).

Conclusion

It appears that the two approaches of morpheme order and developmental sequence focus on different aspects of the total process of L2 acquisition. Therefore, the conclusion cannot be to claim general superiority of one over the other. Morpheme order approaches, if properly extended, may provide for the overall acquisitional order of different structural areas. However, at the present imperfect state of our knowledge, studies on developmental sequences of individual structural areas are indispensable to provide detailed insights into the mechanisms of the acquisitional process. We have attempted to show that it is also fruitful to analyze the acquisition of inflections in this way.

Looking back at the morpheme order studies from the vantage point provided by the data of the present study, it is clear why some researchers have failed to find a universal order of acquisition. In fact, generalizing from the regularities that have become apparent above, one can predict that there can be no universal order of acquisition for English. Since reliance on L1 is an integral part of L2 acquisition, for both the naturalistic and the tutored varieties (Wode 1976a, d, 1977a), it follows that any L2 developmental sequence of a given structural area of English will differ as a function of the L1 acquired previously. This, in turn, is bound to reflect back on the gross overall morpheme order. In addition, there is no reason to assume in advance that such items as the various inflections, prepositions like *in, on,* or the copula, are acquisitionally comparable. In fact we think they are not, since their formal properties (bound vs. free forms) are acquisitionally quite different (Wode 1979). Moreover, if it does not matter what is compared in terms of morpheme order, then there is no reason why one should not determine the order of acquisition for, say /r/ vs. negation.

Notes

* Reprinted by permission from *Language Learning* 28 (1978) pp. 175-185.

ON THE USEFULNESS OF EXPERIMENTAL ELICITATION TECHNIQUES FOR INVESTIGATIONS ON NATURALISTIC L2- ACQUISITION*

Hartmut Burmeister, Detlef Ufert, and Henning Wode

0 Purpose

The revival of interest in research on language acquisition during the early 1960's was marked methodologically by attempts to eliminate observer variables or if this proved impossible at least reduce them or keep them constant. By relying on methods developed in the social sciences researchers tried to control the observer situation. Above all, the diary type of data collection which was the chief method utilized in the early days of language acquisitional research (e.g. Stern & Stern 1907, Leopold 1939) tended to be replaced by more exact methods. Naturally, the desire for more control led to the application of controlled experimentation. Utterances were elicited via various elicitation techniques. The tendency to rely primarily on controlled experimental procedures is also quite noticable in the recent upsurge of interest in naturalistic, i.e. untutored L2-acquisition. There are some studies in which experimentally elicited utterances provide the only data for descriptions of the L2 development (e.g. Bailey et. al. 1974, Dulay & Burt 1973, Mills 1977). These studies do not check whether experimentally elicited data are isomorphic with spontaneous material, i.e. whether experimentally elicited data mirror the child's competence in just the same way as his spontaneous verbalizations do. Of course, to provide spontaneous data requires longitudinal studies, which, as is well known, are much more time consuming. In the past it was impossible to check empirically to what extent both data types are isomorphic, because most studies dealt only with either spontaneous utterances or elicited material. In the long run what is needed is both data types from the same speaker.

Of course, it is almost trivial to say that people behave differently in natural situations than in non-natural ones. Examples of this abound in psychology.

Two recent studies on naturalistic L2-acquisition from the U.S. confirm this, namely, Fillmore 1976 and Rosansky 1976a. However, these studies state only that the data types differ. It is necessary to go further. The main point is to determine what constitutes these differences and to what extent elicited data provide a different picture of the speech development than spontaneous utterances. This is the background that gave rise to the question of the usefulness of data collected with different techniques. To what extent do such data types allow for the same or comparable inference about the development of speech? This point applies to all types of language acquisition.

Below, we contrast experimentally elicited and spontaneous data, each type being gathered from four German children who learned English as their L2 without foreign language instruction. The most characteristic differences between the two data types are worked out by viewing the experimental data in the light of the insights derived from the spontaneous material. The latter are summarized first.

1 Some Insights from the Spontaneous Data

Our data come from a project which aims at establishing an integrated theory of language acquisition. This theory is intended to allow us to capture, in a systematic way, both the commonalities as well as the differences between the various acquisitional types, such as L1 acquisition, naturalistic L2 acquisition, foreign language teaching, etc. (details on this typology of acquisitional types in Wode 1974, Felix 1978b). The comparison of the data for the various acquisitional types produced a large number of commonalities in the way in which children acquire the linguistic structures of a given target language.

We noted in particular that within all the acquisitional types so far investigated, children do not pick up the structures of the target language all at once. Rather, they seem to filter out certain properties of the target structures which are subsequently reintegrated step by step and thus approach the target language via a series of developmental stages (details in Wode 1976d). In doing so they also produce utterances which are ungrammatical in terms of the adult grammar. The sequence of developmental stages and the linguistic structure of the utterance types which constitute these stages is called the developmental sequence (some such developmental sequences can be found, e.g. in Wode 1976a, c, 1977b, c, 1978b, Felix 1978b). These developmental sequences will be our major concern, because as far as we can now determine these sequences derive from the psycho-neurological processes and abilities which enable human beings to acquire natural languages (Wode 1978c).

2 Data

Our data come from a six months longitudinal study of four German children. They were observed how they acquired English during a half year stay in the United States. They were not quite 4, 6, 8, and 9 years old when the investigation began. The children did not receive any English instruction. They acquired the language through daily interaction with their friends and neighbors (details in Wode 1978a).

There are two types of data: on the one hand, the spontaneous utterances of the children were noted; on the other hand, their state of development was checked at 3 to 4 week intervals via experimental elicitation. The data base consits of:

Spontaneous data:
There are approximately 100 hours of tape recordings of spontaneous speech in various situations. In addition, there is a substantial body of notes which were taken directly at the scene of events. They contain, in addition to the children's utterances, phonetic transcriptions, the − most probable − intention of the speaker, as well as indications about the situation, references to previous discourse, etc.

Experimentally elicited data:

Twelve tests[1] were administered to check on the state of development of the four children with respect to various structural areas. The children were tested individually, each session lasting from 20 to 30 minutes. They had to translate German sentences into English and the reverse. As for the content of the sentences, it mirrored activities which were familiar to the children, e.g. fishing or baseball with the boys. At least during the beginning of the stay the children were quite willing to do these tests. The children tended to regard the experiments as a sort of game. Errors were pointed out and/or corrected by the interviewer only when the children asked him to do so. At times it was necessary to supply some vocabulary.

3 Spontaneous vs. Elicited Data: The Case of L2 – English Negation

The utterance types which the children produced in the tests deviated quite markedly from those which were produced spontaneously during the same period. There are five major differences. As opposed to the spontaneous data, the experimental material was characterized by:

1. an increase in the reliance on L1;
2. a greater frequency of archaic structures;
3. an avoidance of certain target structures;
4. many structural types which were not noted in the spontaneous productions;
5. all in all, a much greater heterogeneity in the data, namely,
   a) in terms of the number of different developmental structures, and
   b) in terms of the individual differences between the children.

It will suffice if these differences are represented by referring to one of the children. We choose Lars. In the beginning of the investigation he was slightly less than six years old. His development corresponded closely to that of the other children. The major stages in the developmental sequence of negation in the spontaneous data were the same for all children except for the fact that not all of them progressed equally far. The developmental sequence is summarized in table 1. Note that the stages are characterized by the appearance of specific developmental structures.

It does not seem necessary here to report on all of the tests. The central insights can be illustrated by reference to one of them. We select the test at 2;20 (two months and twenty days of contact). Lars is already fairly advanced (stage V, structural type 4.b of the developmental sequence in tab. 1). This is the point at which Lars begins to produce utterances in which do-support appears in conjunction with full-verbs as well as modals.

Tab. 1 Developmental sequence for the L2 acquisition of English negation by four 4 to 9 year old children with German as L1 (from Wode 1977a). Optional elements in ()

	structural type	example	stage
1	anaphoric: Neg	no	I
2.1	anaphoric: Neg X	no, Kenny	
	X Neg	Tiff, no	
2	non-anaphoric[2]: Neg X	no finish	II
		no play baseball	
		Henning, not home	
		not drink	
3.1	Subj (be) Neg X		III
	that's no Adj	that's no right	
	you not N	you not dummy	
	Subj be not Adv	Johnny is not there	
3.2a	Subj Neg V		IV
	not	I'm[3] not go bed	
	no	me no close the window	
3.2b	Subj V (Pron) Neg X	I'm steal not the base	
		Marylin like no sleepy	
	M Neg X	I cannot say that word	
3.2c	imperative: don't VP	don't broke	
3.2d	imperative: V (Pron) not X	shut not your mouth	
		hit it not over the fence	
4.a	suppletive don't/didn't	no, don't	V
4.b	Subj don't/didn't Aux VP	I don't can eat anymore	
	Aux	you didn't can that	
	VP	I didn't have a snag	

3.1 Increased Reliance on L1

If compared with the spontaneous data, the experimental material shows a relatively greater amount of interference with respect to the total amount of such utterances as well as with respect to the diversity of the (interference) structural types. Apparently this feature is specific to the test situation. It does not only pertain to the test at 2;20, but it is typical of all the tests which were conducted during the 6 month stay.

The experimental data from the session under consideration here show 22% interference structures, whereas the spontaneous productions show very little interference, if any. In the spontaneous utterances, negation in the structural type 4.b is achieved via *do*-support both before full-verbs and modals; spontaneous utterances lacking *do* are rare with Lars around 2;20. In the experimental data *do*-support is frequently omitted. Some examples are given in tab. 2.

Tab. 2: Spontaneous vs. elicited L2 utterances involving *do*-support.

spontaneous		elicited	
(1)	don't touch the ball	(5)	don't hit the ball
(2)	don't broke (=break)	(6)	throw not too far
(3)	I don't want to play catch	(7)	I see not cricket
(4)	Johnny don't go to school	(8)	I want not going fishing

As for the imperatives, at the time of the test they are negated spontaneously target-like via *don't* + VP (cf. (1-2)). In the test the structure is often directly taken over from the German test item. For example, in *throw not too far* the word-order mirrors German *wirf nicht weit.* Furthermore in (7) and (8) the influence of the German test item *ich sehe die Grillen nicht* and *ich will nicht zum Fischen gehen,* respectively, is obvious. It should be noted that the post-verbal position of the negative morpheme *not* as in (7) and (8) was also noted spontaneously, although much earlier, during stage IV, structural type 3.2b. During stage V this type of post-verbal *not* is no longer used spontaneously.

3.2 Backsliding into Archaic Structures

During the tests the children very often fell back on structural types which, according to the spontaneous developmental sequence(s), mark earlier stages of development. That is, the tests led the children to produce structures which they used at an earlier point of time but which at the time of the test itself were no longer employed. Cf. tab. 3.

Tab. 3: Backsliding in the elicitations.

		relapse into stage
(9)	I no can't see	IV structural type 3.2a
(10)	I want no bread	IV structural type 3.2b
(11)	I want not play catch	IV structural type 3.2b

The experimental utterances such as (9) have auxiliaries with pre-posed negative element *no*. This is a structural type which is similar to type 3.2a. There are no spontaneous utterances on record with this negative element in front of the modal. However, it is quite obvious that Lars is relying on an archaic position of the negative morpheme, namely, pre-verbal neg. During stage IV, modal auxiliaries are already negated target-like in the spontaneous productions so that double-negation, as in (9), does not occur. When, in the structural type 4.b, *can* is negated via pre-posed *don't/ didn't* the enclitic *−n't* is not also attached to *can*. In addition, at the time of the tests Lars is also beginning to produce utterances like (12) spontaneously.

(12) I can't do this any longer

Utterances like (10) and (11) were noted during stage 3.2b in Lars' spontaneous speech. At the time of this test, comparable spontaneous utterances have *do*-support.

3.3 Avoidance of Structures

Frequently, there are utterances in the experimental data which suggest that the children avoid certain structures. For example, Lars very often uses copula structures in order to translate full verb sentences. One gets the impression that the boy is attempting to avoid *do*-support which would be required if he employed the full verb. For example, the interviewer once gave the item *Kommt Johnny heute nicht zum Essen?*. At first Lars hesitates. Then he begins with (13a):

(13a) does Johnny ....

Then he stops and continues with the copula structure, which does not require *do*-support (13b):

(13b) is Johnny not coming for dinner today?

Also, there are examples in which negation is avoided altogether. Frequently the meaning of the sentence is not essentially altered (14-16):

L2 rendering	German test item
(14) Johnny, you can stay	Johnny, du musst nicht nach Hause kommen
(15) that's right	das ist nicht falsch
(16) Heiko missed the snag	Heiko hat keinen *snag* gefangen

The fact that the test items are frequently avoided or simplified makes it impossible to determine exactly the child's state of development because the children also avoided structures in the tests which they had already produced spontaneously.

3.4 Structures Occuring only in the Test

There are some observations which are peculiar to the tests. They can only be identified as peculiar by comparing them with the spontaneous material. These are structures which do not occur at all in the spontaneous material and which, consequently, are not entered in the developmental sequence of tab. 1. Cf. tab. 4.

Utterance types like (17-21) which were produced in the test are not recorded spontaneously at all. Modal *cannot* in (17) is used in comparable spontaneous utterances in the sequence Subj + cannot + V + X (as in type 3.2b of tab. 1).

Tab. 4: Some L2 utterances type observed only in the elicitations.

	L2 rendering	test item
(17)	I cannot Barbara see	ich kann Barbara nicht sehen
(18)	don't going to fishing	geh nicht zum Angeln
(19)	I see don't cricket	ich sehe keine *crickets*
(20)	I want don't pitch	ich will nicht *pitchen*
(21)	Heiko is don't the pitcher	Heiko ist nicht der *pitcher*

The post-verbal positioning of *don't* (19-20) appears exclusively in the experimental utterances. *Don't* is here placed after the verb just as the negative morpheme *not* is in the structural type 3.2b. In (21), Lars negates *is* via post-posed *don't* although spontaneously equational sentences are negated via post-verbal *not*. Utterances like (21) were still produced by Lars in the elicitations towards the end of the stay, i.e. 3 months after the test at 2;20 discussed here.

3.5 Increased Heterogeneity of the Experimental Data

On the one hand, both longitudinal as well as interval investigations of children's spontaneous speech have produced a surprising number of commonalities between different speakers. This might suggest that language acquisition is a fairly homogeneous process. Our spontaneous data also show that the development of each of the four children is basically the same. No doubt there were individual differences but they are limited to specific developmental stages and the range of variability was fairly limited.

On the other hand, the elicited data provide a different impression, namely, a much more heterogeneous one, and this in two respects: First, in a given test, the number of different structural types is much greater than in the spontaneous productions. This is due, first and foremost, to those structures which occur only in the elicitations (recall sec. 3.4). This increased range of variation in the experimental elicitation was found with all children and all structural areas. Second, the structures are not necessarily the same for all children. There is a greater range of individual variation among the different children.

4 Additional Studies

There are two recent studies which support our reservations about the relevancy of elicited data. These studies also provide spontaneous as well as experimentally elicited material and they use different elicitation techniques. Rosansky 1976a investigated six Spanish-speaking individuals learning English as L2. In addition to her daily longitudinal observations she also used experimental elicitation techniques. The tests were based on the bilingual syntax measure, an elicitation device developed by Burt et al. 1975. The BSM is a set of cartoons which is shown to children so that the interviewer can ask questions about these pictures. Before the tests can be administered it is necessary to check whether the L2 lexicon is sufficiently advanced so that the children can follow the interviewer's instructions. Burt et al. thought that the validity and the reliability of the BSM was sufficient because there was a high correlation between the results from different investigations which were carried out according to the same methodology. However, the test itself as a data elicitation technique was never seriously questioned, perhaps by comparing the elicited to the spontaneous data from longitudinal studies.

Rosansky notes that for several speakers the structure of the elicited utterances is drastically different from that of the spontaneous data of the same period. She further points out some difficulties that relate to the use of statistical methods, like the BSM, because many of the common statistical evaluation procedures obliterate individual differences.

Fillmore 1976 collected spontaneous and experimentally elicited data for five Mexican children with Spanish as L1 and English as L2. She used various elicitation techniques. Among other things, she attempted to provoke verbal interaction through playing games. Very often pictures and drawings served as stimuli. Initially she used a bilingual method to bridge comprehension difficulties. The question in English was followed by the Spanish equivalent. When the L2 children were advanced enough, lexically as well as syntactically, the repetition in Spanish was omitted. In addition, the stimuli were redesigned to provide more liberty in replying, for instance, via invitations like „tell me about this" or „tell your friend what's happening there". Among other things, the children were shown a series of pictures which belonged together as far as subject matter was concerned. At times, the interviewer provided a target-like sentence for the first picture. Since the following pictures very often differed only in small nuances, the children's task then amounted only to paradigmatic substitutions.

Fillmore analyzes her data types separately. But she does not attempt to specify the differences in any systematic way, as we have attempted in sec. 3. But it is obvious that the elicitation techniques used by Fillmore often only lead to elliptical utterances or to utterances which are not very complex. There was a disproportionately high amount of holophrastic utterances in the elicitation material. In addition to the drastic differences between spontaneous and experimental data Fillmore's investigation also shows that different elicitation techniques lead to different results.

5 Conclusion

As already briefly indicated, the lack of isomorphism between experimentally elicited and spontaneous data not only holds for the structural area of negation. In our files, the same also applies to all those structural areas for which tests were administered, namely, interrogation (Ufert 1980), word order, inflexions (Wode et al. 1978), and phonology (Wode 1977c, 1978a).

It would be premature to conclude that one or the other data type should be totally eliminated. In the long run the task is to determine with more precision the usefulness that the various data collection procedures may have. After all, there must be some relationship between the data types that have been contrasted in this paper, although perhaps only in rather global ways, and the child's/speakers' knowledge about English. This implies that in the future we will have to determine with much more precision exactly what it is that is spontaneous about sponaneous data and what may be test-specific about elicited material. There is no reason to assume that the outcome will be a bipolar division. As long as this is not achieved it remains methodologically dangerous to simply mix the two data types. It is already very clear that it is methodologically erroneous to investigate language acquisition only by relying on experimental elicitation techniques. Such techniques produce a distorted picture, as is clearly indicated by our data as well as by those provided by Rosansky 1976a and Fillmore 1976. It is not yet known to what extent such distortions are specific to individual acquisitional types, for example, to the L2 types. It seems appropiate to recall the study on L1 imitation tests by Slobin and Welsh (1973). They reported that in an imitation exercise an L1 English-speaking child used structures which were not yet used spontaneously but which were to become productive at the next stage. Our L2 subjects did not exhibit anything like this in their L2 development.

Notes

* Reprinted by permission from *Linguistische Berichte* 64 (1979) pp 55-104. Expanded version of a paper delivered at the eight annual meeting of the GAL at Mainz, October 1977. Thanks for comments and criticism are due to Jens Bahns, Ocke Bohn, Sascha Felix and Werner Prauss.
1) The term „test" is used here not in the strict sense of a well-defined experimental design as in psychology. We use the term in a less restricted way to refer to semi-standardized interviews.
2) These utterances are called non-anaphoric because neg, as in *no play baseball*, negates the whole utterance. The meaning is „I/we don't want to play baseball" (Wode 1977b).
3) *I'm* is still monomorphemeic at this stage of development.

Commentary

The two papers, if taken together, indicate that we are still far from possessing reliable procedures according to which acquisitional studies can be conducted and evaluated. The best that can be done at present is to make use of the advantages of the various approaches, i.e. to combine longitudinal with cross-sectional data collection, to couple emphasis on developmental sequences with concerns for the order of morphemes, and to complement experimental data by spontaneous observation.

Part IV

INTERLANGUAGE STRATEGIES

Introduction

There is no doubt, that research on language acquisition has to look first and foremost at the empirically observable facts. Ultimately, however, our interest should not be in learner errors or observable phenomena in a superficial sense. The goal must be to characterize the underlying abilities that enable human beings to produce whatever peculiarities are directly observable. That is, emphasis must ultimately turn to the abilities, strategies, or processes which human beings activate when learning a language. Essentially, this amounts to the question of the nature and functioning of the linguo-cognitive capacities mentioned in the introduction to part II. Current research is beginning to turn to such questions. Various strategies have been proposed. Most of these proposals suffer from the fact that they are far too global and that they do not indicate what is specific about learning languages as against, say, learning to ride a bike or to solve mathematical problems. Some such strategies are: overgeneralization, simplification, strategies of training, strategies of learning, transfer of prior knowledge, etc. (Selinker 1972). All these strategies, one way or another, apply to various learning domains, i.e. they are not specific to learning languages. The crucial problem therefore is not to find more strategies, like those above, but to determine the linguo-cognitive details. For example, how is the phonological system of a target language „simplified"; how is a vowel like English /æ/ „simplified"; or how is the inflectional system of, say, German „simplified" by speakers of English?

The three papers of this part are attempts to identify some linguo-cognitive strategies as minutely geared to handle the formal properties of linguistic devices. The first paper traces such a strategy through L1, naturalistic L2, and FLT. This leads to the suggestion of a new notion of acquisitional universal, namely, one which is no longer restricted to L1 but which refers to all types of language acquisition. It is claimed that some linguo-cognitive strategies are universal in the sense that they are available to the learner in all learning situations no matter which language is being learned, what the age of the learner is, and what the external situation may be.

The other two papers deal with the nature of interference. There are two reasons why these papers are included. The first reason is to show that those current views are wrong which assert that interference does not occur, is unimportant, or that it is a negligible aspect of naturalistic L2 acquisition. The data presented in these papers illustrate that L1 transfer is just as much a developmental phenomenon in L2 acquisition as other regularities. This view is likely to be easily acceptable for phonology. The paper on negation is therefore added to show that the same applies to non-phonological structural areas as well.

The second reason for the inclusion of the papers on L1 transfer is that L1 transfer is not random, but highly systematic. In fact, it lends itself just as much to an analysis in terms of minute linguo-cognitive strategies as the other acquisitional regularities which do not involve reliance on L1.

In addition, the paper on L2 phonology is noteworthy because I show that presently available phonetic/phonological theories are not suited to describe the facts of language acquisition. This weakness is, unfortunately, also true for linguistic theories in general, irrespective of which structural area is concerned.

OPERATING PRINCIPLES AND 'UNIVERSALS' IN L1, L2, AND FLT*

Henning Wode

0 Purpose

In particular, past research on FLT has stressed the distinctness of this type of language acquisition as against, for instance, L1 because of the peculiar situation pertaining in the classroom (cf., for instance, Lane 1962). The observation as such need not be disputed. But emphasizing the distinctness of FLT should not mislead one to regard it as totally unrelated to other types of language acquisition, unless it be assumed that man is endowed with different acquisitional capacities wholly unrelated to each other in that each is strictly limited in its applicability to one specific acquisitional type, i.e. one for L1, another for L2, a third for FLT.

I think a change in focus is necessary. The view that FLT is distinct because of the peculiar external setting, and by implication other acquisitional types as well, should be complemented by detailed investigations (a) as to how and whether these variables affect man's/the student's development in L1, L2, and FLT, and (b) whether there are not developmental parallels in spite of differences in the situational setting. This requires a new approach, i.e. one that does not treat a specific acquisitional type in isolation, but that integrates it with other types of language acquisition, and that seeks to determine differences and parallels in the acquisition of linguistic structures across all types of language acquisition. In fact, the recent upsurge of research on naturalistic L2 acquisition (for summaries see Wode 1974; Felix 1977f, 1978b; and articles and references in Hatch 1978a) has brought to light differences and parallels. I take the view that both differences and parallels in the observable data must reflect the 'operating principles' – whatever their nature – with which the child/speaker acquires a language. For the purpose of this study it will be assumed that parallels between acquisitional types are due to the application and applicability of the same 'principle(s)'. Differences, however, need not be due exclusively to strict non-applicability but they may also be due to applicability in different orders, and, perhaps, to other factors as well.

1 The Data

The bulk of the data come from a long range project of several years' standing. Our main aim is to bring within the scope of one theory both the parallels as well as the differences between all types of language acquisition. (For a typology of such types cf. Wode 1974.) Consequently, we systematically trace the acquisition of selected structural areas of two languages, namely English and German, across various acquisitional types. We now have at our disposal data on L1 German (four children: aged up to 9 years), L1 English, naturalistic L2 German acquired by children with English as L1 (4: 3–7), naturalistic L2 English acquired by children with German as L1 (4: 4–9), FLT-L2 English as taught to German students (34: 10–11).

The project has deliberately been designed around my four children. They were our informants for L1 German (Wode 1976b–c, 1977b, 1980b, Greenhalgh 1976) as well as for L2 English/L1 German (Wode 1976a, 1977a, c, 1978a, Ufert 1980). The data on L2 German/L1 English were collected from American, Australian and British children whose parents had moved to the Kiel vicinity (Lange 1979, Felix 1976b, 1977b, d, 1978a–b). The data on FLT-L2 English were collected from 34 (high school) students attending a Kiel high school during their first 8 months of instruction (Felix 1976a, 1977a–b, d).

The data were collected in much the same way for all the types. They are longitudinal. For L1 German and L2 English/L1 German we have been able to follow a daily routine; for L2 German/L1 English we had to rely on intervals, none, however, longer than 3 days. The FLT data were collected in such a way that 2–3 investigators sat in on every period taught throughout the entire 8 months. For all types we have tape recordings of spontaneous speech as well as notes taken immediately on the scene of action and including phonetic transcriptions, the child's (most likely) intention, comments on the situation, etc. (For more details cf. Wode 1978a).

2 Some Basic Distinctions: Operating Principles, Universals, Developmental Principles

Slobin's (1973) term 'operating principle' is intended as a cover term for "a sort of general heuristic ... which the child brings to bear on the task of organizing and storing language" (1973: 191). Slobin's universals refer to the product of these heuristics, i.e. to the observable speech data. Within this approach the operating principles provide for the predictive capacity. The universals are derived from the principles.

Slobin's original suggestions refer to L1 acquisition. In extending this approach to other acquisitional types it is necessary to refine the notion of universal by reference to the different acquisitional types. Some peculiarities may be universal to L1, but not to L2 or FLT; other universals may relate to L1 and naturalistic L2, and others may yet be restricted in other ways. Two reasons lead me to revise Slobin's original suggestions. First, numerous acquisitional types have not yet been investigated in sufficient detail. Therefore, we do not yet have the empirical data to make it fruitful to initiate a discussion on how universal an alleged universal has to be to deserve being termed a universal. What is needed is a device that allows us to state whether an acquisitional peculiarity is restricted to one, two, etc. acquisitional type(s). Second, Slobin's operating principles are attractive because they provide for the predictive capacity of the approach. It is these principles that predict the universals and that, consequently, make the theory subject to empirical verification. Unfortunately, however, at the present state of affairs Slobin's operating principles are (largely) vacuous since so little is known about the actual psychological and/or neurological processes.

My notion of developmental principle is intended to avoid the above difficulties and yet to retain the desirable effects. A developmental principle is a relationship between the – supposed – input language and the child's/speaker's output such that if the target language L_i has properties a, b, c...n, then the property a will be observable in the child's/speaker's output L_i before (or after, as the case may be) property b. For instance, if a language has intonational questions and pronominal ones, L1 children will produce intonational questions before pronominal ones. Consequently, a principle can be postulated to the effect that intonation questions precede pronominal ones (details in Wode 1976c).[1]

I think that the above version has several advantages. Tying the developmental principles to linguistic structures proper rather than to largely unknown neuro-psychological phenomena has the advantage of, first, not being delayed by lack of progress in that area. Second, it does not require one to amalgamate psychological and linguistic concepts, but it allows one to keep the two domains apart and to interpret the developmental principles psychologically and/or neurologically given adequate progress in that area. Lastly, the debate on how universal a universal has to be, can be avoided by stating to which acquisitional type(s) a given principle applies.

3 Some Differences between the Acquisitional Types

Though the main point of this paper is to show that there are developmental principles that apply to L1, naturalistic L2, and FLT, this is not intended to imply that there are no differences. It is important, therefore, to safeguard against unbalanced views. Consequently, I shall attempt to provide some proper perspectives by outlining briefly the major developmental differences and parallels that have so far become apparent in our research, in particular those that relate to the child/student himself. Five points have so far emerged quite clearly:

(a) Decomposition of target structures

Target structures are not necessarily acquired as wholes. Complex structural areas like, for instance, interrogation or inflections are at first decomposed, as it were, into various elements which are later on, step by step, re-integrated into the target structure.

The acquisitional types differ as to the degree of decomposition. It is highest for L1, less for naturalistic L2, and even less for FLT. That is both in naturalistic L2 and FLT children/students start with fairly complex strings – phonetic, syntactic, etc. – right from the beginning. (The principle discussed in § 4 will further illustrate this point. See also (c) below).

(b) Developmental sequences

Both naturalistic L2 and L1 acquisition are subject to ordered developmental sequences. That is, a structural area like, for instance, negation is acquired in such a way that the children pass through an ordered sequence of developmental stages. Moreover, these developmental sequences are predictable largely on account of the structure of the languages involved. (For such L1 attempts cf. Wode 1976b, c, 1977b; for L2 cf. Wode 1976a, 1977a, c, 1978a, Felix 1978b.)

According to our data, FLT is also subject to developmental sequences in ways not unrelated to either L1 and/or naturalistic L2. The main difference is that FLT developmental sequences are not as strictly ordered as L1 and L2 sequences. But the developmental structures are much the same. (Cf. Felix 1976a, and below).

(c) L1 $\neq$ L2

The L1 and L2 developmental sequences for the same language are not necessarily parallel (Wode 1976d, Felix 1978b). Our evidence is not yet rich enough to say precisely to which extent developmental sequences from FLT parallel those for either L1 or naturalistic L2, though there are undeniable parallels (cf. below).

(d) Formal properties of linguistic devices as variables in developmental sequences

There is strong evidence both from L1 and L2 acquisition that the formal properties of the linguistic devices used in a given language are the major variable(s) determining the L1 and L2 developmental sequences (cf. data in Wode 1974, 1976a–c, 1978a–b). This implies, for instance, that a child with German as L1 will acquire English as L2 in a different developmental sequence observable with a Japanese child acquiring English. (Contrast Milon 1974 vs. Wode 1976a).

It is not yet certain to which extent the same formal structural variables determine the developmental sequences in FLT. However, one point of this paper will be to argue that many errors familiar from FLT are not due to either the teacher or his methodology, but that they are determined by the student's natural capacity for language acquisition. The differences in the L1 and L2 developmental sequences seem to follow from deeper seated regularities related to the child's/student's prior language experience. They do not only carry into the L2 structures from their L1, i.e. traditionally labelled interference. Felix 1978b has argued that L2 children also rely on more basic insights such as, for example, that speech is coded in specific ways, for instance, sequential ordering in syntax. In addition, there does not seem to be a holophrastic stage in L2, and examples with such bizarre word order patterns as in the notorious *all gone shoe* (Braine 1963) are conspicuously missing. Felix' argument applies also to L2 phonology. Such devastating phonological deformations/processes characteristic for early L1 phonology (cf., for example, Edwards 1971, Stampe 1972, Drachmann 1973, Ingram 1976) have not been found for L2 (Wode 1977c, 1978a).

(e) Reliance on prior knowledge

Both in L1 and naturalistic L2 acquisition, children rely on their prior knowledge. For L1 acquisition, there is no prior language knowledge to fall back on, unless bio-genetically pre-programmed. In accord with Bloom 1973 our own data suggest that for L1 acquisition children make use of prior experiental cognitive knowledge. In naturalistic L2 acquisition and in FLT children/students do rely on their prior L1. The main point, however, is not that they do so, but that they do so in a highly systematic way. Namely, L1 structures are only made use of if specific structural prerequisites are met in the child's own L2 development. And this, in turn, seems to be due to the acquisitional processes that the children adhere to (Wode 1977a).

As for FLT the majority of errors that we have found in naturalistic L2 acquisition are – superficially – parallel to those familiar from FLT. Whether this superficial identity can be taken to indicate that the errors in both types of L2 acquisition result from the application of the same acquisitional devices, whatever their nature, is not clear yet. Some cases that leave little room for doubt will be presented in the following paragraph.

4 The Acquisition of Free vs. Bound Forms in L1, L2 and FLT

PRINCIPLE: free forms are acquired before bound forms.[2]

Crucial evidence will be provided by those languages which offer options between bound vs. free forms to signal (much) the same semantic phenomenon. For English and German this would be, in particular:

> English: *not: n't; will: -'ll; would: -'d; have, has, had: -'ve, -'s, -'d; am, is, are: -'m, -'s, -'re.*
>
> German: the indefinite article(s) *ein, einen, einem: -'n, -'m;* the copula *ist: -'s;* the personal pronoun *er: -a.*

4.1 Evidence from L1

English: *not: -n't:* Before children produce or even understand *-n't* they replace both *not* and *-n't* by *no* as in *Kathryn no like celery.* When, later on, they begin to show reflexes of *-n't* as in *don't, can't, couldn't,* these forms are at first monomorphemic, hence free forms for the child (Bloom 1970, Klima & Bellugi 1966).

English: *will: -'ll:* Bellugi 1967 found that the Harvard children at first did not use *-'ll* but produced only the free forms for the auxiliaries. Bellugi points out that these forms were extremely rare in the speech of the mothers. They much preferred the bound variant *-'ll.*

Bellugi's observations show that what is involved is not a crucial frequency ratio to determine which item a child will acquire, but an acquisitional regularity expressible in terms of acquisitional principles (according to my terminology). Its applicability is not dependent upon crucial frequency ratios apart from the fact that an item has to occur at least a few times to give the child a chance to notice it.

German: The free variants of the indefinite articles occur much prior to the bound forms. The same holds for the copula *ist* and the pronoun *er.* Note also that parallel to the English data, the bound forms *-'s, -'n, -'m,* and *-a* are by far more frequent in colloquial German than their free alternants.

This is not to say that reflexes of target bound forms do not occur in early L1. However, forms like English *I'm, that's* and German *wo's* 'where's', *da's* 'there's' etc. are at first monomorphemic for the children. This becomes obvious from child utterances like *wo's ist er* 'where's is he' where the *'s* of *wo's* has no morphemic status.

For L1 there is corroborating evidence from studies on the acquisition of negation and interrogation. For instance, Latvian negation involves the free form *nē* 'no', the free form *nav* 'is not, has not' used for certain types of intra-sentential negation, and the intra-sentential bound negator *ne-*. Latvian children first use the free form *nē*, next *nav* and as long as they do not have *ne-*, it is replaced by *nē* much like English L1 children replace *not: -n't* by *no* (Wode & Ruke-Dravina 1977, Wode 1977b).

The L1 acquisition of interrogation also supports the above principle. For instance, there are intonation questions; word-order questions; pronominal questions, i.e. with free forms as interrogative markers; and particle questions, i.e. with bound forms as interrogative markers such as the postposed *-ko: -kö* of Finnish, the postposed *-li* of Bulgarian, or the preposed *vai-* of Latvian. With L1 children the first to arise is the intonation question, provided the target language has this type; next is the pronominal type; questions involving bound forms are later than the intonational and/or the pronominal type. Particularly illuminating data are available from Latvian, Finnish and Bulgarian.

According to Bowerman 1973, Finnish does not have intonation questions. Yes/no-questions are signalled via the postposed markers *-ko: -kö*. The two children observed by Bowerman used the pronominal type before the particle type. The children did not ask yes/no-questions until they had mastered the latter type.

Latvian presents three options. Yes/no-questions can be signalled intonationally and/or via the preposed bound form *vai-*. The information questions are signalled by interrogative pronouns. Ruke-Dravina 1963 reports that intonation questions were first, then pronominal questions, and *vai-*questions were last.

Bulgarian also offers three possibilities. Yes/no-questions can be signalled via intonation and/or the bound forms *-li*. Gheorgov 1908 reports that intonation questions were first, then pronominal questions, and then questions with *-li*. (For a detailed survey on the L1 acquisition of questions cf. Wode 1976b, c).

4.2 Evidence from Naturalistic L2

The predictions are fully born out both for L2 German/L1 English and L2 English/L1 German. Thus *ein, einem, ist,* etc. as well as *will, have, is* are in productive use far earlier than the bound forms. We have particularly rich evidence from our L2 English/L1 German children. Though phonological reflexes of bound forms do occur quite early, it is clear that they do not yet have any morphemic status, witness, for instance, *that's its (= is) no good* 'that is no good'.

As in L1 the negative *-n't* takes much longer to be used by the children than the correspondig free forms *no, not.* Moreover, *don't, didn't,* though clearly a reflex of the target auxiliary negation, are at first monomorphemic. Thus, in early L2 English/L1 German I found utterances like *no play baseball* 'I/we don't want to play baseball', *that's no right* 'that's not right', *me no close the window* 'I don't want to close the window'. (For details cf. Wode 1976a, 1977a. For additional supporting L2 evidence on negation cf. Huang 1971 L2 English/L1 Taiwan.; Milon 1974 L2 Engl./L1 Japan.; Adams 1974 L2 Engl./L1 Span.; Schumann 1975a L2 Engl./L1 Span.)

4.3 Foreign Language Teaching

Three problems have to be kept in mind as regards the evidence from FLT. (a) Human beings are capable of memorizing/imitating fairly long sequences of speech material as, for instance, in FLT drill sessions. (b) Human beings/students can produce many target-like tokens for/from a given rule if the rule is presented first. (c) Classroom teaching can be regarded as a (more) formal type of learning; whereas naturalistic L2 acquisition has more affinities with informal learning. Point (c) in a way includes point (b). It is to be expected, therefore, that FLT students will produce fairly long, complex, target-like utterances right from the very beginning. Such target-like utterances are likely to be more numerous during immediate practice sessions. What is not known about such data is whether they lead to the acquisition and availability of structures/rules necessary for natural and spontaneous communication.[3] Consequently, it is not only necessary to look at the data produced during immediate practice sessions but also to collect the material when the students are not immediately associated with the actual teaching, i.e. from their more spontaneous or semi-spontaneous contributions.

If, then, the principle discussed here is to be valid for FLT, we would expect to find evidence where (a) the students do not understand bound forms as required by the target; and where (b) they will substitute free forms for bound forms even if the exercise is designed to teach/practice bound forms. These expectations are born out (described in more detail by Felix 1976a, 1977a–b).

In one exercise the students were required to practice negation involving *isn't.* The reading material contained pictures of various situations. The teacher would ask a question and the students were required to answer in accord with the pictures. For instance:

(a) Teacher: Is there a sofa in Peter's room?
     Student: Yes, there isn't.

(b) Teacher: Can you see Mike?
     Student: No, I can.
(c) Teacher: Is it a red bus?
     Student: Yes, it isn't.

Not all exchanges went wrong like the above. But obviously, the students had not yet identified the structural relation inherent in *isn't*. However, up to this time, the students knew that *no* was a negative. The free form *not* had not been (thoroughly) introduced yet. And, sure enough, in a semi-spontaneous contribution that was not directly required by the exercise, one of the boys produced *that's no my comb* 'that's not my comb'. Note that this is exactly the type of utterance that one would expect at a point in the student's development where he did not yet have the bound negative at his disposal. That is, he fell back on the free form *no*.

In another exercise, the students were supposed to learn the bound variants of *have/has got*. The teacher tried hard. However, throughout the entire session there were only two successful attempts on the part of the students. All other student contributions had the free form, like *I have got a pencil, he has got a dog*. In this case the free forms *have, has* had been used in class though not practised extensively. Moreover, in a few cases the children produced *is* as in *she is got a ruler* 'she has got a ruler'. Note that the bound variant *-'s* is the same for the two free forms *has* and *is* and that the children confused this.[4]

5 Conclusions

I take the view that data as above are central for any notion on, approach to, and theory of, language acquisition including FLT. I think such data provide above all a number of challenging perspectives. The crucial factor involved in the regularities of the data is the type of – formal – device used in the languages involved. Consequently, explanatory approaches will fail or will remain unsatisfactory unless they prove suitable in accounting for these formal linguistic properties and the developmental regularities based on them. In this sense, I think, behaviorism, Piagetian cognitivism, approaches based on pragmatics and/or social interaction, Krashen's monitor model (Krashen 1977a–b), socio-economic factors (Heidelberger Forschungsprojekt Pidgin Deutsch 1975, 1976), affectives variables (Schumann 1975b) all fail to explain these central facts of language acquisition. I do not wish to be understood as suggesting that the variables implied by the approaches just mentioned are irrelevant to language acquisition, for instance, age and age-dependent loss of the ability to re-activate acquisitional strategies used for L1, motivation, types of field dependence, types of learning situations, amount of practice, to name just a few. However, I think their impact has, to date, been established only in rather global ways. It seems to me that we are likely to get a clearer understanding of their relevancy, if it is checked whether and to which extent they influence developmental sequences and the linguistic structure of the learner's utterances. As far as I can see there is no evidence available yet that might warrant the conclusion that such non-linguistic variables crucially determine the structure of the developmental sequences.

As a guide line for future research the data of § 4, I think, support the following speculations: There is no reason to assume that all acquisitional principles should apply alike/be carried over to L2 acquisition and FLT. Recall the differences between L1 and L2 as summarized in § 3. These differences cannot be reduced to the application of the same principle(s). On the other hand, the acquisition of bound forms is a fairly low-level/late phenomenon to take place during the three types of acquisition reviewed in this paper. Furthermore, it is obvious that the choice of structures to be acquired by the students in school can be manipulated via the sequence in which the structures are presented. This manipulation is based on the acquisitional fact – also relevant for naturalistic types of acquisition – that children acquire only those structures that are offered by their surroundings. It is further obvious that in FLT students reproduce from the outset much more complex structures than they do in either L1 or naturalistic L2 acquisition. This corroborates with the fact that in a naturalistic situation the learner is faced with the task of identifying from the total speech that impinges on him those structures that he is ready for. In FLT the student's task is different. The teacher will present him with only one or a limited set of structures to be acquired at a time. This may be the reason why the – tutored – students reproduce from the very beginning structures more complex than in either L1 or naturalistic L2. However, even so, it looks as if the structures presented to the students are subject to acquisitional principles (and the psychological processes that must be associated with these – linguistic – statements) which are specific to the various formal properties that a given structure may involve, irrespective of whether it is acquired as L1 or L2. And here it looks as if it is the fairly low level acquisitional principles, i.e. those that to be applicable require already a certain amount of structural competence that are carried over to all three types of acquisition reviewed here. Consequently, one would expect to find that, for instance, functor deletion, so notable in L1 (Brown 1973), should also loom large in naturalistic L2 and FLT. This is what we found: Deletion of the copula, of unstressed prepositions and of articles, abounds in both L2 types. (For FLT data cf. Felix 1976a, 1977a–b). Naturalistic L2 evidence abounds in our unpublished files. For L2 material available in print note the data appendices in Huang 1971 (L2 Engl./L1 Taiwan.), in Itoh 1973 (L2 Engl./L1 Japan.). However, this should not mislead one to conclude that there are no acquisitional principles peculiar to only one type of language acquisition. (Cf. Wode 1977a for a principle apparently related only to L2).

Above all I think the data reviewed in § 4 clearly show that language acquisition research can no longer be carried out by restricting it to one acquisitional type, preferably L1. Man's capacity for language acquisition is, apparently, not sharply compartmentalized, i.e. one for L1, another for L2, and so on. Consequently, insights into one type remain – fairly – unrevealing unless viewed within the context of other types.

Notes

* Reprinted by permission from *International Review of Applied Linguistics (IRAL)* 17 (1979) pp. 217–231.

[1] The basic idea underlying my notion of developmental principle is by no means novel. In one way or another it is implied by many linguistically orientated approaches in spite of differences in theoretical outlook and/or empirical coverage, for instance, Jakobson 1941, Edwards 1971, Stampe 1972, to name just a few.

[2] Note the similarity of my acquisitional principle with Slobin's L1 "Universal E4: when a child first controls the full form of a linguistic entity which can undergo contraction or deletion, contractions or deletions of such entities tend to be absent" (1973: 230). Apart from Slobin's restriction to L1 his universal and my principle agree in that they both predict the priority of free (Slobin's full) forms over the bound (Slobin's contracted) alternants. However, I have also included bound forms that do not have free alternants as in Latvian negation, or as in the interrogative systems of Bulgarian and Finnish. Moreover, it is not at all clear from our data that deletability is crucial for the children's/student's handling of free vs. bound forms.

[3] Elsewhere I have suggested that naturalistic language acquisition and FLT may be based on different types of learning principles (Wode 1974). The latter includes giving rules; having the students learn rules and/or reproduce utterances from such rules; corrections, drills, reproductions, etc. – all absent from naturalistic language learning. Felix 1977e has suggested that the two types of learning result in different sorts of competence: creative language use from naturalistic learning; (largely) reproductive use from FLT. Since, however, naturalistic learning can never be totally avoided even in the classroom, the result tends to be a mixture between the two types of learning. As far as I can see no learning theory whether behavioristic or cognitive is available at present that can accomodate the intricacies of language acquisition. Language learning, I think, requires a learning theory that is different from conceptual learning, visual learning, the learning of common sense, of logical thinking, of bodily skills, etc. (Wode 1978c; cf. also Chomsky 1976).

[4] This approach is, of course, frowned on by many FL teachers. This does not invalidate the point that students can produce fairly complex target-like utterances this way. Moreover, in spite of theoretical biases the actual classroom work that I have witnessed so far has always contained at least some elements of this 'rule approach'.

ON THE SYSTEMATICITY OF L1 TRANSFER IN L2 ACQUISITION*

Henning Wode

0 Purpose

The main concern of this report is the nature of the reliance on prior L1 knowledge in naturalistic, i.e. untutored L2 acquisition. It is suggested that L1 reliance is systematic in that specific conditions have to be met within the learner's L2 development before he will (can?) draw on his previous L1 knowledge. Therefore it should be possible to predict where, within a given developmental sequence, L1 transfer is likely to occur. It seems that, in the long run, these predictions may be statable in terms of acquisitional principles somewhat in the tradition of Jacobson 1941, Slobin 1973, Wode 1979.

The reasoning will require three steps: First, I describe some of the early stages of the naturalistic L2 acquisition of L2 English/L1 German negation. Then I speculate on whether the developmental structures are derived from L1 or L2, if either.

The data come from my children acquiring L2. (Technical details are given in other papers of this volume (notably papers No. 8 and 9)). Certain word order problems in the acquisition of English negation are selected for special scrutiny.

1 Some Developmental Stages for L2 English/L1 German Negation

The major stages of L2 English/L1 German as recorded from my four children are summarized in tab. 1. The chronology of the structural types is as implied by the numbering. Those types numbered by Roman numerals and subgrouped according to Arabic numerals are developmentally ordered as given by the numbering. Those types that are marked by small letters a, b, ... are structurally distinct but may occur at much the same time as indicated by the numerals.

Stage I: The first negative utterances to appear invariably involved *no*. Semantically, this was anaphoric negation, i.e. the negative relationship did not hold between Neg and the items with which it occured in construction.

Stage II: It comprises type II.2. The word order pattern is much the same as in type II.1. Neg is *no*. It is placed externally. Unlike stage I, the negative relationship is now non-anaphoric, i.e. it holds between Neg and the items with which it occurs in construction. For instance, *no play baseball* means ,,I/we don't want to play baseball." (For details on the terms anaphoric vs. non-anaphoric negation see Wode 1977b)

Stage III: With all four children the first sentences with internal placement of Neg were reflexes of target copula structures, i.e. III.1.

Utterances containing a full verb (V) and with Neg placed internally are consistently later than strings reflecting target copula structures. Neg may be *no* and/or

Tab. 1: The major developmental structural types and stages in the L2 English/L1
German acquisition of negation

structural type				illustrative example	stage
I	anaphoric: Neg			no	I
II. 1	anaphoric:	Neg X		no, Tiff	
		X Neg		Kenny, no	
2	non-anaphoric:	Neg	X		II
		no	V	no finish	
			N	no milk	
			Adj	no cold	
			VP	no play baseball	
III. 1	Subj (be)	Neg X			III
	that's	no	Adj	that's no right	
	you	not	N	you not dummy	
		no		it's no Francisco	
III. 2a	Subj Neg V				IV
	not			I'm not go Bett	
	no			me no close the window	
III. 2b	Subj V (Pron) Neg X			I'm steal not the base	
				Marylin like no sleepy	
	M Neg X			I cannot say that word	
III. 2c	imperative: don't VP			dont't broke	
III. 2d	imperative: V (Pron) not X			shut not your mouth	
				hit it not over the fence	
IV. a	supletive don't/didn't			no, don't	V
IV. b.	Subj don't/didn't	Aux VP		I don't can eat anymore	
		Aux		you didn't can that	
		VP		I didn't have a snag	

not. All in all, there were 4 major structures, III. 2a-d, co-occuring at this stage of
development. The type III.2a does not become (very) productive. Among the imperative types III.2c is the more productive one. In non-imperative declarative sentences, then, the children seem to strive for a single Neg placement rule with Neg
placed behind the first verb no matter whether V or Aux. During stage III, therefore,
there is no error regarding the placement of Neg in declarative negative sentences
that contain an Aux or a form of *be*. However, the structural type IV.b clearly
shows that at stages III - IV the children cannot be credited with a proper L2 Neg
placement rule, since they handle both V and Aux alike.

2 Sources for the L2 Developmental Stages

Types I - II.1: These types must go back to English morphophonologically. Whether the syntax is due to English or to German cannot be determined, since, intonation aside, English and German have much the same regularities.

Type II.2: This type has no direct model in either German or English. It seems that the children were overgeneralizing. The question is what the basis for this over-generalization may have been. I can think of four options: the children's own structure II.1; the anaphoric target L2 structure, or, more precisely, the word order pattern of this structure; truncated target L2 utterances like *no ball, no fish;* and the children's anaphoric L1 structure, more precisely the respective word order pattern. The difficulty, especially with the alternatives explaining II.2 as an overgeneralization from the L1 or L2 targets, is why the children do not go straight to the type III.2b. After all, this type will become productive later on; and there can be no question that at the time when one child produced, for instance, *no play baseball,* he did not already know very well that *play* was a verb and *ball* was a noun. He had the structural information available that is needed to place *not* after the full verb as required in German. But why does he not do so? Note, in particular, that this difficulty is not resolved if the origin of the L2 type II.2 is claimed to be in the truncated utterances. I shall suggest an answer below after a discussion of types III.1-2b.

Type III.1 relates to English morphophonologically. Whether positionwise it goes back to English or German is difficult to decide, since both languages place Neg after the copula. Those equational utterances that have *no* after the copula, must somehow be more directly modelled on English in ways unknown as yet.

Type III.2a is fairly close to target English word order in that Neg is placed in front of the full verb. The use of both *no* and *not* in this position also occurs in the L1 developmental sequence of English. This makes it unlikely that III.2a should be explained by reference to German.

It seems that III.2b heavily reflects German word order. For one thing, III.2b is not attested for L1 English.

3 L1 Reliance within L2 English/L1 German

To illustrate the nature of the reliance on L1 I shall single out the types III.2b and IV.b for two reasons: First, to my knowledge, neither one has yet been reported for L1 English, hence they are L2 specific. Second, again to the best of my knowledge, they have been reported only for certain L2 English combinations, i.e. in addition to L2 English/L1 German for L2 English/L1 Norwegian (Ravem 1968, 1969, Wode 1974), but not for L2 English/L1 Taiwanese (Huang 1971) or L2 English/L1 Japanese (Milon 1974). It follows that such L2 peculiarities must be due to the structure of the L1 involved in a given L2 combination. In fact, both German and Norwegian place Neg after the finite verb no matter whether V or Aux. English, of course, requires *do*-support for V with Neg placed before V.

The puzzle of III.2b is threefold: First, why do the children produce such utterances at that particular stage of their development, and not, say, at II.2? Second, by adopting III.2b the children move away from the target, because via III.2a they were already closer to the English pre-verbal *no/not* than they are via III.2b with post-verbal *no/not*. Third, the explanation cannot be that at II.2 the children did not fall back on their L1 rule because they could not distinguish between V and N. This they could as is obvious from the non-negated utterances of that time. There must be other prerequisites that favor L1 transfer.

I like to think that the acquisition of type III.1 creates the prerequisites to enable, and to induce, the children to bring in their L1 Neg placement rule. More generally, a L2 child will draw on his L1 only if crucial prerequisites are met within his own L2 development. Such prerequisites are a sufficient degree of similarity between the structures involved. Apparently, II.2 was outside this crucial range; III.1 was inside it. Namely, the Neg placement rules of German and English are partly the same.

They fully agree with respect to the copula. Hence at II.2-III.2b copula utterances are target-like. Blunders in copula utterances do not involve the position of Neg in relation to the V's. With respect to V-structures German and English differ. The children seem to experiment with both the German and the English rule (cf. types III.2a vs. III.2b). Eventually, L1, i.e. German wins out. There is additional word order evidence to suggest that the above developmental detour is not specific to negation.

Felix 1978b found the acquisition of the VP for L2 German/L1 English as summarized in tab. 2. The structural type III.1 is superficially target-like with V in final position as required by German. Next the children revert to their L1 word order by placing V behind Aux. This is not target-like. German requires such V's in complex VP's at the end. Thus in III.1 the children were already very close to the mark. In III.2 they move away from it. In III.3 they have to approach the target again. That this is likely to be a reflex of a more general regularity is further suggested by our data on the acquisition of the VP in L2 English/L1 German. The four children started out with III.2 of tab. 2, then III.1, and then III.2 again. Utterances like *I want no bei/by you sit,* „I don't want to sit next to you", *I cannot the crickets catch,* „I can't catch the crickets" belong with the intermediate stage(s) of their development.

The type IV.b poses slightly different problems. There is no reason why the children should not use the rise of *don't/didn't* to differentiate Aux from V as required by English. After all, they will do so after stage V. Moreover, that they could distinguish between Aux and V at a time prior to stage V is clear, for instance, from their L2 command of English word order in non-negated utterances, at least at the rise of type III.1. And most puzzling of all, they were already close to such a differen-

Tab. 2: Developmental sequences for the L2 acquisition of the VP in German by children with English as L1 (Excerpted from Felix 1978b)

I   copula structures

   ich sein a baby (I am a baby)

II simple VP

   du kannst blau (you can blue (= you can have the blue ones))

III complex VP

   1.   Subj   Aux   N   V
                      Adv

        ich hat   alles   essen (I have all eaten (=I have eaten all))

   2.   Subj   Aux   V   N
                             Adv

        ich hab   gesehen   du (I have seen you)

   3.   Sub   Aux   N   V
                      Adv

        ich habe dich gesehen   (I have you seen (= I have seen you))

tiation with respect to negation once before, namely via the structural types III.1 and III.2a. The latter type, i.e. pre-V Neg, though not (very) productive, was limited to V-sentences. Instead, throughout the types III.1-IV.b the children seem to prefer to have Aux and V included in one set which is positionally not differentiated with respect to Neg. And the children rely on this rule although it looks as if that way they take a developmental detour. This is in accordance with the children's L1, i.e. the German Neg placement rule.

4 Conclusion: Linguo-Cognitive L1 Transfer Strategies

To talk about developmental detours is, of course, totally misleading; the children are not taking detours. They are following the regularities that govern L2 acquisition and they do so even if the total process may create the impression that it involves detours. These regularities determine the structure of the developmental sequences. L1 reliance is an integral part of this overall development. L1 transfer occurs only at specific points in the learner's development. This implies that the transfer strategies are part of the regularities which lead to the peculiar nature of learner utterances and the developmental sequences within which they occur. It follows that the details of how, when, and where L1 transfer occurs should be statable within the framework of linguo-cognitive strategies and/or developmental principles as proposed for non-L1 transfer regularities in **Wode 1979**.

Notes

* Special version of Arbeitspapiere zum Spracherwerb Nr. 16, Englisches Seminar der Universität Kiel, 1976. This paper was revised for the purpose of this volume. An expanded version appeared under the same title in Henning Wode 1977.

THE BEGINNINGS OF NON-SCHOOL ROOM L2 PHONOLOGICAL ACQUISITION*

A survey of problems and issues based on data from English as L2 with German as L1

Henning Wode

0 Purpose

In the past the acquisition of phonology has been studied extensively for L1 acquisition and for foreign language teaching. Both lines of research have been carried out fairly independent of each other. As far as I can make out, there has been no large-scale attempt to interrelate these two lines of research. It seems to me that a different approach is necessary. Man is unique in that only he can acquire a – human – language. In fact, he can acquire more than one; and he can do so under different circumstances. His capacity for language acquisition, therefore, is not limited to L1 acquisition. A more comprehensive theory is required, i.e. one that will incorporate (a) the commonalities across the various types of language acquisition such as, for instance, L1, L2 acquired in a natural setting, language teaching, pathological language acquisition (cf. Wode 1974 for details on these types) as well as (b) the differences between them. Such an integrated theory will also contain a sub-theory on naturalistic L2 phonological acquisition. It will be pivotal within this integrated theory in two respects: A comparison with L1 acquisition should make clear whether some/all/no L1 acquisitional strategies are still available or re-activated for L2 acquisition; compared with foreign language teaching, naturalistic L2 acquisition will reveal to which extent man's natural ability to acquire a language can be manipulated, i.e. via teaching.

This paper is a first step towards such a sub-theory, though my aim is rather modest, namely: to survey the field and to explore which issues can profitably be raised for naturalistic L2 phonological acquisition. My focus is primarily on the beginning stages, and here it is production rather than discrimination.

The data come from my Kiel University, Germany, project on language acquisition. I shall first describe the design of the project (§ 1). § 2 will contain a brief discussion on previous approaches to the study of phonological acquisition. § 3 will outline my basic hypothesis. The data can then be presented through the grid of this hypothesis (§ 4). § 5 is an attempt to identify the major differences between naturalistic L2 phonological acquisition and other acquisitional types.

1 The Kiel Project on Language Acquisition

Our long-range goal is to work towards an integrated theory of language acquisition. To provide data we trace the acquisition of selected structural areas of German and English across the various acquisitional types.

The first part of the project was to gather data on the acquisition of German as L1. (For details and some results cf. Wode 1974, Wode 1976b–c, 1977b, Wode & Ruke-Dravina 1977.) Next, L2 German was studied as acquired naturalistically by youngsters from Australia, the US, and Great Britain, (cf. Lange 1979, Felix 1976b, Felix 1977b, d, 1978b). The third part of the project deals with L2 English acquired naturalistically by children with German as their L1 (Wode 1976a, 1977a, c, 1978b). For English as L1 we rely on what is available in print.

Subjects

The project has deliberately been devised around my four children Heiko né 1966, Birgit née 1967, Lars né 1969, and Inga née 1971. They were our subjects for L1 German, and to provide the L2 English data the whole family of six moved to Trinity Center, Cal., for not quite six months, i.e. from April through September 1975.[1]

Except for Inga, the children went to the local elementary school and participated in the everyday activities of the community. No attempt was made to subject the children to organized class room foreign language teaching. The teachers were asked not to do so, and they have cooperated magnificently.[2] We just let the children find their own way; be initiated into English by their age mates in whichever fashion they chose to do it; and we answered questions whenever the children had any. At home we used both German and English. The children were never pressured to employ a specific language.

Inspite of the cooperation on the part of the teaching staff, there is one area where the teaching activities of the school had an effect on the linguistic progress of one of the children. It concerns Birgit. She was allowed to actively participate when the native first-graders were taught reading and spelling. Though these activities had nothing to do with the intentional teaching of a foreign language, Birgit is unique among the four children in that she has some phonological peculiarities which seem to relate directly to her reading and spelling attempts. More details will be given in § 4.2.

Data Collecting

I have followed a day-by-day longitudinal type of data collecting coupled with experiments of various sorts. There are three types of data: (a) tape recordings of spontaneous talk; (b) tape recordings of the experimental sessions; and (c) notes taken spontaneously on the scene of action, including phonetic transcriptions, most likely child intentions, situational comments, etc. All types of data are evaluated to safeguard against unintentional biases.

The Languages Involved

Neither Trinity Center (TC) English, nor the four children's L1, i.e. the Kiel variety of High German, are dialectologically exotic. For the purposes of this exposition I shall not go into details here except for the "r"'s. Our children's L1 is a uvular [R].[3] The TC /r/, taking the town as a whole, varied prevocalically from central frictionless continuant [ɹ-] to retroflex [ɹ˞], even with the local children. The vowels in words like *beer, bare, lure* etc. varied from fully retroflex to centering diphthongs [Vᵊ]. Likewise the reduced vowel as in *(moth)er* alternated from retroflex [ə^r] to [ə].

2 Previous Theories on Phonological Acquisition

It is important to place naturalistic L2 phonological acquisition within the perspectives of existing phonological theories for at least two reasons. First, in order to check whether and to which extent naturalistic L2 phonological acquisition parallels other types of phonological acquisition. This can be done by comparing the respective developmental sequences derivable from these theories. The second point is to determine whether L2 acquisition can clarify, confirm, or refute the basic assumptions inherent in these theories. I shall here take a look at three types of theories: the inventory type, like Jakobson 1941; the process type, like Stampe 1972; and behavioristic conditioning, like Olmsted 1971, Mowrer 1952. (For a fuller appraisal of phonological theories see Ferguson & Garnica 1975).

Turning first to L1 theories, it seems that Jakobson 1941 has, for a long time, been the most challenging. The basic idea is that phonological acquisition proceeds in ordered developmental sequences. Children start from simple syllable types, like CV or VC. The subsequent phonological development is viewed as an increase (a) in the complexity of the system of oppositions and (b) in the inventory of phonological elements that enter into these oppositions.

Several weaknesses have been noted for Jakobson's view: (a) some of his claims are not borne out by empirical observation (cf., for instance, Oksaar 1970, v. Raffler-Engel 1970, Olmsted 1971); (b) an inventory type of approach is likely to miss the fact that some of the child's innovations may relate to sets of phonological elements, like, for instance, the stops, rather than to individual items (see, for example, Smith 1973, Ingram 1976); (c) listing of the additions to the inventory will miss syntagmatic aspects of phonological acquisition, i.e. relating to syllables, morphemes, and the like. Apart from the many pertinent examples as summarized in Ingram 1976, cf. the following case from German. German children can be caught at a stage of development when they have already acquired /t, k, l, a, ɛ/, and when they pronounce a word like *Toilette* 'toilet' as /lɛtə/, but a word like *(ich) kletter* '(I) climb' as /lɛka/. Apparently, the medial /-t-/ of the target is ousted in favour of /-k-/, which, quite likely, reflects the target's initial /-k-/.

In order to remedy weaknesses such as above, various proposals have been made to describe L1 phonological acquisition in terms of different types of rules or processes that also take syntagmatic relationships into account and that apply, or that the child is said to apply, in his acquisition of target forms. Such types include, amongst others, reduplication, cluster reduction, assimilations of various types, final devoicing, etc. (Cf., for instance, Edwards 1971, Stampe 1972, Drachmann 1973, Smith 1973, Ingram 1976). Of course, this array of rules/processes is heterogeneous and belongs to different and by no means isomorphic approaches. However, my point is that all these approaches share a crucial weakness: None has been developed to the point where the rules/processes are developmentally ordered in such a way that they correctly predict developmental sequences in phonological acquisition. These approaches describe post hoc what went on. But recall that ordering coupled with the idea that a child's course of L1 phonological development is predictable, was one of the most attractive and stimulating assumptions of Jakobson 1941. And, as will become apparent from the data of § 4, the same assumption must also be made for naturalistic L2 phonological acquisition, though the details are quite different in many respects.

Moreover, naturalistic L2 phonological acquisition should be highly relevant to phonological theories like Stampe 1972. He claims that the child is biologically endowed with an array of processes that he applies in his phonological acquisition. The child's progress is viewed as suppression, limitation, and ordering of phonological processes due to his experience with the target language. L2 phonological acquisition can help determine what it means for a process to be said to be suppressed, limited, etc. Does it mean it cannot be fully re-activated at all for acquisitional purposes?

Much the same inadequacies noted with respect to the predictive capacity of the above theories apply to the approaches based on behavioristic conditioning like, for example, Mowrer 1952, Winitz 1969, Olmsted 1971. L 1 phonological acquisition abounds with examples where the children's productions are difficult to explain in terms of straightforward reinforcement, like, for instance, the early substitution of [h] or [x] for [R] by German children or the replacement of [w] for [ɭ] by English children (Wode 1977c). For behavioristic theories to gain precision and predictive power they have to be enriched such that they will provide ways for identifying minutely the stimulus that the child reacts to in any acquisitional situation.

As for foreign language teaching I am not aware of any attempt that goes beyond claiming or stating more than the obvious, namely, that L2 students rely on their L1. In general, the evidence is interferences of various types. They tend to be explained by strategies like L1 transfer, overgeneralization, and the like. (Cf., for instance, Selinker 1972). In fact, such global strategies do not explain anything unless the conditions are made clear that will lead to these interferences. The data of § 4 will clearly show that L2 children/people will rely on their L1 knowledge only under specifiable conditions. These conditions are not of any vague motivational sort, but they relate to the phonetic/phonological structure of both the prior L1 and the target L2.

3 The Basic Hypothesis: Some outlines of a theory of L2 phonological acquisition in a natural setting

Whatever the ultimate interpretation of the data of § 4, any solution will have to face the fact that the children's evidence is amazingly uniform even from child to child. There must, then, be a principle general enough to be valid for children/people of such diverging age ranges as have provided the data.

I like to think that L2 phonology, at least with children of the age ranges included in this study, is acquired through the grid of the child's L1 phonological system. The major limitations derive from the state of development of the child's L1 system. From the L1 grid the children move towards the L2 targets in ordered sequences. The process can be likened to a matching procedure. The input is L2 as spoken by the L2 environment the child is exposed to. L2 phonological elements are scanned for equivalencies and for non-equivalencies. That is the L2 elements are checked as to how similar they are to the L1 elements at the child's disposal. There seems to be a crucial measure. A L2 element that falls within that crucial similarity range is substituted by the respective L1 element, i.e. by its L1 equivalent. Any L2 element that falls outside this crucial range, undergoes other developments. The data that we have so far for this latter type suggest that in such cases the child passes through a developmental sequence that is (fairly?) parallel to the L1 sequence of that respective element.

The main difficulty with this claim at the present state of affairs is chiefly one relating to phonetic theory. Namely, to give the notions equivalence and non-equivalence precise enough definitions so that they can be used to predict L2 developmental sequences. This is primarily an empirical issue. And we need many more contrastive data to determine in detail what may count as equivalent to what. But the data of § 4 do suggest strongly, it seems, that some such principle is involved.

4 Some L2 Phonological Developments

The survey is based on a complete sampling of the spontaneous notes plus extensive back checking against the tapes. I shall take a glance at a variety of structural areas.

4.1 Initial Inventory

A sizeable portion of the data is inconclusive as to the above claim. These are the segments/features which are, or sound, the same in L1 and L2. Cf., for instance, /m, n, ŋ, f, v, s, z, ʃ, ʒ, p, t, k, g, d, b/ etc. With these, it is hardly possible to tell whether the child is using his L1 or L2. I shall not discuss this type any further here.

The second type of evidence is more telling. There are those segments/features that are equivalent for L1 and L2 as far as their place in the vowel or consonantal system is concerned, but which, nonetheless, differ phonetically. Cf., for instance, the stressed vowels. It can reasonably be argued that, for example, the /i/'s in L1 and L2 are systemically equivalent, i.e. equivalent as to their place in the vowel system. But they are nevertheless phonetically different. The same is true for other vowels. In general, the lax vowels, for example, tend to be slightly more open in TC English than in German. Still, the children at first substituted these L1 pronunciations for the L2 equivalents. Cf. Tab. 1.

There is a certain type of exception to the trend summarized in tab. 1, which probably supports the above claim rather than that it contradicts it. This most notably concerns L1 /ɛ/ vs. L2 /ɪ/ and /ɛ/. Some of the equivalents or near equivalents like, for instance, the L2 /ɪ/ which the children were exposed to, were more open than their L1 German equivalent /ɪ/. I have, in fact, noted several instances of overlap where the children used their L1 /ɛ/ instead of L2 target /ɪ/. For some examples cf. tab. 2.

Tab. 1: Some substitutions of L1 segments for systemically equivalent L2 segments but differing slightly in phonetic quality (for the phonetic transcription cf. footnote 3).

L2 Target		Child L2	Time of Exposure[4]	Child
/ɪ/	pitcher	pʰɪtʰʃa	0;6	Heiko
/ɛ/	ready	ɹɛdi	1;11	Heiko
/ʊ/	pushing	pʰʊʃɪŋ	0;5	Heiko
/ə/	home run	hom ɹan	0;6	Heiko
/i/	please	pʰliz	1;11	Heiko

Tab. 2: Substitutions for L2 /ɪ/ by L1 /ɛ/.

Clint	kʰlɛnt		0;6	Heiko
Ginger	ðɪnða[5]		0;12	Inga
	quickly ousted by ðɛnðo			
milk	mɛłk – mɪłk		0;22	Lars
milk	mɛłk		0;30	Heiko
sit	sɛt*		1;0	Lars
Rick	ɹɛk – ɹɪk		1;1	Lars
fence	fɪns – fɛns		1;13	Heiko

* in commands to dogs to sit down, which the child would only have heard as /sɪt/, never as /sɛt/.

Not all four children employed the same substitutions in the same lexical items. The /ɛ/ for *sit* was peculiar to Lars. Inga and Birgit, for instance, only said [sɪt] and [θɪt],[5] respectively, even when playing together with Lars with the same dog at the same time.

In *Ginger* only Inga had /ɛ/. Some substitutions did not persist for long. Lars' [sɛt] for *sit* lasted fairly long. Heiko's and Lars' [mɛłk] for *milk* not quite as long. Heiko's other pair [fɛns] and [fɪns] both for *fence* existed alongside each other for quite a while. The same holds for Lars' pair [ɹɪk – ɹɛk] for *Rick*.

Also, there is what on the face of it might look like a countercase. A little 5 year old boy named Kenny was pronounced by three of our children [kʰɪni]; Lars at first had [kʰɛni]. From the local children and from the adults around town I have heard both [kʰɪni] and [kʰɛni]. What seems noteworthy is the fact that the children should settle for one alternative and not adopt the two from the very beginning.

It seems then, that some L2 targets may come within the equivalence range of two L1 elements, for instance, /ɪ/ and /ɛ/. Apart from cases of this sort, the children pick the nearest L1 equivalent. In the subsequent course of their L2 phonological development the children move towards the L2 targets in ordered sequences. I shall illustrate this briefly with the third type of major evidence.

Tab. 3: Some substitutions for the L2 target /æ, ʌ, w, θ/, [ɬ, əʳ — ə]

Target L2	Child L2	Target L2 form	Child L2	Time of Exposure	Child
/æ/	[ɛ]	Hank	[hɛŋk]	0;7	Heiko
		thank	[θɛnkʰ ju]	0;9	Inga
		catch	[kʰɛtʰʃ]	1;16	Birgit
		catch	[kʰɛtʰʃ]	1;16	Lars
/ʌ/	[a]	come on	[kʰam ɔn]	0;8	Heiko
		come on	[kʰam ɔn]	0;13	Inga
		this one	[tɪθ wan]	0;19	Lars
		shut up	[ʃat ap]	0;26	Birgit
/w/	[v]	sandwich	[sɛ·ntvɪtʰʃ]	0;7	Heiko
		Weaverville	[vivavɪl]	1;8	Inga
		wet	[vɛt]	1;8	Birgit
/θ/	[s]	thank you	[sɛŋkʰ ju]	0;15	Birgit
		thanks	[sɛŋkʰs]	0;28	Lars
[ɬ]	[l]				
		killer	[kʰɪla]	0;12	Heiko
		clock	[kʰlɔk]	0;23	Inga
		little	[lɪtl]	0;26	Lars
		cold	[kʰoʊl]	0;28	Birgit
[əʳ-ə]	[a]	pitcher	[pʰɪtʰʃa]	0;6	Heiko
		(Trinity) Center	[θɛnta]	0;5	Inga[5]
		(Trinity) Center	[θɛnta]	0;5	Lars[5]
		Weaverville	[vivavɪl]	1;9	Birgit

This third type of data comprises those L2 segments/features which differ drastically from L1, or which have no equivalents in L1 at all. English /æ, ʌ, w, θ, ð/, [ɬ], the – sometimes – retroflex vowels, [ɻ,–ɭ], and the reduced vowel [əʳ-ə], are cases in point. This type of evidence is crucial in that it seems to show that not all L2 phonological elements are acquired through the grid of the L1 repertoire. Some pertinent data are summarized in tab. 3. I have singled out the L2 targets /æ, ʌ, w, θ, əʳ/ and [ɬ]. The rise of L2 /r/ is discussed separately in § 4.2. I shall use the data on /r/ to illustrate L2 phonological developmental sequences. In § 4.2 it will be argued that the first non-zero substitute for prevocalic /r/ is [w]; next is the fairly frictionless continuant [ɭ]; and, finally, retroflex [ɻ] emerges. Some examples are given in tab. 5.

The substitutions for L2 /θ, w/ require additional comments, because it is not immediately clear whether the children's [s, v] derive from their L1 repertoire or whether these segments should be regarded as analoguous to the [w] substitution for L2 /r/.

There is, of course, a segment [v] in the children's respective L1 repertoires. But the substitution of [v] for adult /w/ also occurs with children acquiring English as L1. I have noted many instances of this sort with a L1 girl aged appr. 2;6.

However, she moved into the community at a time when our four children were well past the stage of substituting [v] for /w/. Note also that our children had [w] in their L2 repertoires at the time when they were substituting [v] for L2 /w/. But [w] was their substitute for L2 /r/. I am undecided whether the [v]:/w/ substitutions are due to L1 or to some more autonomous regularity.

The case of L2 /θ/ is quite similar. [s] substitutions for /θ/ are part of a child's developmental sequence of L1 English, though not the earliest reflex. On the other hand, it may be that our children's substitutions for L2 /θ/ stem from their L1 repertoire. Consider the evidence: Among the four children only Birgit did not develop a lisp in her L1. Heiko had overcome his without therapeutic treatment when we came to Trinity Center, except for a few occasional dropbacks. Lars used his L1 /θ/ and /ð/ in cases where German required /s/ or /z/, respectively. For /ʃ, ʒ/ Lars employed target-like /ʃ, ʒ/. In fact, the boy had already begun to lessen the degree of his lisp so that he already had the odd [s] or [z] in his German.

Inga's lisp was still strong, and she had not yet developed either /ʃ/ or /ʒ/. She used [θ, ð] for target German /s, ʃ/ and /z, ʒ/, respectively, as in Inga's [θön] for /ʃön/ schön, [Raðə] for /kaRaʒə/ Garage, [ðɔl] for /zɔl/ soll, [vaɪθ] for /vaɪs/ weiß.

In their attempts at L2, Birgit at first never hesitated to replace /θ/ by /s/. Heiko may have noted some difference fairly quick. But still at 1;8 he complained to me that he could not get nor do the funny (komisch) way in which people said the word for Germ. Ding, [sɪŋ, fɪŋ] or so, as he put it. He opted for [s] for a short time, and then came up with targetlike [θ]. Lars did not use his lisp in L2 to the same extent as he continued to employ it for his L1. Without having carried out detailed statistics, I had the impression that Lars was using more [s]'s and [z]'s in his L2 attempts than he was in his German at that time. And for quite a while he sometimes even used [s] for the L2 target /θ/ as in thank you or thanks. In fact, I frequently had the impression that even when Lars produced [θ, ð] for L2 /θ, ð, s, z/ he was trying to reduce the degree of his lisping. Of course, his L1 [θ] is systemically German /s/.

The L2 evidence from Inga (tab. 4) makes me inclined to assume that our children's L2 [s] or lisping is due to their respective L1 repertoire, and that these phenomena are not comparable to the use of [w] for L2 /r/. Recall that when

Tab. 4: Inga's usage of /θ, ð/.

L2 Target	Child L2	L2 Item	Child Form	Time of Exposure
/(d) ʒ/	[ð]	Johnny	ðɔni	0;4
		Ginger	ðɪnða	0;9
/s/	[θ]	yes	jɛθ	0;18
		sit	θɪt	1;0
/(t)ʃ/	[θ]	much	matʰθ	0;27
		Shasta	θaθta	0;27
		fishing	fɪθɪŋ	0;30
		English	ɛŋiθ	1;7
/z/	[θ]	guys	gaɪθ	1;2
		please	pʰliθ	1;15

Inga was first exposed to L2, she had no reflex of the /ʃ, ʒ/ vs. /s, z/ distinction of German yet; she substituted [θ, ð] for both pairs. In her English she used [θ, ð] for the L2 targets /(t)ʃ, (d)ʒ, s, z, θ/. I have no evidence for L2 target /ð/ because of lack of appropriate lexical items. Words like *that, this, the*, etc. will not do. Most of the L1 children at Trinity Center did not have /ð/ initially in these words, or at least they had variants that did not contain /ð/. Other items were not available. Cf. tab. 4 for some examples. Note that the only early reflexes of L2 /z/ are all syllable-final and hence show up voiceless as [θ].

I like to think that in particular the data of the Inga-kind emphasize and underline that the state of development of the L1 phonological system sets the major limitations for the start towards acquiring the L2 /θ/. For one thing, neither Inga nor the other three children did go back wholesale to [f], the early substitute for /θ/ in L1 English, and so often noted in the L1 literature. However, I did note a few occasional instances from Inga where the L2 target /θ/ was substituted by [f]. The only stabilized instance, though an isolated one, is from Heiko. For some time he pronounced *nothing* with medial [-f-] instead of [-θ-] (1;7/1;24).

4.2 A Developmental Sequence: The case of L2 /r/

To illustrate developmental sequences within L2 phonological acquisition, I shall briefly summarize the rise of L2 /r/. The facts are too many to be presented here in detail. They are discussed in Wode 1977c. In particular I restrict the summary to L2 /r-V/ and /Cr-V/ sequences.

With our four children, there were four major types of enunciations for L2 /r/: the uvular [R] stemming from L1; the bilabial continuant [w]; the (fairly) frictionless central continuant [ɻ]; and the retroflex [ɻ]. Cf. tab. 5.

Tab. 5 Developmental types in the acquisition of L2 target [ɭ]/[ɹ]

I: Use of uvular [R]

L2 Form	Child L2	Time of Exposure	Child
Redding	Rɛdɪŋ	0;12	Heiko
right here	Raɪtʰia	0;24	Lars
Trinity Center	tʰRɪnɪtʰi θɛnta	0;5	Inga
drink	dRɪŋk	0;28	Birgit

II: Use of [w]

---	---	---	Heiko
Craig	kʰwɛ·k	0;5	Lars
Craig	kʰwɛɪk	0;5	Inga
Craig	kʰwɛk	1;8	Birgit

III: Use of a central frictionless continuant [ɹ]

(home) run	ɹan	0;6	Heiko
Grief	kɹif	0;18	Lars
friend	fɹɛ·nt	1;28	Inga
crickets	kʰɹɪkʰɪtʰs	2;8	Birgit

IV: Use of retroflex [ɭ] proper

Swift Creek Trail	swɪft kʰɭik tʰɭɛɪl	1;7	Heiko
strike	stɭaɪk	1;25	Lars
Craig	kʰɭɛɪk	3;0	Inga
Redding	ɭɛdɪŋ	3;8	Birgit

In Wode 1977c, I have argued that the [R] substitutions of type I are not part of the truly naturalistic process of the acquisition of L2 [ɭ] or [ɹ]. The [R] substitutions are systematic only with Birgit. At her own wish she was allowed to take part in the reading and writing exercises of the first graders. With the other three children the [R] substitutions were sporadic. I think that the naturalistic L2 developmental sequence has the type II [w] substitutions as the first productive non-zero substitute for L2 target [ɭ] or [ɹ]. The next stage is marked by type III, use of the central (fairly) frictionless continuant [ɹ]. After that comes the retroflex [ɭ].

Birgit's development is especially telling in this respect. After school had recessed at the beginning of June, which meant the end for her reading and spelling exercises, Birgit gave up her [R]'s, adopted [w], and then she went through the same developmental sequence as did the other three children.

As for the "origin" of these substitutions I have looked at the L1 and the L2 acquisition of the various "r"s in other languages. The available evidence is highly fragmentary. However, there is not a single instance on record where the respective L1 /r/ was at first regularly substituted for the L2 /r/.

Furthermore, what evidence there is for the L2 /r/'s, largely parallels the developmental sequences of the respective "r"'s when acquired as L1. That is, our four L2 subjects did what L1 children do: substitute [w] for the English target [ɭ] and [ɹ]. And just the same, no L2 child is on record that has systematically substituted [w] for the L2 German target uvular [R]. But there is one that at first substituted [h] (Denison 1958), which is what happens with L1 German. (For details cf. Wode 1977c.)

Birgit's [R] within her developmental sequence for L2 [ɭ] or [ɹ] is enlightening in one more very important respect: At least some developmental sequences characteristic of L2 phonological acquisition in a natural setting are not immune against manipulations based on other variables, for instance, reading and spelling.

4.3 Morphophonology, Phonotactics, String Phonetics

The study of morphophonology, phonotactics, and the phonetics of strings, like phrases, sentences, etc., does not seem to be as rewarding for L2 as it has proved to be for L1. The details will be reviewed in a separate paper. I shall here mention, very briefly, only the major highlights.

There are some confusion phenomena when children get mixed up as to where goes what in words with multiple recurrences of a segment. For instance, the town *Weaverville* was pronounced by the same child in the same conversation like this: [wivavɪl – wiwavɪl – vivavɪl – wivawɪl].

Phonotactically, the children had no problem with clusters, including those that do not have any direct equivalent in German like /θr-, sm-, sn-, sl-, sw-/. Except for the developmental sequences of the individual segments, these clusters were produced target-like from the beginning.

However, the final voicing distinction of English proved a major obstacle. It took Heiko, the child who progressed furthest, more than half of our stay to produce final voiced fricatives and plosives. Till then they were all voiceless. The other three children struggled even longer with the voicing distinction. Of course, in German, final fricatives and plosives are voiceless only.

Occasionally, target front vowels were substituted by back vowels in words like *twelve* [tʰwɔlf], *help* [hɔlp], *milk* [mɔlk], and others. Such substitutions are probably prompted by the phonetic quality of the velar [ɫ]. But even in words of this sort the children more often than not had the expected front vowels. In fact, none of these forms with a back vowel ever turned into a stabilized pronunciation with any of the children.

As one would expect from the preceding §§, the notorious glottal stop [ʔ] of German was in many cases carried over to L2. In German [ʔ] can be inserted in front of a (or most) stressed syllables beginning with a vowel. Consequently, the children would at first say, for instance, [wɔt ʔɪz ɪt] *what is it*, [juə ʔaʊt] *you're out*.

5 Naturalistic L2 vs. Other Types of Phonological Acquisition

L2 vs. monolingual L1

In terms of surface forms my data offer no clues that L2 phonological acquisition is like L1 acquisition. Nor do the respective L1 theories seem to be able to account for L2 phonological acquisition.

There is no support in my data that children recapitulate wholesale the developmental sequence derivable from Jakobson 1941, even if amended according to more recent evidence. For one thing, the children's first attempts at pronouncing L2 lexical items are not limited to front plosives and more or less open vocoids/vowels. Phonetically the strings can be very complex right from the outset. The syllabic structure is more complex and more varied than CV, VC, or CVC, so characteristic of beginning or early L1 phonology. Clusters are likely to occur right away. Reduplication, so prevalent in early L1 speech, was not encountered at all, unless inherent in the target item, like, for instance, in *bye-bye*. And those cases, like the L2 acquisition of /r, w/, which parallel the one for L1, present the type of data that Jakobson's theory cannot handle. That is Jakobson's theory being an inventory type of approach cannot explain why the L2 children use [w] to substitute for /r/, whereas they fail to use it for the L2 target /w/, which they replace by [v] at a time where they have the [w] at their disposal, namely as a substitute for /r/.

Though one might be tempted to suggest that the gradual move from the initial substitutes for vowels, i.e. [ɛ] for target /æ/, [o] for /əʊ–ɵ/, etc., may proceed according to behavioristic S-R principles, no such explanation will do for the data as a whole. In particular, the acquisition of L2 /r, w, θ/ seems to be beyond the reach of any reinforcement interpretations. Recall in particular that Lars did not take his lisp, i.e. [θ], straight into L2.

There are several types of observations that one might want to relate to L1 acquisition via what in § 2 I have called rule/process types of approaches.

Namely the L2 developmental sequence for TC /r/, the use of back vowels before [ɫ], the devoicing of final fricatives and stops.

It seems to me that the first two cases might well be regarded as resulting from the application of processes also operative in the L1 acquisition of English. My reason is that there is nothing in the structure of the children's L1 German that could plausibly explain these facts. On the contrary, it seems that these processes do not simply die away once they have been used for L1 acquisition.

The devoicing of the TC final plosives and fricatives, however, seems to me to be due to the children's L1. Of course, such devoicing is familiar from L1 English (see Ingram 1976 for data). But the reverse also occurs in L1 English, namely the weakening or voicing of initial voiceless plosives (Ingram 1976: 33). I do not have a single instance of this latter sort in my L2 files, so that the curious fact would arise why it is that among the L1 processes relating to voicing only the syllable-final one is reactivated. And above all, instances like the *kletter*-case of § 2 are conspicuously absent from my L2 data.

L2 vs. L1 Bilingualism and L2 Schoolroom Acquisition

Turning, then, briefly to other types of phonological acquisition, it seems that L1 bilingualism complies with L1 acquisition (for data see Leopold 1939–49).[6]

Foreign language teaching, i.e. L2 acquisition in the classroom is closer to naturalistic L2 acquisition. At least our children's errors are all familiar from teaching English to German children in school. What we do not know is whether there are any parallels to the developmental ordering so characteristic of naturalistic L2 acquisition.

6 Summary and Outlook

In the preceding §§ I have presented various types of data and I have offered some hypotheses in an attempt to explain some aspects of this material. All in all, I have stayed close to "surface structure". Unfortunately, the core of the hypothesis, namely, the equivalence relationships (§ 3), could not be worked out in sufficient detail. What is needed are statements to the effect that, apparently, [R] or [r] are not equivalent to [ɭ] or [ɭ] due to their respective phonetic properties; but that, at least in the L2 situation reviewed above, [ɛ] is equivalent to [æ]. The fact that the children's behaviour was so uniform can be taken as an indication that these equivalencies are not idiosyncratic. They probably reflect universally valid similarity relationships between phonetic/phonological elements relative to (a) man's perceptual capacity and (b) his prior language experience. Therefore, to develop the theory of L2 phonological acquisition we need general statements that specify which phonetic/phonological elements are equivalent to each other in any L2 acquistional situation. Such general statements should enable us to predict that, and explain why, for example, in a situation with L1 German and L2 English, [ɛ] will be the initial substitute for L2 [æ]; but that [R] or [r] will not substitute for L2 [ɭ] or [ɻ]. It is obvious that we need many more studies involving a wide range of typologically diverse phonetic/phonological systems, until the details can be worked out in any satisfactory way.

Notes

* Reprinted by permission from *International Journal of Applied Linguistics (IRAL)* 16 (1978) pp. 109–125. – Revised version of Arbeitspapiere zum Spracherwerb Nr. 8, 1975, Englisches Seminar der Universität, Kiel. Thanks are due to several people on our research group, notably Jens Bahns, Werner Praus, Dietrich Lange and Sascha Felix.
1 I gratefully acknowledge a special grant by the Landesregierung Kiel towards meeting part of the expenses of this trip.
2 Special thanks are due to Mrs. Cleo Carpenter and Mr. John Cain. They have never hesitated to go to great troubles to make our children feel at home and to integrate them into their classes.
3 The transcription is basically IPA: [R] uvular /r/; [ɻ] retroflex /r/; [ɭ] central frictionless continuant; [ɵ] tense rounded back vowel slightly more open than [o]; the lax, front, rounded vowel as in German *Köcher,* 'quiver', *Knöchel* 'ankle', *Wörter* 'words' is transcribed as [ø].
4 The time of exposure is given in months and days.
5 Both Lars and Inga had a lisp at that time.
6 Leopold 1939–49 is widely quoted as a source for the acquisition of L1 English, for instance, by Ingram 1976, Ferguson & Garnica 1975, and many others. However, it should not be overlooked that, strictly speaking, Leopold's classic study concerns L1 bilingualism. As long as we do not know what the differences are, if any, as against other types of language acquisition, we do well to treat this acquisitional type separately, until we can be sure, that in fact it works (much?) like monolingual L1 acquisition.

Commentary

The three papers in this part have important implications for a theory of language acquisition that is not arbitrarily restricted to individual types but which attempts to incorporate all types of acquisition. The main problem, therefore, is whether there are acquisitional regularities that are universal in the sense that they apply to all age groups and to all types of language acquisition, apart from the three acquisitional types surveyed in paper no. 8. In conjunction with this notion of acquisitional universal it is important to determine which regularities are restricted to specific types. The two papers in the following part deal with these issues.

Part V

UNIVERSALS

Introduction

The term universal is current in at least two fields, language typology and language acquisition. Typological universals govern the restrictions on the structure of all natural languages. Acquisitional universals are regularities which occur in all situations in which languages are learned. What is the relationship between these two types of universals? The two papers of part V present attempts to approach such issues empirically.

As for the language acquisitional universals, the first step to take relates to the goals of an integrated language learning theory that incorporates all types of language acquisition. There should be at least some — non-trivial — properties which relate to all acquisitional types. That is to say, there should at least be some acquisitional strategies which occur no matter what the acquisitional type, what the language being learned, or what the age of the learner. But there is no reason to assume that all strategies should be equally universal. Some may be more restricted in various ways.

The fascinating aspect of such issues is that their solution requires that the limitations traditionally imposed on the study of language acquisition are given up and that phenomena are included which so far have not been considered from the point of view of language acquisition. This includes the structure of pidgin and creole languages, the nature of linguistic borrowing, (imperfect) code-switching by bilinguals and/or bi-dialectals. This view almost inevitably leads to speculations about the relationship between language typology and language acquisition.

On the other hand, such a vantage point naturally forces one to recognize that phenomena which used to be regarded as totally disparate turn out to be related and resultant from the same neuro-psychological mechanism(s). This, in turn, makes it necessary to examine the empirical data for what is suggested about the nature of such mechanism(s), especially man's language learning system.

This methodological development is reflected in the two papers reprinted in part V. The first paper deals with the structure of pidgins and creoles. Two negation structures are traced through all acquisitional types for which data are presently available, including foreign language teaching and the relearning of a language. Note that these two structures occur in all acquisitional types and that they also conform to two negation types which are quite frequent from a typological point of view.

The second paper reviews phonological data for various L2 types. It summarizes, and builds on, the beginnings of L2 phonological acquisition (presented in paper no. 10), and then contrasts them with various other types of L2 English, including foreign language teaching. The main result is that the various phonological errors are highly comparable. There are systematic differences as a function of the L1 involved in the respective L2 combination, irrespective of the age of the learner. This means that L1 reliance must be regarded as a linguo-cognitive ability available to any human being throughout his lifetime.

LANGUAGE ACQUISITION, PIDGINS, AND LANGUAGE TYPO—LOGY*

Henning Wode

Surely, one fundamental assumption of linguistics is that a language can be structured only in such a way that it is learnable by human beings. It follows, first, that languages can change historically only in such a way that they remain learnable by humans, and, second, that newly created or developing languages can only be structured such that they are learnable by humans. Learnability, it seems, provides for the limitations on the range of different structural types to be found in natural languages and as embodied in the typological universals of language structures.

It appears that the best way to study such relationships empirically is to compare language acquisition, the rise and the structure of pidgin and creole languages, and language typology. What needs to be determined is whether learner structures parallel certain pidgin structures and whether both types conform to the typological restrictions that emerge from the examination of a large number of different languages. If such parallels can be established, then it seems that the typological universals can be explained psycholinguistically as a function of, and as resulting from, the language processing abilities of the human brain.

As regards the structure of pidgins, the essential questions to pose are: Why are pidgin utterances structured linguistically the way they are? And why, as has often been noted, do the linguistic structures of different pidgins tend to be more similar to each other than to the structure of the original languages involved in the specific pidginization process? This has been noted as all the more surprising since these similarities also occur in cases where totally unrelated languages are involved, where borrowing must be excluded, or where historical explanations cannot apply because there was never any contact in the past at all. I suggest that these similarities result from the way people learn languages, in particular, from the way they learn L2's, L3's, etc.

Researchers on language acquisition, particularly those who have investigated naturalistic, i.e. untutored L2 acquisition, have often noted many parallels between the linguistic structures found in early pidgins and creoles and those utterances employed in naturalistic L2 acquisition, irrespective of the languages involved, notably, such negation structures as *neg X,* or *Subj neg VP,* as in *no shoot Buffalo,* or *baby name, me no like* (for instance, Schumann 1975a). There have also been some suggestions that such parallels may result from the way human beings learn languages (for example, Todd 1974). In addition, Kay & Sankoff 1974 speculated that the structure of pidgins should relate to language universals in the typological sense.

These individual issues, i.e. the relationship between pidginization, language acquisition, and typological universals can now be substantiated by empirical evidence.

It seems that certain peculiarities of the three domains derive from the same language learning/processing abilities of the human brain/mind.

My suggestions primarily derive from the research at Kiel University, Germany, on various types of language acquisition. Ultimately, our aim is to develop an integrated theory that characterizes people's capacity for language acquisition. The design of the project, the methodology, the data base, and various other details are described in other papers in this volume (see in particular paper no. 1). This paper expands our data base through the addition of pidgins and creoles.

Systematic comparisons across the various acquisitional types reveal that some acquisitional peculiarities occur in all of them which means that these commonalities are due to non-age specific non-language specific, hence, universal strategies; peculiarities that are restricted to individual acquisitional types must be due to strategies more restricted in their applicability. Given such strategies the structural peculiarities of pidgins and early creoles can be predicted from the structure of the languages involved.

To illustrate, I trace the two negation structures *neg X ~ X neg* and *Subj neg VP* through various types of language acquisition. I first show that the two structures occur early in language acquisition. This will be concluded from their occurence in the developmental sequences for L1 English, L1 German, L2 English/L1 German, and L2 German/L1 English (tab. 1). Next will be a survey of the two negation structures in various acquisitional types in addition to those of tab. 1 and including pidgins and early creoles (tab. 2). Only a few comments are required.

The data of tab. 1 clearly show that the types *neg X* (or its less frequent positional variant *X neg*) and *Subj neg VP*, are among the first non-anaphoric negation structures used by naturalistic L2 learners. If these utterance types are to have a universal status, they should also be found in other L1 and L2 types as well as in re-learning a language and in foreign language teaching (FLT). Tab. 2 fully supports this conclusion.

In tab. 2 the source studies have been added. As for L1 monolingualism, additional data on other languages are summarized in Wode 1977b. They all point to the same conclusion. The L1 trilingual data come from research in progress on a boy growing up in Paris, with his German mother, Hungarian father, and the family's French servant. Additional data on naturalistic L2 acquisition involving other languages than those listed in tab. 2 are available. They are not given because they point to the same general conclusion. This also applies to the pidgin-like German spoken by migrant workers (Gastarbeiter) in Germany. For them, the two negation types have been reported in abundance, though with *nicht* „not" or *nix* „nothing" as neg (for instance, Heidelberger Forschungsprojekt Pidgin-Deutsch 1975). But the same types have not been reported to involve *nein* „no" in place of *nicht, nix*. How-

Tab. 1 Early stages in some development sequences for the acquisition of negation
adapted from Wode 1976a, 1977b).

1.) *L1 German*   *L2 German/L1 English*

I   nein   I-II   nein
    „no"   „no"
                                               nein, da
II nein, Milch   „no, (it is) there"
    „no, (I want) milk"

III nein hauen   III   nein helfen
    „no bang (i.e. don't bang on   „no help (i.e. don't help
            the table)"   me)"

IV Heiko nicht essen   IV   Katze nein schlafen
    „Heiko not eat (i.e. doesn't eat)"   „the cat no sleep"
    die nicht kaputt
    „this not broken"   Milch nicht da
                                               „milk not there"

2.) *L1 English*   *L2 English/L1 German*

I   no   I-II   no
                                               no, you
II no, mom

III no close   III   no play baseball
    „don't close the door"   „let's not play baseball"

IV Katherine no like celery   IV   that's no good
                                               lunch is no ready
                                               me no close the window
                                               "I'm not going to close the
                                                               window"
    Katherine not quite through   John go not to the school
                                               "John is not going to school"

ever, we have collected many such examples, i.e. involving non-anaphoric *nein,* in
ongoing research at Kiel that was designed to check whether or not such *nein*-types
occur.

The data on L2 re-learning come from a recent study in which the four German
children described in Wode 1976a were taken back to the United States in 1977 to
be observed as they re-learned English, most of which they had forgotten since their
first stay in 1975.

In order to check whether the negation types under scrutiny here also occur in
FLT, we have sent a questionaire to some 50 teachers in the Kiel vicinity. They re-

Tab. 2: Negation structures *neg X* ~ *X neg* and *Subj neg VP* in various types of language acquisition, including pidgins and early creoles.

acquisitional type	negation type		
	neg X	X neg	Subj neg VP
L1 monolingualism			
English (Bloom 1970, Bellugi 1967)	no close		I no want envelope
German (Wode 1977b)	nein schaff ich „no manage I"	Kaffee nein „coffee no"	Heiko nicht essen „Heiko not eat"
Swedish (Lange/Larsson 1973)	nej kossa „no cow"		Embla inte ha täcket „Embla not have quilt"
Latvian (Wode/Ruke-Dravina 1977)	nē minimi „no pencil"	gib nē „will no"	inupu nē ĩta „bath no go"
L1 trilingualism (Kadar-Hoffmann 1977)			
German	nein Hanno kann „no Johannis can"		das nein geht „that no works"
Hungarian	nem jo „no good"		itt em jön atró „from here no come subway"
French	non Hanno aime „no Johannis like"		après Daniel non ouvre „afterwards Daniel no open (the door)"

naturalistic L2 acquisition		
L2 English/German (Wode 1976a, 1977a)	no play baseball	me no close the window
L2 English/Spanish (Schumann 1975a)	no like coffee „(I) don't like coffee"	I no can see „I can't see"
L2 English/Japanese (Milon 1974)	no my turn	me no win
L2 German/English (Felix 1978b)	nein meine „no mine"	ich nein hat eins „I no have one"
re-learning L2		
L2 English/German (Wode, unpublished data)	no sit here „don't sit here"	I no want to play „I don't want to play"
pidgins/creoles		
Ewondo Populaire (Todd 1974)	ke bo „don't go"	me ke bo „I don't do"
Freetown Krio (Todd 1974)	nɔ du „don't do"	a nɔ du „I don't do"
Hawaiian Pidgin (Carr 1972)	my father, no take care me „my father, (he) didn't take care of me"	baby name, me no like „I don't like my baby name"
Tok Pisin (Bauer 1974)	(not mentioned)	mi no lukim „I haven't seen him"
Chinese Pidgin (Bauer 1974)	can do? no can do? „can't you do that?"	he no belong handsome „he isn't handsome"
Jamaican Creole (Bailey 1966)	no sliip pan da bed „don't sleep on that bed"	nobody no gaan a puos yet „nobody has gone to the post-office yet"

port that the two negation structures do not occur frequently; but if they do occur it is typically during the initial stages of instruction.

The pidgin data of tab. 2 are taken from what I could find in the literature available to me. The difficulty is that the sources I was able to consult are not developmental; almost all are scant and in most cases the examples had to be extracted from running texts or they were mentioned only in passing. Obviously, these data cannot be interpreted developmentally in any adequate way. However, if the two negation structures result from universal strategies involved in language acquisition, then they should occur in pidgins and, perhaps, in early creoles, even if their chronological status within a developmental sequence cannot be established. This view is fully supported by the data that I have been able to find. Some have been listed in tab. 2.

As for the linguistic structure of pidgin utterances it seems that they are as they are, because pidgins arise as a particular type of language acquisition, namely, as L2's. Consequently, the acquisitional regularities that govern L2 acquisition also apply to pidgins. This makes them similar among each other no matter which languages are involved, and no matter whether there is any contact between them. Moreover, since some regularities are universal in the sense that they apply to all acquisitional types, pidgins necessarily have specific properties that they share with all languages as these develop acquisitionally. Though I have here used negation to illustrate my point, the arguments can also be supported by evidence from other structural areas, for instance, phonology and inflections (see Wode 1981). Whether one interpretes these acquisitional regularities as simplification in terms of traditional approaches to pidgins, is a different matter. I doubt that *no like coffee* can be regarded as a simplification in any reasonable way. Moreover, it can also be assumed that certain aspects of the structure of the process of creolization/decreolization is also largely governed by language acquisitional regularities.

As for the relationship of pidgins and language acquisition to typology and typological universals, reference is made to Dahl 1979. He compared the negation systems of approximately 240 languages across the world. He reported that there are many genetically unrelated languages around the world in which negation is expressed by placing neg after the subject and before the predicate. To place neg in sentence-initial position is also attested in a few languages. It seems, then, that the developmental structures *neg X* and *Subj neg VP* do not go counter to the universal constraints on the structural options permitted by the typology of natural languages Indeed, if this insight can be substantiated by further empirical investigations, we may eventually be able to explicate more fully what now reads like a truism, namely, that language typology and language acquisition are both constrained by the language processing abilities of the human brain.

Note
* Based on Arbeitspapiere zum Spracherwerb Nr. 21 (1980), Englisches Seminar der Universität Kiel, 20-29, which appeared in *Studies in Second Language Acquisition* 3 (1981), 193-200.

PHONOLOGY IN L2 ACQUISITION*

Henning Wode

This paper contrasts the acquisition of phonology within various L2 types, such as naturalistic L2 and foreign language teaching (FLT), and L1 acquisition. The aim is to determine parallels and differences between these types. The focus is on how the learner − child or adult − acquires a sound system rather than what differences there are in the external setting. The survey will show that there are numerous parallels in the available data in spite of drastic differences in the external settings and in the age ranges of learners. It will be proposed that such data leave little room for suggestions other than that these parallels − in the data − derive from the way the human brain processes phonological information for the purpose of acquisition. In particular, such data dispel claims that learning a language in FLT is totally different from other acquisitional situations in terms of those neuro-psychological mechanisms that enable man to learn languages.

O Purpose

How does man acquire languages? Does he learn the second like the first? Does he learn a second language in school as he does without school room tuition? Such questions are central for any theory of language acquisition that is not unjustifiably restricted to L1 acquisition, but that seeks to characterize man's overall capacity for language acquisition, whatever the acquisitional type. The recent upsurge of research on naturalistic L2 acquisition now makes it possible to begin to approach such questions empirically.

This paper reviews phonological acquisition from such a comprehensive point of view. The main aim is to determine whether various L2 types are or are not governed by the same acquisitional regularities. I take the view that a profound understanding of L2 phonological acquisition is possible only if it be shown how it differs from, and/or agrees with, other types of language acquisition. But even so, this will remain fragmentary as long as phonological acquisition is not incorporated into a theory including the acquisition of the other structural systems of a language apart from phonology. It would have to be shown in which way phonological acquisition is like or unlike the acquisition of these other structural systems of natural languages.

Naturalistic L2 acquisition will be of central concern in this paper. I shall begin with a review of some proposals about the nature of language learning, even if they relate only to restricted areas of language structures. Then I shall summarize the major insights for naturalistic L2 acquisition and ask whether FLT L2 is different or not. Next I shall draw attention to some differences and parallels between the L2 types and L1 acquisition. Lastly, this will lead to some speculations about the nature of man's language learning system.

1 Some Alternative Views on Language Acquisition

It is very unlikely that all formal devices of natural languages, or that the various structural subsystems of a language, should be learned in the same way. It is important, therefore, to check any proposals about the acquisition of restricted areas of language structures as to whether and to which extent they can be generalized to other areas for which they were not expressly devised. Several alternative views have to be considered, ranging from Jakobson 1941 via contrastive analysis hypotheses, as Lado 1957, through proposals based on Chomsky (1959, 1976), like, for instance, McNeill 1970a, to Dulay & Burt 1973, 1974a-c. In spite of vast differences, these views basically agree in regarding the learner as actively acquiring a language through specific cognitive abilities rather than being passively shaped or conditioned as implied by behavioristic approaches, as in Winitz 1969 or Olmsted 1971.

Some of the above proposals are restricted to L1, like Jakobson's and Olmsted's; others relate to L2, e.g. the contrastive analysis hypothesis, or Dulay & Burt's creative construction hypothesis. The latter focuses on naturalistic, i.e. untutored, L2 acquisition; the former was primarily developed from/for teaching a L2.

Jakobson's theory was proposed for phonological acquisition. It views the L1 child as proceeding via universal abilities that operate on the phonological structure of the target language. Hence the variables that determine the developmental sequence is the target phonological system. Chomsky and those who have built on him have claimed that these (or some of these?) abilities are inborn and universal. Such views were put forth with reference to L1 acquisition, though not restricted to phonology. But do these abilities also function in L2 as well? Perhaps in all acquisitional types? Are they independent of age? Can they be manipulated via teaching? Such problems have never been investigated empirically apart from the critical age issue. Lenneberg 1967 has strongly argued that, at puberty, man loses the ability to fully acquire the phonology of a language. But Lenneberg did not consider appropriate L2 data.

The contrastive analysis hypothesis as proposed by Lado 1957 maintains that the L2 is acquired such that all L2 targets are substituted by elements of the learner's L1 system. More precisely, they are substituted by those elements most similar to them. It is well known that this view does not account for all errors that can be observed in L2 acquisition (see Richards 1974 for a survey of such error types from foreign language teaching and other situations).

Dulay's & Burt's creative construction hypothesis links with Jakobson and the Chomsky tradition rather than with the contrastive analysis hypothesis. Dulay & Burt maintain that in learning a L2 children make use of „universal cognitive mechanisms" of which reliance on L1 is not a central part. This is said to explain why — according to them — children from different L1 backgrounds use target items from English target-like in much the same chronological order. These claims were developed from L2 data about the acquisition of a few grammatical morphemes, such as inflections, prepositions, articles. But these few items do not make a language. It has already been shown that the creative construction hypothesis as explicated by Dulay & Burt, does, in general, not fully hold either for those structural areas not covered by them, for instance phonology (Wode 1978a) or for the grammatical morphemes of their original studies (Wode et al. 1978).

Other proposals could have been discussed. But they all share the same basic weakness. As they stand, they are non-integrated isolated fragments, i.e. a fragment from syntax, a bit on phonology, patches on L1, patches on L2, etc. But such attempts fail in two ways. First, they fail to show how these fragments fit into a theory of language acquisition covering a language as a whole. For instance, the details of a theory like Jakobson's (1941) obviously apply only to phonology. His more general claims, however, such as the notion of ordered developmental sequences, apply to many (all?) structural areas. Likewise, Jakobson's proposals relate to L1 acquisition. But do none of his insights carry over to the acquisition of other structural areas?

Second, such non-integrated proposals are fairly unenlightening for determining the nature of man's language learning system. Such non-integrated proposals give the impression as if man's capacity for learning languages is to be viewed as strictly compartmentalized into totally unrelated acquisitional mechanisms: one geared only for L1 acquisition, another for L2, still another for the class room, etc., with further compartmentalization according to structural areas, like phonology, morphology, and so on. — And all this as if there were no general properties and principles to apply beyond the individual compartment. I have rejected this view as inadequate elsewhere. And I have instead argued that man's capacity for language learning must be regarded as a unified learning system flexivle enough to cope with the differences in the acquisitional setting (Wode 1974, 1978a, 1978c, 1978e).

From this point of view it is particularly deplorable that the acquisition of phonology has so far received very little attention from researchers on naturalistic, i.e. untutored, L2 acquisition, because rich data sources are available for other types such as L1, foreign language teaching (FLT), and immigrants' speech. This evidence, if considered together, would have clearly shown that such restricted views as cited above cannot be upheld and that, instead, a compromise in terms of a more comprehensive approach is quite feasible. By looking at phonological acquisition in various acquisitional settings I shall show that certain aspects from the alternatives discussed above can be retained and integrated such that a unified view of man's capacity for learning languages begins to emerge.

2 Some Methodological Considerations

Acquisitional types

To be able to investigate differences and parallels requires that the acquisitional types

and the respective data first be kept separate to allow for inspection and evaluation. The following typology will be adopted (from Wode 1974, 1981):
— number of languages learnt: monolingualism, bilingualism, etc.
— chronological sequence: first language (L1), L2, L3
— Application vs. non-application of school room instruction:
    instruction applied: language teaching
    instruction not applied: naturalistic acquisition.

Phonological substitutions

The main points of this paper can be established by discussing the data in terms of fairly unsophisticated approaches. For the sake of brevity I shall rely on the traditional substitution approach tied to word phonology. (For L2 analyses in terms of more sophisticated approaches cf. Wode 1977c, 1978a, 1981)

„Typical errors"

Not every substitution ever reported for a given target can be included. Instead, I shall concentrate on those that are traditionally regarded as being the „typical errors" for, say, a German learning/talking English, or the Frenchman attempting the same. It should be borne in mind throughout, though, that it may be difficult to determine exactly and in detail what a typical error is. Yet it is also clear that, empirically, there are specific error types that are simply characteristic of a given L2/L1 combination. More important, such „typical errors" tend to be reported no matter which methodology is used. It must also be remembered that there is a good deal of variation in the pronunciation not only of L2 learners. The substitutions, as in the tables below, should therefore be interpreted more as marking the range of the phonological variation of the learners. If, for instance, German L2 learners of English are said to substitute [e] for English /ɛi/ this means that the range of variation is between [e] and [ɛi] with a preponderance towards [e] -like productions.

3 Naturalistic L2 Acquisition

Apart from fragmentary hints scattered in the literature, there is only Chamot 1972 and Itoh 1973 (summarized in Itoh & Hatch 1978). Chamot studied her son's acquisition of English. It was his third language, having learnt Spanish and French before. Chamot devotes one chapter to phonology applying the methods of traditional error analysis. Itoh 1973 includes some observations on a 2 1/2 year old Japanese boy learning English. Among other things, both studies note some differences from L1 acquisition. Yet, neither makes any attempt to construct a theory of L2 phonological acquisition, or to show systematically if and how naturalistic L2 phonological acquisition differs from phonological acquisition within other acquisitional types, say, L1 acquisition or foreign language teaching. The only such studies to date are Wode 1977c, 1978a.

These two papers focus on the naturalistic L2 phonological acquisition of English by four children aged 4-10, with German as L1. Brief hints are given about the major differences between L1 and naturalistic L2 acquisition. Below I shall draw heavily on the evidence from these children (cf. Tab. 1-2). The English the children were exposed to is that of Trinity Center, Northern California. Amongst other peculiarities this variety tends to have [ɔʊ~ ɵ ~ ɵʊ] in words like *no, go, showed;* [ɵ] in *gold, mould, old*; mostly low back rounded [ɒ] in *not, shot, dog, dock,* and the like, but occasionally also a low back unrounded vowel, notably from newcomers to the area; words like *cot* and *caught, not* and *naught* tend to be homophonous; the vowels in *bear, beer, car, start,* and the reduced vowels as in *(butt)er, (moth)er, (Eleon)or,* may alternate between fully retroflex and non-retroflex, the latter pronunciation occurring perhaps slightly less frequently.

Table 1: Phonological substitutions for the free and the checked vowels for natural-istic L2 English/L1 German. Four children aged appr. 4 - 10 (adapted from Wode 1977c, 1978a.)

/č

L2 target	child L2 substitute	illustrative example
i	i	me, Weaverville, Creek
ι	ι	Bill, Ginger, cricket
ɛ	ɛ	bed, better, seven
æ	ɛ	catch, thank you, Hank
u	u	shoe, you, stupid
ʊ	ʊ	good, hook
ɵ ~ ɵʊ~ ɔʊ	o	pole, boat, home run, throw
ɒ	ɔ	not, caught, song, Bob, saw
α	α	father
ʌ	a	shut up, someone, truck
e ~ ɛι	e	lake, game, chain, say
ɔι	ɔι	boy, noisy
aʊ	aʊ	house, out
aι	aι	strike, my, bike
ər	ø ə	German, first bird
ʋr ~ ʋe	ʋe ͺ ʋa	beer, bear, lure, porch, our

Table 2: Main phonological substitutions for selected English consonants in naturalistic L2 English/L1 German. Conventions, transcriptions and sources as in tab. 1.

L2 target	child L2 substitute	illustrative example
w	v	Weaverville, wet, sandwich
θ	s	thank you, three, this
ð	d	that, the
	z	mother, weather, brother
ł	l	Bill, hill, cold, please, milk
r	w	Redding, Craig, truck

The L2 substitutions were amazingly uniform accross the four children. The bulk of the vowel substitutions were as summarized in tab. 1. In addition, there were some peculiarities reflecting phonological peculiarities of the target. For instance, high or front vowels before the target's retroflex/velar [ɫ] were occasionally replaced by lower and/or back vowels, as [mɒlk] for *milk,* [hɔlp] for *help.*

The English consonants /p t k b d g m n ŋ f v s z ʃ z h j/ were produced target-like from the beginning, except that the voiced fricatives and plosives were devoiced in syllable-final position. Moreover, due to a speech defect, /s z ʃ ʒ/ at times were produced as a lisp (details below).

One child's favorite substitute for the retroflex target /r/ was [R]; with the other children it was [w]. This one child was allowed, at her own request, to take part in the first grade reading exercises in school. As soon as school stopped for the summer recess, [R] was given up in favor of [w]. In Wode 1977c I have argued at length that this [R] is due to orthography and that it should not be considered as part of the naturalistic L2 development proper.

To account for these empirical data I have suggested the following hypothesis: In naturalistic L2 acquisition phonological systems are acquired through the grid of the learner's L1 system, or the stage of development that his system may have reached. Those elements of the L2 target system that are sufficiently similar to elements in the learner's L1 repertoire will at first be substituted by these elements. Those L2 elements that fall outside these crucial similarity measures are not substituted by the learner's L1 elements but they undergo autonomous developments similar to (identical with?) those which the respective elements undergo in L1 acquisition. An instance of the latter sort is [w] substituting for English /r/. Instances of the former sort are [ɛ] for /æ/, clear [l] for velar/retroflex [ɫ], [s z] for /θ ð/, or the devoicing of the voiced fricatives and plosives in final position. That these substitutions are due to the children's L1 German is suggested by the fact that their German does not have /æ/, that their L1 /l/ is clear in all positions, and that the opposition between voiced vs. voiceless stops and fricatives in German is limited to word-initial and word medial positions with neutralization via the voiceless one in final position.

Moreover, the fact that such substitutions are due to the learner's L1 stage of development is most drastically illustrated by the occurrance of [θ ð] in the speech of the children. Only one of the four children had not developed a lisp in her L1 German. She most confidently at first replaced English /θ/ by [s]. The 10 year old had overcome his lisp. He produced [θ] and [ð] fairly soon after a few productions of [s], and, rarely, [f] in place of [θ]. The third child's lisp was still strong, though he had begun to use [s] and [z] in his German for target German /s z/. In his English he produced many more [s z]'s in his attempts at words involving English /θ ð/ than he did in his German. The fourth child, aged 4, had not yet developed the German contrast between /s z/ vs. /ʃ ʒ/. She employed [θ ð] for all of them in her German. And she did just the same for her English /(t) ʃ (d) ʒ θ ð s z/.

4 FLT L2 English

In the next two sections I shall review evidence from FLT L2 situations to show that phonological acquisition within this acquisitional type is governed by much the same regularities as naturalistic L2 acquisition. The argument will have two parts. The first is to illustrate that the error types of naturalistic L2 acquisition recur in FLT. FLT L2 English acquired by German students will serve for this purpose. The second part is to show that the substitutions differ systematically as a function of the L1 acquired previously. For this purpose I shall present a survey on different L2 Englishes as acquired by speakers from various L1 backgrounds. It will not always be clear whether it is FLT L2 English or naturalistic L2 English.

FLT L2 English/L1 German

Tab. 3 contrasts and summarizes the data from naturalistic L2 English/L1 German from several sources that list „typical" errors heard from German talking/learning English in school. These studies are hardly comparable with respect to methodology, notably, data collection, data evaluation, speakers sampled, age range of speakers, linguistic theories/models employed, and above all, with respect to the variety of English offered as the target. For FLT the latter varies from native speakers with different regional accents to the FLT English of German school teachers. The most detailed among the sources cited in tab. 3 are Schröder 1979 and Weiher 1975. Schröder analysed in great detail the productions of 34 10-11 year old students

Table 3: FLT error types for selected L2 English targets from students with German as L1 compared to naturalistic L2 English/L1 German. Less frequent substitutions in ( ); – not investigated

L2 target	substitutions for L2 English/L1 German						
	natural-istic L2	Gimson 1970	Jones 1972	Kufner 1971	Keutsch 1974	Arnold/Hansen 1968	Schröder 1979	Weiher 1975
θ	s (f)	s t (f)	s f	s (f)	s	s (t)	θ	s f
ð	z d	z d (v)	z v (θ)	θ d (z)	z	z (d)	z (d)	z
r	w	ɾ R ʁ	R ʁ	R ɾ	R	ɾ R ʁ	R (w ɾ)	w (ʁ)
w	v	ß v	ß (v)	v (ø)	v	v	v	–
ɬ	l	l	l	l	l	–	l	–
æ	ɛ	ɛ	ɛ	ɛ	ɛ	ɛ	ɛ	ɛ
ʌ	a	a (œ)	a ɑ œ	a	a ɑ	a œ	a	--
ɔᏉ~ɵ~ɵᏉ	o	œᏉ Ᏽ	o ɔᏉ	–	o	ɔ	o (ɔᏉ)	–
ɛι	e	e	e	–	e	–	eʼ	–
əʳ~əː	œ	ø œ	œ ø	ø œ	ø œ	ø œ	œ (əa œa) –

from a high school in Kiel, Germany, during their first 8 months of instruction. The students were followed in a day-by-day longitudinal routine. Weiher also used students from the Kiel vicinity. His data were elicited experimentally via a number of carefully devised tests aiming at both production and perception.

As for the errors, complete uniformity across all studies cannot be expected, because of the methodological differences. Therefore, the actual amount of agreement is all the more impressive, first among the FLT studies; and, second, between the FLT studies and naturalistic L2 acquisition. The majority of error types is the same for either acquisitional subtype. Moreover, some of the heterogeneity will further diminish on closer inspection. For instance, the use of [f] for /θ/ also occurs in naturalistic L2 acquisition, though somewhat rarely. Moreover, it is prone to occur for the target clusters /θr- sw-/ as in *three, swift,* and the like. Front rounded vowels like [œ] may be used for /ʌ/ if the vowel in the target item is pronounced mid-central or higher. This rounded substitute is particularly frequent with older German people who were taught English before world war II. And, lastly, some substitutions like Gimson's 1970 [œɷ ~ ɸɷ] and others are simply unique and it is not clear at all where such observations were made.

In addition to the substitutions of tab. 3 the parallels between naturalistic L2 and FLT acquisition increase further if phonotactic peculiarities are considered. They are basically the same, notably the devoicing of final voiced plosives and fricatives, or the excessive use of the glottal stop which tends to be reported in all those studies that are not limited to isolated words (e.g. Schröder 1979).

Differences, though, do occur. The chief source seems to be teaching methodology, and, above all, stimulation via channels other than the auditory one, namely, orthography and reading, as highlighted by the use of [R] by one child in the naturalistic L2 English/L1 German data of sec. 3. Note also that [w] as a substitute for English /r/ is mentioned for FLT only by Schröder 1979 and Weiher 1975, the most detailed studies. And even in their data [w] is much rarer than the L1-based [R].

5 Other L2 Englishes

Do L2 learners make the same errors for a given L2 irrespective of their L1 backgrounds? Recall that this was one of the claims of the Dulay & Burt hypothesis (cf. sec. 1). Tab. 4 contrasts typical errors in the acquisition of selected phonological elements for various L2 Englishes based on different L1's, including naturalistic L2 English/L1 German. In fact, in some sources to be quoted it is not clear whether a neat separation of FLT vs. naturalistic L2 acquisition can be adhered to. In many situations, for instance, those in Africa, the spread of L2 English is by no means limited to the activities of the schools. Sec. 4 has already shown that the distinction between FLT and naturalistic L2 is not extremely sharp and that, consequently, it can be neglected for the purpose of this section.

Table 4: L2 substitutions for selected English vowels by speakers from various L1's.
? indicates unclear cases

types of L2 English	English targets and their substitutions source
	i ɩ ɛ æ u ⊙ ʌ aɩ ɛɩ ɔɩ a⊙ əⵔ
naturalistic	
L2 English/L1 German	i ɩ ɛ ɛ u ⊙ a aɩ e ɔɩ a⊙ o (Wode 1978a)
FLT	
L2 English/L1 German	i ɩ ɛ ɛ u ⊙ a aɩ e ɔɩ a⊙ o (Schröder 1979)
L2 English/L1 French	i i ɛ a u u ? aɩ e ɔɩ a⊙ o (O'Connor 1967)
others	
Hindi	i ɩ æ/ɛɩ æ u ⊙ a aɩ e ɔɩ a⊙ o (O'Connor 1967)
Arabic (Cairo)	i ɛ ɛ ? u ⊙ ɔ aɩ e/ɩ ɔɩ a⊙ o (O'Connor 1967)
Spanish	i i ɛ a u u a aɩ ɛɩ ɔɩ a⊙ ɔ (O'Connor 1967)
Twi	i i ɛ a u u a aɩ e ɔɩ a⊙ o (Sey 1973, own observations)

Without going into details, it is obvious from tab. 4 that the „typical" errors differ systematically as a function of the structure of the respective L1. Thus, speakers of French substitute [i] for /ɩ/ and [u] for /⊙/, lacking [ɩ ⊙] in their L1 repertoire. Germans tends to have [ɩ ⊙] for /ɩ ⊙/, both being available in their phonological L1 system. On the other hand, Germans tend to have [ɛ] for /æ/; but Frenchmen mostly [a] and less frequently [ɛ] for /æ/; and a speaker of Twi will have [a] in place of /æ/. German and French agree in that neither one has /ɛ/ opposed to /æ/. Twi has /i e ɛ a/, but these vowels function in different subsets, namely, /i e/ belong to the „tense" series, /ɛ a/ with the „lax" series. The vowel harmony of Twi treats these and other vowels as different sets (Redden & Bongo 1963). I shall here not go into the problem of which properties among the elements involved govern these substitutions. That is why, for instance, the German tends to replace English /æ/ by [ɛ] and not, say, by [a], though both are available in his L1; whereas French speakers prefer [a] for /æ/, though both [ɛ] and [a] are available via their L1. (For some suggestions concerning such explanations cf. Wode 1977c). But even so it is obvious that such regularities are highly systematic.

It is important to note that apparently not all phonological elements are substituted by L1 elements. Consider the diphthongs of tab. 4. English /aɩ ɔɩ a⊙/ tend to be produced fairly target-like irrespective of whether the L1 also has them or not. For instance, French does not have these diphthongs. Yet speakers of French tend to have no difficulties with them when learning English. On the other hand, English /əⵔ/ and /ɛɩ/ are redularly substituted by monophthongs in L2 English, if the L1 does not have them, as happens with Germans, Frenchmen, Arabs, and others.

6 L1 vs. L2 Phonological Acquisition

L1 phonological acquisition is neither totally like L2 nor totally unlike it. For instance, it has been shown in Wode 1978a that L2 speakers' first attempts are not limited to front plosives and to more or less open vocoids/vowels as in L1 acquisition. Phonetically the L2 productions can be very complex right from the outset. The L2 syllabic structure is more complex and more varied than CV, VC, or CVC, so characteristic of early L1 phonology. Clusters are likely to occur in L2 right away. Reduplication, so prevalent in early L1 speech, is not characteristic of early L2 speech unless inherent in the target item, like in *bye-bye*. And, above all, L2 learners do not, as L1 children do limit their initial attempts at one or at a few elements at a time.

On the other hand, parallels have also been found, notably the use of [w] for /r/, or [v] for /w/. These and other substitutions also occur with L1 learners of English. In addition, a survey on the acquisition of the various types of „r" 's (Wode 1977c) has shown that such parallels between L1 and L2 also hold for other L2 combinations involving other languages and other types of „r" 's than the ones involved in L2 English/L1 German.

7 Towards a Comprehensive Theory of L2 Phonological Acquisition

To conclude, this survey indicates, so it seems to me, that the data on the whole should be subsumable into one comprehensive theory. That is, inspite of gaps in the data, inspite of vast methodological differences, and inspite of drastic differences in the exposure situations, there is no empirical evidence in these studies to substantiate any conclusions to the effect that the basic neuro-psychological processes involved in phonological acquisition differ between naturalistic L2 and FLT L2 acquisition. In fact, they seem to be basically the same except those directly related to special teaching materials, and, above all, to visual presentation via orthography. Moreover, the case of the L2 „r" 's, and other items indicate that some L1 regularities carry over to L2, which clearly calls for rejecting any views that maintain that L2 is totally different from L1 acquisition.

The view that begins to emerge for phonological acquisition agrees, in its general outlines, with that for other structural areas, such as syntax, morphology, semantics. Man is equipped with species-specific cognitive capacities geared especially to the acquisition of languages. This capacity can be regarded as a learning system, much in a way repeatedly outlined by Chomsky though never substantiated by him empirically (1959, 1976).

Phonological acquisition relates to a particular subsystem of natural languages. The nature of this system determines the way languages can be learned. Therefore the developmental sequences and the error types reflect the mode of operation of this system and, above all, they reflect the fact that the learner actively re-builds the target language for himself, whatever the acquisitional type.

This learning system is triggered to function on adequate stimulation, primarily via the auditory channel. But stimulation is also possible via other channels, such as visual stimulation, and perhaps others.

It is still largely unknown, how the data are processed in terms of neuro-psychological mechanisms, how language knowledge is stored, how stored knowledge is re-organized and modified to approximate target structures, as reflected in developmental sequences. But it seems clear that these neuro-psychological mechanisms which the human brain utilizes to process language structures for acquisition, function on a categorical basis rather than on a gradual one, as implied by behavioristic conditioning (for details of this argument cf. Wode 1978c).

It seems reasonable to me to assume that the various formal devices used in natural languages require cognitive abilities that are structured especially for processing them. Thus I would like to think that to process phonological data requires different cognitive abilities than to process word order information. Nonetheless, it seems that these minute processes and strategies can be grouped into more global sets which can be said to be applicable in various subparts of the whole language learning system, for instance, decomposition of target structures, re-integration of decomposed elements into target-like structures via developmental sequences (for details on these notions see Wode 1977a, 1979), overgeneralization, L1 transfer, etc. However, such in part wellknown global groupings remain meaningless unless the conditions of applicability are specified in several ways, namely, in terms of the structural device/area they are to apply to; in terms of the acquisitional type in which they may operate; and in terms of prerequisites that relate to the state of development of the learner. Consider the case of L1 transfer. The details of L1 transfer in phonological acquisition will be different from those in the acquisition of word order. L1 transfer can only take place in the L2, L3 . . .types. And, lastly, it is obvious from the data of sec. 3 on the use of [θ] in the L2 speech of the four German children that L1 reliance occurs only, if certain prerequisites are met within the state of development the learner has reached (for details cf. Wode 1976a, 1977a, Wode et al. 1978).

The hypothesis suggested here builds on, and incorporates certain aspects of, the theories reviewed briefly in sec. 1. My view is that the learner is actively acquiring the target language/structure(s) via cognitive abiblites available to him. From the traditional contrastive analysis hypotheses, such as Lado 1957, I retain the notion that the L2 is acquired through the grid of the prior L1. My proposal deviates from the traditional contrastive views in two ways. First, in that only certain L2 elements are substituted by L1 elements, namely, those meeting specifiable similarity requirements. Second, in that those elements which do not meet the similarity requirements are acquired via developmental sequences similar to (identical with?) L1 acquisition.

As for the Dulay & Burt hypothesis, I differ by including L1 reliance as an integral part of the creative acquisitional mechanism at man's disposal. It follows from all this that traditional contrastive analysis is inadequate in that it has not been provided with any component that specifies/predicts how a given learner will solve the clash he is confronted with between his L1 and the new target L2. The above data clearly show that learners do follow predictable developments. For the contrastive analysis approach to be useful it has to be amended by an acquisitional component that specifies how learners resolve such structural clashes (Wode 1978e).

All in all, so it seems to me, this language learning system, though equipped with abilities peculiar, and very likely unique, to the task of acquiring the formal devices used in natural languages is not totally unlike other of *homo sapiens'* learning systems. Such global strategies like decomposition, re-integration via developmental sequences, overgeneralization, reliance on prior knowledge, are well known to occur also in other learning domains. It is the details relating to the specific learning domain, namely, how the formal devices of natural languages are processed for acquisition, that we know so little about and that it is an urgent research task to uncover.

Note
* Reprinted by permission from Sascha W. Felix, ed., *Second Language Development. Trends and Issues.* Tübingen: Gunter Narr, 1980, pp. 123-136.

Commentary

These two papers mark the extremes which any comprehensive theory of language acquisition must encompass. There seem to be some linguo-cognitive strategies/abilities which apply to all acquisitional types, and which are available to all age groups, for example, the two negation types *neg X ~X neg* and *Sub neg VP*. Other strategies/ abilities, such as reliance on L1, may be restricted to individual types. However, at least the phonological data suggest that the ability to rely on L1 as well as the systematicity of the individual linguo-cognitive transfer strategies do not vanish or change as a function of age. This implies that both types of strategies/abilities, i.e. the negation types above and reliance on L1, are universal non-age dependent properties of man's language learning system. The difference is that if there is no prior L1, then there is no linguistic knowledge on which to fall back. Hence, the transfer strategies must be innate since there is no place where the learner could have learned them independently, nor are they taught.

It further seems that these language acquisitional strategies determine the typological universals observable in natural languages. The papers presented in the concluding part are the first attempt to integrate these insights into the basic outlines of a comprehensive theory of language acquisition.

Part VI

TOWARDS AN INTEGRATED VIEW OF LANGUAGE ACQUISITION

Introduction

The first paper presents the major outlines of an integrated theory of language acquisition that is directed to the mastery of the formal properties of the linguistic devices. It was especially revised and expanded for this volume to function as a summary of the various points raised in the papers of parts I through V. This paper also includes a brief review of various applied issues which appear in a different light if placed within the integrated perspective adopted in the papers of this volume. A number of applications for foreign language teaching are considered in the final paper. The central issue is the role of contrastive analysis for language learning and foreign language teaching.

AN INTEGRATED VIEW OF LANGUAGE LEARNING*

Henning Wode

0 Purpose

How do human beings learn languages? What enables them to do so? Do they have a different and totally unrelated neuro-psychological mechanism for learning a first language (L1), another one for the second (L2), yet another one for learning a language in a classroom, as in a foreign language teaching (FLT), and still others for every different situation in which an individual may acquire a language? The answer to these questions can only be *no:* There are infinitely many different situations. This would require infinitely many neuro-psychological mechanisms. This, in turn, would imply that the capacity of the human brain is infinite, which it clearly is not. Man's ability to learn languages must therefore be thought of as a finite learning system flexible enough to cope with different situations. Consequently, if a theory of language acquisition is not to be ad hoc and anecdotal, it must take as its domain all types of language acquisition, and it must state the commonalities as well as the differences among these types. The main questions to ask are: First, are there any acquisitional regularities which are universal in the sense that they apply in all types of language acquisition irrespective of the variables that may be involved including the age of the learner? Second, are there any acquisitional regularities which are more restricted in that they apply only in some situations, with certain age groups, etc.? Third, to what extent do learners vary individually when acquiring the same language? Fourth, to what extent can the language learning abilities, particularly the neuro-psychological language processing abilities, be manipulated, as is hoped, for example, in FLT? And fifth, what type of learning theory is required to describe language learning?

These issues are taken up below. Since some of them represent drastic departures from the ways in which language acquisition has been studied in the past, it is important to indicate how these questions fit into the history of the field.

1 Past Research

In the past, research on language acquisition was centered on individual types. Consider the situation during the late 1960's, which marks a point of renewed interest. The research activities were centered on L1 acquisition and on FLT. Studies focussing on L1 acquisition (ranging from, for example, Jakobson 1941 to Slobin 1970, and McNeill 1970a) claimed that there were universal acquisitional regularities; studies centered on FLT considered FLT as something totally unrelated to L1 because of the teaching situation (e.g. Lane 1962, Littlewood 1974, Burgschmidt & Götz 1974). The L1 acquisition studies failed to determine how universal the alleged universals really are. It never occured to these researchers to consider L2 acquisition, FLT, or other acquisitional types as worthy of consideration. On the other hand, researchers working on FLT failed to see that a human being could not possibly have an infinite number of acquisitional mechanisms, one for every new language situation a learner might find himself in. Worst of all, FLT researchers made no attempt to investigate empirically in which ways FLT differed from learning a language outside the classroom. That is, long lists have been given enumerating differences between natural learning situations and those pertaining in the classroom (for example, Hüllen & Jung 1979). But no studies were undertaken which determine whether and to what extent this has any effect on man's language processing abilities as utilized in language learning. Are these abilities different for the different learning situations? Do the various abilities function differently?

The situation improved during the early 1970's, due to the rise of research on naturalistic, i.e. untutored L2 acquisition. (Surveys in McLaughlin 1978, Felix 1978b, Wode 1981) Among other things, this research has from the beginning been concerned with the extent to which naturalistic L2 acquisition may parallel L1 acquisition. This L2 research has also always stressed its implications for FLT. However, it is necessary to advance further and consider all types of language acquisition and to check them all for differences and commonalities, if we are ever to arrive at a satisfactory understanding of how human beings learn languages.

2 Research Designs

The only research design proposed so far for such comprehensive investigations as suggested above comes from the Kiel project. The core is a typology of acquisitional situations providing for monolingualism, bilingualism, etc.; L1, L2, L3 ..., i.e. non-simultaneous acquisition; language teaching vs. naturalistic, i.e. untutored acquisition; re-learning of languages; and others. The acquisitions of a given structural area is traced across the various acquisitional types. (For details see, in particular, Wode 1981)

Methodologically, it is important to insist on two points: On the one hand, the way in which linguistic structures are learned, i.e. processed by the brain, must be distinguished from the level of proficiency achieved by a given learner. On the other hand, the crucial point is not to give long lists of co-occurring variables, but to determine which variable(s) control(s) which property in the observable learner data.

Learning vs. learner proficiency

Consider two L2 learners who do not reach the same level of proficiency, i.e. they do not progress equally far. This need not imply that their brains process language data in different ways. It is quite likely that both learners possess the same neuropsychological processing mechanisms, but that for various reasons other psychological mechanisms block their application.

Co-occurrence of variables

Many researchers insist on identifying every variable involved in a language learning situation to provide the fullest possible picture (for example, Oksaar 1977). This is of little help. Such lists state co-occurrences, but they do not tell us which variable determines what in the speech of the learner. The same is true for more sophisticated approaches which determine the statistical significance for these co-occurrences. But this still does not tell us what determines what. The issues concerning how the human brain processes language data for the purpose of acquisition are far too complex to be solved by correlation statistics.

3 The Domain of a Language Learning Theory

It is a truism that a language is, generally, not acquired for its own sake. People learn languages for social reasons, namely to be able to communicate, to take part in social interactions, to be a member of a group. This does not mean that a theory of the development of communication and/or interactional competence also automatically accounts for the way in which the linguistic structures are learned. In particular, the papers of Part II have shown that such a view would be highly erroneous. The initial truism merely indicates that the learner does not discover the input to his learning system, i.e. the linguistic structures in a vacuum, but that, instead, the language data to be learned occur together with, and are a part of, complex social events. Since there can be no communication via speech unless the speakers know the linguistic structures, it follows that a language learning theory must be centrally directed to the linguistic structures. I think Chomsky is correct in insisting on this point. He is also correct, it seems to me, to insist on the fact that such a language learning theory must relate to human beings learning natural languages. No learning theory is adequate which does not state in detail what the difference is between, say, maze-running by rats and language learning by humans (Chomsky 1976). It is still true today, as I pointed out years ago (Wode 1974), that no learning theory is yet available which adequately describes in detail the facts empirically observable in the speech of learners. On the other hand, it is obvious that a language learning theory must also indicate how the learners sort out the complex social events, and how interactional, communicative, and other variables interact with the acquisition of the linguistic system in the narrower sense. Language acquisition must be studied within an interactional/communicative framework.

4 Three Basic Characteristics

To charactize language learning in a comprehensive way, as envisioned by the Kiel project, requires a common frame of reference with respect to which the acquisitional types can be said to differ and/or agree. There seem to be three basic characteristics which apply to all types of language learning, namely, decomposition of target structures, developmental sequences, and individual variation. The first two were developed in Wode 1976d and expanded in Wode 1979. The notion of individual variation needs to be explained in greater detail here.

Decomposition of target structures

Whatever the type of acquisition, target structures are not necessarily acquired all at once. Complex structural areas, e.g. interrogation, or inflections, are first decomposed, as it were, into various elements which are later reintegrated, step by step, into the target structure. This is reflected, among other things, in the errors observable in the speech of language learners. The acquisitional types differ as to the degree of decomposition. It is highest for L1; less for naturalistic L2, including pidgins; it is much alike in naturalistic L2 and naturalistic relearning of L2; but it is drastically less in FLT.

Developmental sequences

The notion of developmental sequence refers to the chronological order in which the structural elements of a given language are acquired. The naturalistic types, in contrast to the tutored ones, are marked by a much stricter chronological sequence in which the elements of a structural paradigm (e.g. the interrogative pronouns), or a particular structure or structural area (such as negation, the vowel system) is acquired. Note that this includes the pre-targetlike developmental structures.

As an illustration for the notions of decomposition and developmental sequence note tab. 1. It contrasts some early stages and developmental structures when English and German are involved in various combinations of L1 and/or naturalistic L2 acquisition. (Additional illustrations for developmental sequences/decomposition are found in papers no. 3, 4, 5, 6 and 10 of this volume.)

Individual variation

With very few exceptions (for example, Ferguson & Farwell 1975, Clahsen 1980, Pienemann 1980), studies on language acquisition have so far largely neglected to investigate the most important type of individual variation among learners. Of course, it is well known that onset of acquisition, speed, fluency, and the like, may vary drastically. Less is known about structural variation, i.e. individual variations within the developmental sequences in terms of variations among the linguistic structures used by learners, including pre-targetlike errors. Such variations occur in all acquisitional types. But they seem to be much greater in FLT than in either L1 or naturalistic L2 acquisition. These variations are not infinite. Their range is limited relative to the acquisitional type(s) and the target structure(s).

To give an example, I return to the free vs. bound form principle proposed in Wode 1979 (paper no. 8). Suppose a learner of English has learned both *no* and *not*. The free vs. bound form strategy allows him to use either one. This is exactly what we found in our data on L2 English/L1 German, for example in the *Subj neg VP*

Tab. 1 Early stages in some developmental sequences for the acquisition of negation (adapted from Wode 1976a, 1977b).

1.)	*L1 German*		*L2 German/L1 English*
I	nein „no"	I-II	nein „no" nein, da „no, (it is) there"
II	nein, Milch „no, (I want) milk"		
III	nein hauen „no bang (i.e. don't bang on the table)"	III	nein helfen „no help (i.e. don't help **me**)"
IV	Heiko nicht essen „Heiko not eat (i.e. isn't eating) die nicht kaputt „this not broken"	IV	Katze nein schlafen „the cat no sleep" Milch nicht da „Milk not there"

2.)	*L1 English*		*L2 English/L1 German*
I	no	I-II	no no, you
II	no, mom		
III	no close „don't close the door"	III	no play baseball „let's not play baseball"
IV	Katherine no like celery	IV	that's no good lunch is no ready me no close the window „I'm not going to close the window"
	Katherine not quite through		John go not to the school „John is not going to school"

structures. The type *Subj not VP* occurred, and so did *Subj no VP*. Both structures may be found with one speaker; other learners may prefer one over the other. In sec. 5 I suggest that this type of structural variation results from the structure of the language processing strategies of the human brain. (For further details on individual variation of the structural sort and for a review of the issue see Wode 1981).

5 Linguistics vs. Psychology: Linguo-Cognitive Strategies

There is no need to formulate the three global characteristics proposed in sec. 4 in terms of a linguistic framework. Obviously, these characteristics are the product of behavior on the part of the learner. They must result from learner strategies. To be more precise, they result from the language processing mechanisms of the human brain/mind. Consequently, linguistic formulations must be complemented by (neuro-)psychological ones and/or (neuro-)psychological interpretations. The task is to characterize these acquisitional strategies.

I assume that a characteristic like the decomposition of target structures presents a set of strategies minutely geared to process the formal properties of linguistic devices. They are structure-specific in that it should require different strategies to handle, say, phonology, word order, free vs. bound forms, and so forth. Consequently, the three global characteristics above remain rather uninformative unless these minute strategies are identified and unless their domains, i.e. the conditions of their applicability, are made clear both in terms of the formal structures they operate on and in terms of the acquisitional type for which they are available.

The domain of acquisitional strategies

Recall the acquisition of free and bound forms as surveyed in Wode 1979 (paper no. 8), i.e. English *will: -'ll, have: -'ve, no/not: -n't,* or German *er: -a, ist: -'s, ein: -n.* The principle suggested was that free forms are produced productively before the bound forms.

If interpreted as an acquisitional strategy the domain is specified first in terms of the formal property involved, namely, the item has to be a free form. Second, the domain is specified by the acquisitional situation, i.e. the acquisitional type to which it applies. As suggested in Wode 1979 (paper no. 8) and paper no. 11, the free-over-bound-form strategy is applicable in all types of language acquisition.

In principle at least, the domain of a given strategy can be specified further by reference to various parameters, for example, age, communicative task (recall the differences between experimentally elicited and natural data (paper no. 7), commucative setting, brain maturation, development of cognition, development of memory, etc. This leads to various applied issues (some of which are reviewed in sec. 6).

L1 transfer strategies

At the present state of our knowledge, it appears that the strategies governing L1 transfer fit the general framework proposed above. It is obvious, for example, from the L2 phonological data of Wode 1978a (paper no. 10) and Wode 1980a (paper no. 12) that the domains of such phonological transfer strategies are marked by the phonetic/phonological properties of the given target items, the difference being that the domains must be established with reference to L1, the target L2, and the state of the learner's development (as illustrated for L2 phonology in Wode 1978a (paper no. 10), and for word order problems in conjunction with negation in paper no. 9).

Individual variation and linguo-cognitive strategies

If the notion of linguo-cognitive strategies is to be valid it should also incorporate individual variations among the developmental structures of learners. Consider, again, the free-over-bound-form principle/strategy. I pointed out above that data are available which show that L2 learners of English may use *no* or *not* in such developmental structures as *Subj neg VP* and others. Most L1 learners of German start with *nein* „no"; but occasionally a child uses *nicht* „not" very early. During their early stages of development, L2 learners of German may have *nein* „no", *nix* „nothing", *nie* „never". In L1 English and L1 Russian, children generally start with *no* and *njet* „no", respectively. However, one English-speaking child on record first used *nomore* (Bloom 1970). Gvozdev 1949 reported that his son started with [nɑda]. The two forms *nomore* and [nɑda] were reflexes of poly-morphemic forms of the target, i.e. *no more* and *ne nado*. Both target strings may occur in isolation, hence as free forms. In the speech of the two children the forms were monomorphemic.

Similar data could be cited about the range of structural variation in L1 transfer. It seems, therefore, that the range according to which the developmental structures may vary across individual learners is determined/constrained by the nature of the strategies themselves (Wode 1981).

Universals

In my previous work I have suggested that some acquisitional regularities are universal in the sense that they are available in all acquistional types irrespective of the age of the learner and/or the language being learned. Recall, for example, the developmental negation structures *neg X ~ X neg* and *Subj neg VP* (Wode 1979 (paper no. 8) and paper no. 11). In addition I have proposed that there are other acquisitional regularities which are restricted in their occurrence. For example, L1 reliance is limited to the L2 types. (Recall, for example, Wode 1979 (paper no. 8), Wode 1978a (paper no. 10), Wode 1981) These earlier conclusions were primarily motivated by concerns for the linguistic structure of the empirically observable facts.

Looking at the same data from the point of view of the availability of processing abilities suggests some clarifications. While it is still true at the linguistic level that L1 transfer is restricted to the non-L1 types, this need not imply that the ability to transfer is not universal in much the same way as the linguo-cognitive strategies underlying, for example, the negation types *neg X ~ X neg* and *Subj neg VP*. The constraints in the occurrence of L1 reliance, namely, being restricted to the non-L1 types, is accounted for by the domain (of applicability) of the transfer strategies. If there is no prior knowledge to fall back on, as in L1 acquisition, then these strategies do not apply, hence non-occurrence of interference in L1. On the other hand, I am not aware of any reliable empirical evidence at all which suggests that the ability to rely on L1 is not available for specific age groups, or that the nature of this transfer is different as a function of age, education, ethnicity, or the like. Nor, and this is perhaps the most important point, am I aware of any evidence whatsoever which implies that L1 reliance is learned in the course of the child's speech development. I like to think that the ability to rely on L1 including the systematicity of the individual linguo-cognitive L1 transfer strategies is innate to the human being and that it does not change, at least not drastically, as a function of age.

6 Applied Issues

It would be premature to attempt to outline all the implications that the application of such a comprehensive view of language acquisition might eventually have. However, there are a few problems of long standing which require a good deal of reconsideration given the insights developed in the papers of this volume, i.e. if one relates such problems to the distinctions between learning as reflected in the developmental structures vs. learner proficiency as reflected in the learner's progress. The range of issues includes: age and language learning; the critical period hypothesis; the relevance of IQ, motivation, aptitude, and other non-linguistic personality variables for language learning; long-range intellectual effects of bilingualism; the effect of socio-economic and social variables; neurological implications; the effect of foreigner talk; the inadequacy of the presently available linguistic theories for language learning; and, above all, FLT. The implications for FLT are so enormous that I include a separate paper to indicate some of them. The other issues are taken up briefly below.

Optimal age

One view widely current among laymen and professionals asserts that young children are more successful language learners than adults and that, consequently, the former also learn differently. This assessment is derived primarily from comparisons of adult and child L2 learners (for example, Lenneberg 1967).

This view is incorrect. First, there is no evidence to suggest that the *how* of language learning differs drastically. The error types committed by the various age groups are much the same. (Recall the evidence from paper no. 11 on the developmental negation types, and paper no. 12 on phonology.) Second, I know many adult L2 learners who acquired nativelike control of a L2 after puberty. Third, various experiments have been conducted which indicate that different age groups perform optimally on different tasks (summaries in McLaughlin 1978, Wienold 1973. See also Snow & Hoefenagle-Höhle 1978). There is, then, no overall optimal age for (second) language learning. Future research must develop more refined techniques for the study of such issues. Above all they should be investigated with respect to all acquisitional types.

The critical period hypothesis

This issue is closely linked with the issue of age in language learning. Lenneber 1967 proposed that a human being has to be exposed to a natural language/speech during a critical period, namely before puberty, if the language is to be learned in the natural way, i.e. as children do. Lenneberg asserted that during puberty changes take place in the brain which lead to the loss of the sort of plasticity required for the native-like mastery of a second language. The crucial point is the establishment of hemi-spheric dominance. Lenneberg's argument was built, first, on evidence about the resti-tution of speech/language with people who had suffered brain injuries, and, second, on the common view about the successful L2 child vs. the unsuccessful L2 adult. The second argument fails as pointed out above. The first argument has also lost its force, since Krashen 1973 reanalyzed the data on brain damage originally used by Lenneberg. Krashen concludes that, according to this material, hemispheric dominance should be completed by approximately age 5. But children older than 5 generally have no trouble in achieving native-like mastery of additional languages. Above all, if there is anything to the original critical period hypothesis it should be made more precise by including the whole range of acquisitional types.

(Non-linguistic) Personality variables: IQ, motivation, aptitude, and others

There is the common view that some people are more talented for learning languages, and that general intelligence, high motivation, as well as various other personality traits promote the mastery of a language.

If there is anything so such views, it must be admitted that researchers have so far failed to make precise what the exact impact is. Different linguo-cognitive strat-egies? Different developmental sequences? Different developmental structures? Dif-ferent learning speed? Far from it: there is no evidence to suggest that differences in personality traits correlate with the availability of different linguo-cognitive stra-tegies. As far as we can determine today, the developmental sequences and the error types are the same despite personality differences. As for the speed of acquisition, in many cases on record the child with the highest IQ developed slowest. For ex-ample, Schaerlaekens 1973 studied a set of Dutch triplets. All three made the same developmental errors and their developmental sequences agreed. But the child with the highest IQ developed slowest. On the other hand, there are many well designed studies which report that adequate motivation promotes second language learning and teaching (see, for example, papers and references in Solmecke 1976). Obviously, future research must develop much more sophisticated approaches to study such problems before the intricacies posed by personality variables can be solved.

Long-range intellectual effects of bilingualism

There is a wide spread anxiety among parents and educators that the mastery of an additional language will drain the child's intellectual resources. Bilingualism and bi-lingual education, it is feared, may have detrimental affects on the intellectual devel-opment and the performance in other school subjects. That this is not so, has been convincingly demonstrated again recently by Canadian immersion programs. In the long run, i.e. after 3-4 years, the participants in such programs were well ahead of the non-participant control groups in terms of their command of the new language as well as in terms of their general intellectual achievements (summary in McLaughlin 1978).

Social and socio-economic variables

Some sociologists and social psychologists maintain that membership in a lower social class, as characterized by socio-economic status, leads to cognitive deficiencies which hinder such children/people in learning a language in the way individuals from the higher social ranks can (for example, Bernstein 1971/1973).

There is no evidence at all in support of this view. As far as one can determine today, the developmental structures and the developmental sequences are highly comparable across different social groups. This implies that the linguo-cognitive strategies are the same despite vast differences in the social setting (Wode 1981).

On the other hand, a learner's social distance from the social group which speaks the language to be mastered, i.e. the degree to which the learner wants to identify/ integrate himself with the culture and the value system of this group may promote his ultimate success (Schumann 1975a, b, 1976).

Foreigner talk

When more competent speakers of a given language talk to the less competent, they tend to modify their speech in ways which they assume makes communication easier. This applies to baby talk addressed to L1 children (see, for example, articles in Snow & Ferguson 1977) as much as to foreigner talk addressed to L2 learners of all age groups (Hatch 1978b), Peck 1977, 1978; Katz 1977). One would think that learners exposed to such simplified input should fare better, or that this exposure situation should be reflected in their speech.

No conclusive evidence is available to indicate in detail the effect of such simplified input. L1 children universally produce the same developmental structures irrespective of whether they are exposed to baby talk or not. The surprizing fact about L2 learners is that their developmental errors are so similar despite obvious differences in the exposure situation. Future research should not only study the peculiarities of foreigner talk and discourse directed at learners but these findings must be related systematically to the learner's neuro-psychological processing as reflected in his speech.

Linguistic theories and language learning

Despite the indisputable advances of linguistics since the 1950's no linguistic theory is presently available that adequatly accounts for the facts observable in learner speech, whatever the type of acquisition. The properties which learners so obviously react to first and foremost in the learning process very often figure much less prominently in the linguistic description or they do not appear in them at all. Any attempts to formulate such simple matters as the regularities of L1 reliance and the similarity relationships on which they are based pose tremendous difficulties. The linguistic theories should be revised to fit the facts of language learning.

7 Conclusion

It is obvious that man's capacity for language acquisition is not strictly compartmentalized such that there is one acquisitional mechanism for L1, another totally unrelated one for L2, and so on. Rather, man seems to be invested with a unified mechanism flexible enough to handle various differences in the external settings. This learning system operates on the formal properties of the linguistic devices used in natural languages. On the one hand, man's language learning system constitutes a special type of cognitive capacities which are especially geared to the acquisition of language structures. The details of these capacities cannot be equated with cognitive concepts, the development of logical thinking, of perception, of pragmatics, or how to handle the complexities of social interaction, and the like. On the other hand, man's language learning system seems to agree with at least some of the general properties of other learning systems. The notion of developmental sequences, including individual variation, recurs elsewhere in the maturational development of human beings. So does reliance on prior knowledge, and the decomposition of complex phenomena for the purposes of learning.

As for L2 acquisition, whether one looks at the various types of L2 bilingualism in terms of language contact or conflict, loyalty, shift, intellectual advantages or disadvantages, or in terms of purist attitudes, interference, borrowing, or pidginization and de-creolozation, all these issues, it seems to me, cannot be studied in any truly profound way unless the language acquisitional aspects are given due consideration. All these phenomena one way or another fall within the range of L2 acquisitional regularities.

This also implies that FLT must be seen within such a perspective. It is true, as pointed out in Wode 1979 (paper no. 8), that one difference between FLT and naturalistic L2 acquisition is the lack of chronologically ordered developmental sequences in FLT. However, this does not mean that both types are totally unrelated since the error types are much the same despite this difference. This means that man's natural processing abilities also operate in FLT. Moreover, these abilities can be manipulated only in limited ways, because they recur even in classroom drills conducted with the intent to avoid these error types. Consider the utterance *doesn't John go home.* It is one among many like it in our FLT data. Such utterances occurred while negation was being learned/practised. They are not intended as interrogatives, but as negated statements. They cannot be explained by the teaching methodology, nor by L1 reliance. Rather, such utterances are due to the free-over-bound-form strategy, with *doesn't* being used as a free form. The word order is that of the type *neg X,* familiar from naturalistic L2 (cf. tab. 1 of this paper and tab. 1 of paper no. 11). (For more details on these FLT data see Felix 1982)

All this clearly shows that in any teaching situation man's natural language learning abilities cannot be freely disregarded, suppressed or manipulated. Teaching a foreign language can only be successful if the student's natural language learning abilities are duely taken into account.

Note

* Revised and expanded version of a paper delivered at the 2nd Nordic Conference on Applied Linguistics, Hanasaari, ESpoo, Finland, Nov. 23-25, 1979. A shorter version appeared in K. Sajavaara, A. Räsänen & T. Hirvonen, eds., AFinLA Yearbook 1980, Jyväskylä, Finland.

CONTRASTIVE ANALYSIS AND LANGUAGE LEARNING*

Henning Wode

Abstract

This paper is an attempt to integrate contrastive analysis within a comprehensive theory of language acquisition, in particular, a theory of L2 acquisition. It is argued that, although contrastive analysis is not a language learning theory in itself, it is an indispensable component of any language learning theory that is to cope adequately with the observable facts.

1 Introduction

For the purposes of this paper, two types of contrastive analysis (CA) are distinguished: CA for typological purposes, and CA as a language learning theory. I think that it is fair to say that CA for typological purposes is, at present, generally accepted as fully legitimate by linguists and scholars in related disciplines. Typological contrastive linguistics provides the basis for comparative studies not only in historical linguistics but also in synchronic typology; as such, CA is at the heart of linguistics and linguistic methodology.

In contrast, CA as a language learning theory has become quite controversial, due primarily, it seems, to research by Dulay and Burt (1972, 1973, 1974a-c). These researchers found very little evidence for L1 transfer when they analyzed the data obtained from approximately 150 Chinese- or Spanish-speaking children learning English. Dulay and Burt's conclusion was that since there was so little evidence for L1 transfer, reliance on L1 was an unimportant variable in language acquisition. Consequently, they rejected CA as a language learning theory and banned it completely from further consideration. Dulay and Burt's findings supported earlier criticism. Many researchers prior to Dulay and Burt found that the error predictions provided by traditional CA, i.e. as a language learning theory, were not confirmed by empirical observations. (See, for example, Brière 1966, Dušková 1969, Richards 1971 to name just a few of the many studies which pointed out such inadequacies.)

Although the conclusions of Dulay and Burt and those who followed them may be quite justified given the limited amount of data available to these researchers, I think that a modification of their drastic view is required if the data base is extended and if other types of structures are taken into consideration. My aim in this paper is to reintroduce CA into a comprehensive theory of language acquisition to whatever extent may be necessary given the empirical data presently available. The point of departure will not be another theory/model. Nor shall I add another layer of theoretical speculations. Instead, I shall inspect learner utterances to determine in which way learners solve the conflict with which they are faced if they learn an additional language (L2, L3, etc.). It is hoped that this procedure will provide the empirical basis for an indication of the extent to which CA must be incorporated into an empirically adequate theory of language learning.

The main results are: there is nothing wrong with CA as such, except that it is not a language learning theory. If it is to be turned into one, it requires the addition of a language learning component that specifies in which way learners resolve the clash between the linguistic structures of language(s) learned previously and the subsequent one(s). In the past, CA has been used to describe differences and commonalities between languages. This aspect will be retained. But proponents of CA as a language learning theory have made the wrong claims about how learners learn these differences and commonalities. It is here that the language learning component is postulated to predict the way learners resolve such conflicts. In psychological terms, CA as a language learning theory was reduced basically to a transfer theory. This is empirically unjustified. It will be argued that transfer of prior knowledge is only one part of the way additional languages are learned. On the other hand, despite recent claims to the contrary, such a transfer can be shown to be involved in learning additional languages, although not in the ways previously suggested.

The procedure to be followed is this: first, I present a review of the major issues relevant to the points to be made. This involves views of language learning. In particular, views about the role of L1 transfer must be discussed. These views are then contrasted with some data on language learning, notably from L1 acquisition, naturalistic L2 acquisition, and L2 acquisition within foreign language teaching (FLT) situations. I then return to the major issues outlined above. The review of the data will, it is hoped, suggest which aspects of traditional CA should be retained and which rejected.

2 Major Issues in Traditional CA as a Language Learning Theory

There is no need to go back further than Fries 1945, Weinreich 1953, or Lado 1957, since it is not my intention to present a complete history of the development of CA. The important point here is that studies like the three mentioned above are often interpreted to the effect that an additional language is learned by carrying/transferring the previous language into the new one. This, it is suggested, affects all structures. I do not wish to discuss whether this interpretation is correct or not. The important point to note here is that this interpretation leads to a language learning theory which makes the prediction that *all* learner utterances result from L1 transfer. That is to say, all learner structures/utterances should show L1 influence. As for the empirical verification of such claims, if two languages have identical structures, there is no way to tell on which language the learner utterances are based. If, however, two languages have different structures, then L1 influence should be noticeable in the learner structures.

It has long been established that these predictions are not confirmed by the empirical evidence. That is, not all error types predicted by this type of CA have been found; and those errors that have been found cannot always be explained by this type of traditional CA (recall, as one of many such articles, Richards 1971). There have been several attempts to deal with the resulting problems. One was to reject CA as useless for a theory of language learning, as done, for instance, by Dulay and Burt, and those who followed them. Another approach was to distinguish between various types of CA, as proposed, for example, in Wardaugh 1970. Wardaugh distinguishes between strong and weak versions of CA. Strong versions are those were CA is used as a predictor of learner structures. Such versions are no longer advocated seriously because of the difficulties outlined above. Instead, one frequently finds what Wardaugh calls weak versions of CA. Here CA is not used to predict learner structures but to explain post-hoc the errors/learner structures that have been observed. Unfortunately, weak versions are not very helpful either. Whereas the strong versions of CA make predictions albeit the wrong ones, the weak versions make no predictions at all. This means, simply, that these versions cannot be regarded as, or incorporated into, any language learning theory, since the aim of a language learning theory must be to predict learner structures.

3 CA and Transfer Theory

Throughout its development as a language learning theory, CA has always been strongly linked to transfer theory, notably behavioristic versions thereof. There is no need to go into great detail about various versions of behavioristic transfer theories. One type implies that learning a behavior pattern proceeds in such a way that the new pattern replaces the old one. This implies that the old behavior pattern must be extinguished so that the new one can take its place. Obviously, this type of transfer theory does not apply to language learning, because while learning an additional language people do not necessarily forget the previously learned language(s). Any language learning theory therefore requires a different notion of L1 transfer, namely, a type that does not require the extinction of what was learned before. This is, in effect, the notion of transfer familiar and popular in FLT. It is this type of L1 transfer that is at issue in the discussion of whether transfer does, or does not, occur in L2 acquisition.

4 Some Recent Views About L1 Transfer in Language Learning

Two groups of studies can be distinguished. On the one hand, there are studies, like Richards 1971 and many others, which report that not all learner structures/errors can be explained by reference to L1. These studies, at least by implication, suggest that L1 transfer does occur, although it is not the only acquisitional regularity which learners follow when learning additional languages.

On the other hand, there is the view most typically represented by Dulay and Burt. Their claim, as will be recalled from the preceding sections, is that L1 transfer occurs only rarely in learner data, hence, it is unimportant for language acquisition and it is not part of the „creative" neuropsychological mechanisms which enable man to learn languages. This was called the Creative Construction Hypothesis (Dulay & Burt 1974 a, b). It was concluded from this hypothesis that CA as linked to L1 transfer should be banned from teacher training requirements and that it should not have a place in a theory of language learning. As already suggested, this view appears to conflict with the empirical evidence available other than the data that Dulay and Burt chose to consider. I think, their view is too narrow. A brief review of their experimental design and the type of structures considered in their investigations are required to illustrate this. The result will be that reliance on L1 is just as much part of man's „creative" language learning mechanism as those regularities which do not involve L1 transfer.

Morpheme Order: The Creative Construction Hypothesis

The experimental design which later came to be known as Morpheme Order was originally devised by Cazden 1968 and Brown 1973. They chose 14 morphemes (some inflections, the articles, some auxiliaries, some prepositions, and the copula *be*). They determined the point at which, chronologically, these various items were used target-like, i.e. correctly, by L1 learners. Correctness was determined in terms of adult grammar. An item was said to be „acquired" if the learner used it target-like in 90% of the environments where required by the (adult) grammar. Brown and Cazden, and later de Villiers & de Villiers 1973 reported much the same sequence for a number of L1 learners.

Dulay and Burt applied the same framework to a study of L2 learners of English. They reduced the number of morphemes to 11, and they used an elicitation instrument called the Bilingual Syntax Measure (BSM) to elicit speech. The subjects in the Dulay & Burt studies on L2 English-speaking children spoke either Spanish or Chinese as their L1. Dulay and Burt found that their L2 morpheme order differed from the L1 order. However, the L2 orders were much the same irrespective of the L1 involved. Furthermore, they found only approximately 5 % of the errors to be traceable to L1 transfer. It should be noted, however, that they used a narrow definition of what should be regarded as L1 transfer. Nonetheless, the same order has subsequently been found in numerous other studies. Some employed the same design, others introduced modifications, for example, different elicitation techniques, different age groups, etc. In short, there is a large body of data available related to a limited number of morphemes which were acquired in much the same chronological order and with little evidence of L1 transfer. (See summary in Burt & Dulay 1980.) Studies of this sort were taken to confirm Dulay's and Burt's original suggestion that L1 transfer was unimportant and that there was no need to deal with this problem in FLT.

This view is inappropriate and it was just as inappropriate during the early 1970's for a number of reasons. First, L1 transfer did occur in the Dulay & Burt data. The important points to determine, therefore, are not only the extent of L1 transfer, but also whether it does or does not occur at all, and the conditions under which it occurs. Second, the morpheme order approach does not examine pre-targetlike errors. Consequently, a good amount of evidence may have been disregarded from the very beginning. (For more details on the methodological weaknesses of the morpheme order approach, see Wode et al. 1978.) Third, the notion of transfer is far too narrow in that it is limited to surface structures. We know far too little about how what may be transferred in language acquisition. Last, and most important, the data base is extremely weak. It may be bold to base generalizations about language learning in general on the inspection of one language. It is even bolder to base them on the evidence from 11-14 morphemes. It should be remembered that 11-14 morphemes do not make a language. And if these morphemes are limited to the structural types as in the Dulay/Burt material, that is inflections, a few prepositions, articles, auxiliaries, and the copula, then it is difficult to see how generalizations based on them can be extended to phonology, the lexicon, word order, and other areas of language structure. In fact, the data available during the early 1970's produced reliable evidence that L1 transfer did occur (recall, for example, the data provided by Ravem 1968, 1969, 1970, 1974).

An Integrated Alternative: A Developmental View of L1 Transfer

Any theory of language acquisition, if it is to be empirically adequate, will, of course, have to incorporate evidence from the morpheme order studies. But at the same time, the theoretical claims, notably the creative construction hypothesis, must be revised in such a way that they do not contradict the evidence available elsewhere, including the data obtained both before and after the morpheme order studies. It seems to me that reliance on L1 must be regarded as creative and developmental in language acquisition just as those regularities which do not involve L1 transfer. In fact, the next section will show that L1 transfer does occur very extensively in other structural areas. One area, phonology, has been chosen for closer inspection.

5 Some Phonological Data

The phonological data are summarized in tabs. 1-4. The data are largely derived from research at Kiel University. We are attempting to develop a comprehensive theory of language learning which is not restricted to isolated acquisitional types, such as L1 or L2 acquisition. Our aim is to devise an integrated theory of language learning that incorporates all types of language learning. Such a theory should describe both the commonalities and the differences among the various acquisitional types. The main result so far has been that some acquisitional regularities occur in all acquisitional types. These regularities are truly universal in the sense that they are available to the learner irrespective of the acquisitional situation in which he learns a language, and irrespective of the age at which he does so. Other acquisitional regularities are more restricted in that they apply only to certain acquisitional types. Our data suggest that man is endowed with specific linguo-cognitive abilities which are specifically geared to the acquisition of the formal properties of linguistic devices. That is to say, the empirically observable peculiarities in the linguistic structure of learner utterances cannot be explained by any presently available learning theories that build on general cognition, on the development of logical thinking, or the like. We assume instead that the human brain is equipped with specific cognitive abilities which we call linguo-cognitive abilities. It is these linguo-cognitive abilities that enable human beings to process the formal properties of the linguistic devices used in natural languages, such as word order, free vs. bound forms, supra-segmental vs. segmental marking, etc. (Wode 1979, more details in Wode 1981).

Tabs. 1-4 are intended to illustrate some of these regularities for phonological acquisition. The approach used in this presentation need not be very sophisticated. It suffices to rely on the traditional substituation approach and simply check what kind of substitutions learners make for particular target phonological items.

Tab. 1 illustrates that four German children, ages 4 to 10, used essentially the same substitutions in their L2 acquisition of English vowels.

L2 target	child L2 substitute	illustrative example
i	i	me, Weaverville, Creek
ι	ι	Bill, Ginger, cricket
ε	ε	bed, better, seven
æ	ε	catch, thank you, Hank
u	u	shoe, you, stupid
℺	℺	good, hook
θ ~ θ℺ ~ ǝ℺	o	pole, boat, home run, throw
ɒ	ɔ	not, caught, song, Bɔb, saw
ɑ	ɑ	father
ʌ	a	shut up, someone, truck
e ~ ει	e	lake, game, chain, say
ɔι	ɔι	boy, noisy
a℺	a℺	house, out
aι	aι	strike, my, bike
ǝ r	ø ǝ	German, first bird
vr ~ vᵉ	vᵉ ˍ vª	beer, bear, lure, porch, our

Table 1: Phonological substituations for the free and the checked vowels for naturalistic L2 English/L1 German. Four children aged appr. 4-10 (adapted from Wode 1977c, 1978a, 1980a)

Tab. 2 illustrates the same for a selected subset of consonants. Note the following: The substitutions are systematic and not random. L1 transfer undoubtedly occurs, for example, the [s] substituting for /θ/, or the clear [1] substituting for the velar [ɬ]. But not all target items are replaced by L1 items. For example, the children under scrutiny here do not replace the L2 English target /r/ with their uvular L1 German [ʀ]. Instead, they use the bilabial [w] for the target's somewhat retroflex /r/. Note that L1 children learning English also at first substitute [w] for the retroflex /r/ (Wode 1977c, 1978a).

L2 target	child L2 substitute	illustrative example
w	v	Weaverville, wet, sandwich
θ	s	thank you, three, this
ð	d	that, the
	z	mother, weather, brother
ɬ	1	Bill, hill, cold, please, milk
r	w	Redding, Craig, truck

Table 2: Main phonological substitutions for selected English consonants in naturalistic L2 English/L1 German. Conventions, transcriptions, and sources as in tab. 1

Tab. 3 summarizes various studies on the L2 acquisition of English in the classroom. These data are contrasted with the evidence from naturalistic L2 English of

L2 target	naturalistic L2	Gimson 1970	Jones 1972	Kufner 1971	Keutsch 1974	Arnold/Hansen 1968	Schröder 1979	Weiher 1975
θ	s (f)	s t (f)	s f	s (f)	s	s (t)	θ	s f
ð	z d	z d (v)	z v (θ)	θ d (z)	z	z (d)	z (d)	z
r	w	ɾ ʀ ʁ	ʀ ʁ	ʀ ɾ	ʀ	ɾ ʀ ʁ	ʀ (w ɾ)	w (ʁ)
w	v	ß v	ß (v)	v (ø)	v	v	v	–
ɬ	1	1	1	1	1	–	1	–
æ	ɛ	ɛ	ɛ	ɛ	ɛ	ɛ	ɛ	ɛ
ʌ	a	a (œ)	a ɑ œ	a	a ɑ	a œ	a	–
əʊ–ɵ~əʊ	o	œʊ ʊ	o ɔʊ	–	o	ɔ	o (ɔʊ)	–
ɛɪ	e	e	e	–	e	–	e	–
əɾ–əː	œ	ø œ	œ ø	ø œ	ø œ	ø œ	œ (ɔa œa) –	

Table 3: FLT error types for selected L2 English targets from students with German as L1 compared to naturalistic L2 English/L1 German. Less frequent substitutions in ( ); – not investigated. Sources as in tab. 1.

tab. 1-2. Note that the substitutions are much the same in all studies despite methodological and other differences involved in the various studies from which the data
were compiled.

Tab. 4, which contrasts various types of L2 English, is central to the issue of
whether or not L1 transfer occurs in L2 acquisition. The important points here are:
First, the substitutions for naturalistic L2 English/L1 German are the same as for
FLT L2 English/L1 German. Second, the L2 English substitutions differ systematically as a function of the L1 acquired previously. Compare, for example, the substitutions for English /ɪ/ as in *sit* and /æ/ as in *fat* in L2 English/L1 German with
those in L2 English based on L1 French, Hindi, Arabic, Spanish, or Twi. Perhaps
the most important point to note is the fact that although some substitutions obviously derive from the L1 acquired previously, there seem to be some targets that
are not subject to L1 transfer even though the same element does not occur in the
L1. Consider, for example, the English diphtongs. Diphtongs like /eɪ/ and /əꭥ/ tend
to be replaced by monophtongs if the L1 does not have such diphtongs. The English
diphtongs /aɪ ɔɪ aꭥ/, however, tend not to be replaced by monophtongs even if the
L1 acquired previously does not have /aɪ ɔɪ aꭥ/. French speakers of English have no
difficulty in producing these diphtongs more or less target-like despite the fact that
these diphtongs do not appear in French. The same is true for Twi, and in various
ways, for the other language combinations shown in tab. 4.

types of L2 English	English targets and their substitutions source
	i ɪ ɛ æ u Ꝺ ʌ aɪ ɛɪ ɔɪ aꝺ əꝺ
naturalistic	
L2 English/L1 German	i ɪ ɛ ɛ u Ꝺ a aɪ e ɔɪ aꝺ o (Wode 1978a)
FLT	
L2 English/L1 German	i ɪ ɛ ɛ u Ꝺ a aɪ e ɔɪ aꝺ o (Schröder 1979)
L2 English/L1 French	i i ɛ a u u ? aɪ e ɔɪ aꝺ o (O'Connor 1967)
others	
Hindi	i ɪ æ/ɛɪ æ u Ꝺ a aɪ e ɔɪ aꝺ o (O'Connor 1967)
Arabic (Cairo)	i ɛ ɛ ? u Ꝺ ɔ aɪ e/ɪ ɔɪ aꝺ o (O'Connor 1967)
Spanish	i i ɛ a u u a aɪ ɛɪ ɔɪ aꝺ ɔ (O'Connor 1967)
Twi	i i ɛ a u u a aɪ e ɔɪ aꝺ o (Sey 1973, own observations)

Table 4:   L2 substitutions for selected English vowels by speakers from various L1's. ? indicates
      unclear cases. Sources as in tab. 1.

6 *Some Conclusions*

Several conclusions can be drawn from data such as I discussed above. One relates to the linguo-cognitive basis of L1 transfer; the second pertains to whether L1 transfer is „negative"; and the third has to do with the implications for CA within a theory of language learning.

The Linguo-Cognitive Basis of L1 Transfer

Note that the substitutions discussed in section 5 do not seem to be due to chance. There must be a basis for this usage so strikingly systematic across languages as well as across learners. One part of the explanation for this systematicity relates to the formal properties of the linguistic items themselves; the other part pertains to the way man's linguo-cognitive processing abilities operate on these formal properties.

As for the first part of the explanation, I have suggested elsewhere (Wode 1978a) that crucial similarity measures must be met between the L2 target items and the previously acquired L1 items before L1 transfer can take place at all. Just what the crucial properties are, is, at present, a matter for future research to determine. The nature of this task, however, can most impressively be illustrated by the handling of /θ/ as in *thick, three,* etc. in various L2 combinations of English. Germans tend to have [s]. L2 learners with Hindi as L1 tend to replace English /θ/ with an aspirated [t^h], although they contrast /t/ and /t^h/ in their L1 system. Japanese are said to use [s]. Speakers of those varieties of Spanish which have /θ/, like Castilian Spanish, use [θ]; speakers of varieties of Spanish which lack /θ/, replace the English target /θ/ by [s] (for such data see Weinreich 1953, Lado 1957, Ritchie 1968, Wode 1981).

The second part of the explanation for the systematic and non-random character of the L2 substitutions is a corollary to the first. I assume that it takes linguo-cognitive processing abilities that crucially react to and operate on, the phonetic/phonological properties so obviously involved in the data discussed above. It remains for future research to work out in detail the nature of these linguo-cognitive abilities. But it seems to me, that there can be no doubt at all that the linguo-cognitive regularities governing L1 transfer can be formulated with as much rigor and precision as those that govern the processing not related to L1 transfer (for some such attempts see Wode 1979, 1981).

„Negative" vs. „Positive" Transfer

Certain aspects of L1 transfer are commonly regarded as undesirable, as implied by the familiar distinctions between „negative" and „positive" transfer. Transfer is negative if it leads to non-targetlike learner structures; positive transfer leads to targetlike ones. The former is regarded as in need of eradiction; the latter is acceptable and is encouraged. This view needs to be abandoned, because it fails to take into account the developmental nature of L1 transfer. In particular the data on naturalistic L2 acquisition clearly show that reliance on L1 is an integral part of how human beings learn L2's, L3's, etc. Terms like „negative/positive transfer" are inadequate categorizations. We have learned to accept the fact that young children at a certain stage of their development do not make the proper judgements, for example, about volume constancy. Nobody would classify such behavior as „negative" or „positive". We accept it as developmental. The attitude required towards reliance on L1 in language acquisition should also be developmental. We have to accept L1 transfer as developmental as much as we accept other types of acquisitional regularities commonly regarded as developmental.

Moreover, although so far the basic insights were developed through phonology, extensive data are available on other structural areas, for example, negation (Ravem 1968, 1969, 1974; Wode 1976a, 1977a), interrogation (Ravem 1970, 1974; Wode 1978b; Ufert 1980), inflections (Wode et al. 1978), the lexicon (Wode 1981), conversational skills (Keller-Cohen 1979), signalling the topic (Schachter & Rutherford 1979), socio-linguistic and stylistic variation (Schmidt 1977), etc.

Implication for CA and for a Theory of Language Learning

To sum up and to return to the question of CA's place in a language learning theory, there can be no doubt that the traditional all-or-nothing view of CA, as well as the Dulay/Burt view which bans L1 transfer from consideration, are inadequate. Rather, several types of regularities interact and complement each other. This requires a perspective about language learning which integrates both views. This leads back to the original problem of how to reintegrate CA into a language learning theory.

The view that emerges is roughly this: typological CA specifies the structures of the languages involved and points out differences and commonalities. It describes the structural conflict with which the learner is faced when he is learning an additional language. The language learning theory proper predicts and specifies how learners solve these conflicts acquisitionally. Obviously then, CA cannot be a language learning theory, nor can a language learning theory be based exclusively on CA.

How do we incorporate CA into a language learning theory? There seem to be two possibilities. From the point of view of language learning, typological CA can be incorporated as one component that specifies the domain that is to be learned. This implies that it is CA that is incorporated into a language learning theory. The alternative would be to start from the typological point of view and build into such a CA a language learning component that specifies how the learner will resolve conflicts. Which of the alternative solutions is chosen may be a matter of personal preference. I prefer the solution in which CA is regarded as a result of language learning. After all, the typology of natural languages can only be such that the various language structures remain learnable. In other words, the language learning capacity of the human brain constrains the typological variety that can be found in natural languages. From this point of view, typological CA and language learning are complementary, i.e. they are two sides of one and the same coin.

Note

* Paper delivered at the International Seminar on Contrastive Grammar at Stanford University, March 15-16, 1980.

Concluding Remarks

The central topic throughout the 14 papers of this volume is the remarkable capacity which human beings have for learning natural languages. It is emphasized that the study of this capacity requires a unified view contrasting all types of language learning in all age groups. The various papers were focused on individual aspects — structural, methodological, and applied. To be sure, we are still far from a comprehensive assessment or understanding of the total range of phenomena. But in spite of the patchy nature of our overall understanding of these phenomena, the general impact, it seems to me, is promising and worth pursuing in more detail and on a larger scale in future research, because, irrespective of which aspect was selected for study, numerous traditional views current among either laymen or scholarly specialists were shown to be in need of revision and refinement if reviewed within an integrated perspective such as that advocated in this volume.

As for methodology and subject matter, the 14 papers are clearly rooted in linguistics, with emphasis on linguistic structures in the narrower sense. Obviously, the range of phenomena has to be broadened such that the development of linguistic competence is integrated within the overall development of the ability to communicate and interact using a given language and including non-verbal means as well. The empirical evidence presently available on such issues clearly shows that our understanding of the interrelationship of language acquisition with other cognitive domains can be advanced considerably if such problems are explored from the proposed comprehensive perspective, i.e. by carefully contrasting the evidence from different acquisitional types.

It is highly likely, therefore, that the most important long-range consequence of the comprehensive approach to language acquisition as advocated here will turn out to be methodological. That is, comparing different acquisitional types presents a new research paradigm with great potential for various disciplines. It seems that a new understanding of many issues in cognitive and developmental psychology can be achieved by exploiting this new paradigm. Its potential can be illustrated most easily for L1 acquisition and the cognitive development of children. Traditional approaches to the study of child development look at the L1 monolingual, or, at best, at the L1 bilingual child. Methodologically, the difficulty with such subjects is that both linguistic and non-linguistic developments co-occur. They cannot be separated empirically. Within this traditional approach it is difficult to determine whether this is a relationship of co-occurrence, or whether and to what extent language development determines general cognitive development, or whether and to what extent general cognitive development determines linguistic development. The comprehensive approach advocated in these papers promises to offer a new way of looking at such issues. If, for example, the same developmental peculiarities with respect to the same items occur both in the very young L1 child and in the more advanced L2 child or even in a cognitively mature adult L2 learner, then it can no longer be argued that these acquisitional characteristics are determined by the maturational processes governing the development of general cognition. Rather, such evidence would suggest clearly that certain linguistic aspects develop independently of cognitive aspects. Or, to put it differently, this research paradigm allows one to analyse in much more detail exactly what may be due to general linguistic developments and what may be due to general cognitive development.

Such methodological advances provide new points of interest for other disciplines or for interdisciplinary research. It seems that the comprehensive approach advocated here offers a much richer data base for future research in psychology, neurology, and, in particular, for brain research, than was available thus far utilizing the more traditional methodologies. For example, if it is possible to state in more detail whether and to what extent linguistic and general cognitive development — although co-occurring — nevertheless develop independently, these data would have important consequences for psychology and neurology, in particular, for problems concerning the development and functioning of the human brain. Such issues as brain maturation, specialization of brain functions, restitutability of brain functions after loss due to brain injuries, critical periods for the development of various brain functions, etc. can be investigated with much more sophistication.

BIBLIOGRAPHY

Abrahamsen, A.A. 1977: *Child Language. An Interdisciplinary Guide to Theory and Research*, Baltimore, London, Tokyo.

Adams, M.S. 1974: *Second Language Acquisition in Children*, M.A. Thesis, University of California at Los Angeles.

Ament, W. 1899: *Die Entwicklung vom Sprechen und Denken beim Kinde*, Leipzig.

Andersen, R. 1977: „The Impoverished State of Cross-sectional Morpheme Acquisition/Accuracy Methodology, or, the Leftovers are More Nourishing than the Main Course", Working Papers on Bilingualism 14, 47-82.

Andersen, R.W. 1979: „Expanding Schumann's Pidginzation Hypothesis", Language Learning 29, 105-121.

Anisfield, M. & Tucker, G.R. 1967: „English Pluralization Rules of Six Year Old Children", Child Development 38, 1201-1218.

Antinucci, F. & Volterra, V. 1973: „Lo sviluppo della negazione nel linguaggio infantile: uno studio pragmatico", Istitutio di Psicologia, CNR, Rome.

Arnold, R. & Hansen, K. 1968: „Phonetik der englischen Sprache. Eine Einführung", Leipzig.

Asher, J.J. & Garcia, R. 1969: „The Optimal Age to Learn a Foreign Language", The Modern Language Journal 53, 334-341.

Asher, J.J. & Price, B.1967: „The Learning Strategy of the Total Physical Response: Some Age Differences ", Child Development 38, 1219-1227.

Atkinson-King, K. 1973: „Children's Acquisition of Phonological Stress Contrasts", Working Papers in Phonetics 25, University of California at Los Angeles.

Bailey, B.L. 1966: *Jamaican Creole Syntax. A Transformational Approach*, London.

Bailey, N., Madden, C. & Krashen, S.D. 1974: „Is There a ‚Natural Sequence' in Adult Second Language Learning?", Language Learning 24, 235-243. Reprinted in: Hatch, E.M. 1978a: 362-370.

Bar-Adon, A. & Leopold, W.F. (eds.) 1971: *Child Language. A Book of Readings*, Englewood Cliffs, N.J.

Bauer, A. 1974: *Das melanesische und chinesische Pidgin-Englisch. Linguistische Kriterien und Probleme*, Regensburg.

Bellugi, U. 1967: *The Acquisition of Negation*. Doctoral Dissertation, Harvard University.

Bellugi, U. & Brown, R. (eds.) 1964: „The Acquisition of Language", *Monographs of the Society for Research in Child Development* 29 (1), Lafayette, Ind.

Berko, J. 1958: „The Child's Learning of English Morphology", Word 14, 150-177.

Bernstein, B. (ed.) 1971/73: *Class, Codes, and Control*, 2 vols., London.

Bloom, L.M. 1970: *Language Development: Form and Function in Emerging Grammars*, Cambridge, Mass.

Bloom, L.M. 1971: „Why not Pivot Grammar?", Journal of Speech and Hearing Disorders 36, 40-50. Reprinted in: Ferguson, C.A. & Slobin, D.I. 1973, 430-440.

Bloom, L.M. 1973: „One Word at a Time. The Use of Single Word Utterances before Syntax", Janua Linguarum Series Minor 154, The Hague.

Bowerman, M. 1973: *Early Syntactic Development*. A Cross-linguistic Study with Special Reference fo Finnish, Cambridge, England.

Braine, M.D.S. 1963: „The Ontogeny of English Phrase Structure. The First Phase", Language 39: 1-13. Reprinted in: Ferguson, C.A. & Slobin, D.I. 1973: 407-421.

Brière, E. 1966: „An Investigation of Phonological Interference", Language 42, 768-796.

Brown, H.D., Yorio, C.A. & Crymes, R.H. (eds.) 1977: *On TESOL '77: Teaching and Learning English as a Second Language: Trends in Research and Practice*, Washington D.C.

Brown, R. 1968: „The Development of wh-Questions in Child Speech", Journal of Verbal Learning and Verbal Behavior 7: 279-290.

Brown, R. 1973: *A First Language: The Early Stages*, Cambridge, Mass.

Brown, R. & Fraser, C. 1963: *The Acquisition of Syntax*, Cofer, C.N. & Musgrave, B.S.: 158-197. Reprinted in Bellugi, U. & Brown, R. 1964: 43-79.

216

Burgschmidt, E. & Götz, D. 1974: *Kontrastive Linguistik:Deutsch/Englisch*, Theorie und Anwendung, München.

Burling, R. 1959: „Language Development of a Garo- and English-speaking Child", Word 15, 45-68. Reprinted in: Ferguson, C.A. & Slobin D.I. 1973, 69-90.

Burt, M.K., Dulay, H.C. & Hernándes-Chavez, E. 1975: *Billingual Syntax Measure*, New York.

Burt, M.K. & Dulay, H.C. 1980: „On Acquisition Orders", Felix S.W. 1980: 265-328.

Burt, M.K., Dulay, H.C. & Finocchiaro, M. (eds.) 1977: *Viewpoints on English as a Second Language*, New York.

Carlson, P. & Anisfield, M. 1969: „Some Observations on the Linguistic Competence of a Two-Year-Old Child", Child Development 40, 569-575.

Carr, E. 1972: *Da Kine Talk. From Pidgin to Standard English in Hawaii.* University of Hawaii Press.

Cazden, C.B. 1968: „The Acquisition of Noun and Verb Inflections", *Child Development* 39, 433-448. Reprinted in: Ferguson, C.A. & Slobin, D.I. 1973, 226-240.

Chamot, A. 1972: *English as a Third Language: Its Acquisition by a Child Bilingual in French and Spanish*, Doctoral Dissertation, University of Texas at Austin.

Chomsky, C. 1969: „The Acquisition of Syntax in Children From 5 To 10", Research Monograph 57, Cambridge, Mass.

Chomsky, N. 1959: „Review of B.F. Skinner, Verbal Behavior. New York 1957", Language 35, 26-58.

Chomsky, N. 1965: *Aspects of the Theory of Syntax*, Cambridge, Mass.

Chomsky, N. 1976: *Reflections on Language*, New York.

Christian, J.M. 1971: *Developing Bilingualism in a Two-Year-Old Gujarati-English Learning Child*, Department of Anthropology and Sociology, University of Alabama, Mimeo.

Clahsen, H. 1980: „Psycholinguistic Aspects of L2 Acquisition", Felix S.W. 1980, 57-59.

Clark, E.V. 1971: „On the Acquisition of ‚before' and ‚after' ", Journal of Verbal Learning and Verbal Behavior 10: 266-275.

Clark, E.V. 1973: „What's in a Word?", Moore, T.E.: 65-110.

Clark, H.H. 1970: „The Primitive Nature of Children's Relational Concepts", Hayes, J.R.: 269-278.

Clyne, M. 1968: „Zum Pidgin-Deutsch der Gastarbeiter", Zeitschrift für Mundartforschung 35, 130-139.

Cofer, C.N. & Musgrave, B.S. (eds.) 1963: *Verbal Behavior and Learning: Problems and Processes*, New York.

Corder, S.P. 1967: „The Significance of Learner's Errors", International Review of Applied Linguistics 5, 161-170.

Crystal, D. 1973: „Non-segmental Phonology in Language Acquisition. A Review of the Issues", Lingua 31, 1-45.

Dahl, Ö. 1979: „Typology of Sentence Negation", Linguistics 17, 79-106.

Dato, D. 1971: „The Development of the Spanish Verb Phrase in Children's Second Language Learning", Pimsleur, P. & Quinn, T., 19-33.

DeCamp, D. & Hancock, I.F. (eds.) 1978: *Pidgins and Creoles: Current Trends and Prospects*, Washington, D.C.

Denison, N. 1958: „Comment on Haugen", Sivertsen, F., 803-804.

Detering, K. & Högel, H. (eds.) 1978: *Festschrift für Käthe Lorenzen*, Hannover.

Drachmann, G. 1973: „Some Strategies in the Acquisition of Phonology", Kenstowicz, M. & Kisseberth, C., 145-159.

Drachmann, G. (ed.) 1976: *Akten des 1. Salzburger Kolloquiums über Kindersprache*, Tübingen.

Drachmann, G. (ed.) 1977: *Salzburger Beiträge zur Linguistik 4: Akten der 3. Salzburger Jahrestagung für Linguistik*, Tübingen.

Dulay, H.C. & Burt, M.K. 1972: „ ‚Goofing': An Indicator of Children's Second Language Learning Strategies", Language Learning 22, 235-252.

Dulay, H.C. & Burt, M.K. 1973: „Should We Teach Children Syntax?", Language Learning 23, 245-258.

Dulay, H.C. & Burt, M.K. 1974a: „Natural Sequences in Child Second Language Acquisition", Language Learning 24, 37-53.

Dulay, H.C. & Burt, M.K. 1974b: „A New Perspective on the Creative Construction Process in Child Second Language Acquisition", Language Learning 24, 253-278.

Dulay, H.C. & Burt, M.K. 1974c: „Errors and Strategies in Child Second Language Acquisition", TESOL Quarterly 8, 129-136.

Dušková, L. 1969: „ On Sources of Errors in Foreign Language Learning", International Review of Applied Linguistics 7, 11-36.

Edwards, M. 1971: „One Child's Acquisition of English Liquids", Papers and Reports on Child Language Development 3, 101-108.

Ervin-Tripp, S.M. 1966: „Language Development", Hoffmann, L.W. & Hoffmann, M.L., 55-105.

Ervin-Tripp, S.M. 1973: *Is Second Language Learning Like the First?*, Paper Read at the TESOL Symposium, Puerto Rico, May 1973.

Felix, S. 1976a: „Entwicklungsprozesse im gesteuerten Zweitsprachenerwerb", Kühlwein, W. & Raasch, A. 1977, 134-145.

Felix, S. 1976b: „Wh-Pronouns in First and Second Language Acquisition", Linguistische Berichte 44, 52-64.

Felix, S. 1977a: „Natürlicher Zweitsprachenerwerb und Fremdsprachenunterricht", Linguistik und Didaktik 31, 231-248.

Felix, S. 1977b: „Entwicklungsprozesse im natürlichen und gesteuerten Zweitsprachenerwerb", Anglistik und Englischunterricht 1: Sprachdidaktik, 39-60.

Felix, S. 1977c: „Repetitive Orders of Acquisition in Child Language", Lingua 41, 25-51.

Felix, S. 1977d: „Interference, Interlanguage, and Related Issues", Molony, C. Zobl, H. & Stölting, W., 237-258. Reprinted in: Felix, S.W. 1980, 93-107.

Felix, S. 1977e: „Kreative und reproduktive Kompetenz im Zweitsprachenerwerb", Hunfeld, H., 25-34.

Felix, S. 1977f: „Natürlicher Zweitsprachenerwerb: ein Überblick", Studium Linguistik 4, 25-40.

Felix, S. 1978a: „Some Differences Between First and Second Language Acquisition", Waterson, N. & Snow, D., 469-479.

Felix, S. 1978b: *Linguistische Untersuchungen zum natürlichen Zweitsprachenerwerb*, München.

Felix, S.W. (ed.) 1980: *Second Language Development. Trends and Issues,* Tübingen.

Felix, S. 1982: *Psycholinguistische Aspekte des Zweitsprachenerwerbs*, Tübingen.

Ferguson, C.A. & Slobin, D.I. (eds.) 1973: *Studies of Child Language Development,* New York.

Ferguson, C.A. & Garnica, O.K. 1975: „Theories of Phonological Development", Lenneberg, E.H. & Lenneberg, E., 153-180.

Ferguson, C.A. & Farwell, C.B. 1975: „Words and Sounds in Early Language Acquisition", Language 51, 419-439.

Fillmore, L.W. 1976: *The Second Time Around: Cognitive and Social Strategies in Second Language Acquisition.* Doctoral Dissertation, Stanford.

Flores d'Arcais, G.B. & Levelt, W.J.M. (eds.) 1970: *Advances in Psycholinguistics,* Amsterdam.

Fries, C.C. 1945: *Teaching and Learning English – as a Foreign Language*, Ann Arbor, Mich.

Gheorgov, I.A. 1908: „Ein Beitrag zur grammatischen Entwicklung der Kindersprache", Leipzig. Reprinted in: Archiv für die gesamte Psychologie 11, 242-432.

Gimson, A.C. 1970: *An Introduction to the pronunciation of English*, London.

Grebe, P. (ed.) 1973: *Der große Duden, Bd. 4, Grammatik der deutschen Gegenwartssprache.* Mannheim.

Greenberg, J.H. 1966a: „Some Universals of Grammar with Particular Reference to the Order of Meaningful Elements", Greenberg, J.H. b, 73-113.

Greenberg, J.H. (ed.) 1966b: *Universals of Language,* Cambridge, Mass.

Greenhalgh, S. 1976: *Erwerb und Entwicklung der Interrogativpronomina in der Kindersprache am Beispiel des Deutschen,* M.A. Thesis, Kiel University.

Grégoire, A. 1937: *L'apprentissage du language 1, Les deux premières années,* Paris.

Grégoire, A. 1947: *L'apprentissage du language 2, La troisieme annee et les annees suivantes, Paris.*

Grimm, H. 1973: *Strukturanalytische Untersuchung der Kindersprache.* Bern.

Gutfleisch, I., Rieck, B.-O., Dittmar, N., Bialystock, E., Chaudron, C. & Fröhlich, M. 1979/80: „Interimsprachen- und Fehleranalyse. Teilkommentierte Bibliographie zur Zweitsprachenerwerbsforschung 1967-1978", Linguistische Berichte 64, 105-142, Linguistische Berichte 65, 51-81.

Gvozdev, A.N. 1949: *Formirovaniye u rebenka grammaticheskogo stroya russkogo yazyka.* Akad. Pedag. Nauk RSFSR, Moscow.

Hakuta, K. 1974: „A Preliminary Report on the Development of Grammatical Morphemes in a Japanese Girl Learning English as a Second Language", Working Papers on Bilingualism 3, 18-43.

Halliday, M.A.K. 1967: *Intonation and Grammar in British English*, The Hague.

Hartig, M. & Wode, H. (eds.) 1978: *Kongreßberichte der 8. Jahrestagung der Gesellschaft für Angewandte Linguistik GAL e. V. Mainz, 1977*, Vol. 4, Stuttgart.

Hatch, E.M. (ed.) 1978a: *Second Language Acquisition: A Book of Readings*, Rowley, Mass.

Hatch, E.M. 1978b: „Discourse Analysis and Second Language Acquisition", Hatch, E.M. 1978a, 401-435.

Hayes, J.R. (ed.) 1970: *Cognition and the Development of Language*, New York.

Heidelberger Forschungsprojekt Pidgin-Deutsch 1975: *Sprache und Kommunikation ausländischer Arbeiter. Analysen, Berichte, Materialien*. Kronberg/Ts.

Heidelberger Forschungsprojekt Pidgin-Deutsch 1976: *Arbeitsbericht III: Untersuchungen zur Erlernung des Deutschen durch ausländische Arbeiter*, Germanistisches Seminar der Universität Heidelberg.

Henning, C. (ed.) 1977: *Proceedings of the Los Angeles Second Language Research Forum*, Los Angeles, Cal.

Hockett, C.F. 1958: *A Course in Modern Linguistics*, New York.

Hoffmann, L.W. & Hoffmann, M.L. (eds.) 1966: *Review of Child Development Research*, New York.

Hornby, P.A. 1971: „Surface Structure and the Topic-Comment Distinction", Child Development 42, 1975-1988.

Hornby, P.A. & Hass, W.A. 1970: „Use of Contrastive Stress by Preschool Children", Journal of Speech and Hearing Research 19, 395-399.

Huang, J.S.F. 1971: *A Chinese Child's Acquisition of English Syntax*, M.A. Thesis, University of California at Los Angeles.

Hüllen, W. & Jung, L. 1979: *Sprachstruktur und Spracherwerb*, Düsseldorf, Bern, München.

Hunfeld, H. (ed.) 1977: *Neue Perspektiven der Fremdsprachendidaktik. Eichstätter Kolloquium zum Fremdsprachenunterricht*, Kronberg/Ts.

Hyltenstam, K. 1977: „Implicational Patterns in Interlanguage Syntax Variation", Language Learning 27, 383-411.

Hyltenstam, K. 1978: *Variability in Interlanguage Syntax. Working Papers*, Phonetics Laboratory Dept. of General Linguistics, Lund University.

Ingram, D. 1976: *Phonological Disability in Children*, London.

Itoh, H.T. 1973: *A Child's Acquisition of Two Languages – Japanese and English*, M.A. Thesis, University of California at Los Angeles.

Itoh, H.T. & Hatch, E.M. 1978: „Second Language Acquisition: A Case Study", Hatch, E.M. 1978a, 76-88.

Jakobson, R. 1941: *Kindersprache, Aphasie und allgemeine Lautgesetze*, Uppsala. (Reprinted 1969, Frankfurt/Main).

Jones, D. [9]1972: *Outline of English Phonetics*, New York. ([1]1918).

Kadar-Hoffmann, G. 1977: „Der Erwerb der Negation bei einem dreisprachigen Kind", Hartig, M. & Wode, H. 1978, 47-53.

Kaper, W. 1959: *Kindersprachforschung mit Hilfe des Kindes: Einige Erscheinungen der kindlichen Spracherwerbung, erläutert im Licht des vom Kinde gezeigten Interesses für Sprachliches*, Groningen.

Kaper, W. 1975: „Negatie in de Kindertaal", Forum der Lettern 16, 18-44.

Katz, J.T. 1977: „Foreigner Talk Input in Child Second Language Acquisition: Its Form and Function over Time", Henning, C. 1977, 61-75.

Kay, P. & Sankoff, G. 1974: „A Language Universal Approach to Pidgins and Creoles", DeCamp, D. & Hancock, I.F. 1978, 61-72.

Keller-Cohen, H. 1979: „Systematicity and Variation in the Non-native Child's Acquisition of Conversational Skills", Language Learning 29, 27-44.

Kenstowicz, M.J. & Kisseberth, C.W. (eds.) 1973: „Issues in Phonological Theory", *Proceedings of the Urbana Conference on Phonology*, The Hague.

Kenyéres, E. 1938: „Comment une petite hongroise de sept ans apprend le français", Archives de Psychologie 26, 521-566.

Kessel, F.S. 1970: „The Role of Syntax in Children's Comprehension from Ages Six to Twelve", Monographs of the Society for Research in Child Development 35, 6.

Keutsch, M. 1974: *Praxis der englischen Aussprache*, Tübingen.

Klein, W. & Dittmar, N. 1979: *Developing Grammars. The Acquisition of German Syntax by Foreign Workers,* Berlin, Heidelberg.

Klima, E.S. & Bellugi, U. 1966: „Syntactic Regularities in the Speech of Children". Lyons, J. & Wales, R.J., 183-208. Reprinted in: Ferguson, C.A. & Slobin, D.I. 1973, 333-355. Revised Version: Bar-Adon, Adon, A. & Leopold, W.F. 1971, 412-424.

Krashen, S.D. 1973: „Lateralization, Language Learning, and the Critical Period: Some New Evidence", Language Learning 23, 63-74.

Krashen, S.D. 1977a: „The Monitor Model for Adult Second Language Performance", Burt, M.K., Dulay, H.C. & Finocchiaro, M., 152-161.

Krashen, S.D. 1977b: „Some Issues Relating to the Monitor Model", Brown, H.D., Yorio, C.A., Crymes, R.H., 144-158.

Kühlwein, W. & Raasch, A. (eds.) 1977: *Kongreßberichte der 7. Jahrestagung der Gesellschaft für Angewandte Linguistik GAL e.V. Trier, 1976,* Vol. IV, Stuttgart.

Kühlwein, W. & Raasch, A. (eds.) 1978: *Kongreßberichte der 8. Jahrestagung der Gesellschaft für Angewandte Linguistik GAL e.V. Mainz, 1977,* Vol. I, Stuttgart.

Kufner, H.L. 1971: *Kontrastive Phonologie, Deutsch-Englisch,* Stuttgart.

Lado, R. 1957: *Linguistics across Cultures. Applied Linguistics for Language Teachers,* Ann Arbor, Mich.

Lane, H. 1962: „Some Differences Between First and Second Language Learning", Language Learning 12, 1-14.

Lange, D. 1979: „Negation im natürlichen englisch-deutschen Zweitsprachenerwerb: Eine Fallstudie", International Review of Applied Linguistics 17, 4, 331-348.

Lange, S. & Larsson, K. 1973: *Syntactical Development of a Swedish Girl Embla, between 20 and 42 Months of Age, Part I: Age 20-25 Months,* Stockholm.

Larsen-Freeman, D.E. 1975: „The Acquisition of Grammatical Morphemes by Adult ESL Students", TESOL Quarterly 9, 409-419.

Lenneberg, E.H. 1967: *Biological Foundations of Language,* New York, London, Sidney.

Lenneberg, E.H. & Lenneberg, E. (eds.) 1975: *Foundations of Language Development,* Vol. 1, New York.

Leopold, W.F. 1939-1949: *Speech Development of a Bilingual Child: A Linguist's Record,* (4 Vols.) Evanston, I11.

Leopold, W.F. 1952: *Bibliography of Child Language,* Evanston, I11.

Leopold, W.F. 1959: „Kindersprache", Phonetica 4, 191-214.

Lindner, G. 1898: *Aus dem Naturgarten der Kindersprache: Ein Beitrag zur kindlichen Sprach- und Geistesentwicklung in den ersten vier Lebensjahren,* Leipzig.

Littlewood, W. 1974: „A Comparison of First Language Acquisition and Second Language Learning", Praxis des neusprachlichen Unterrichts 4, 343-348.

Lyons, J. & Wales, R.J. (eds.) 1966: *Psycholinguistics Papers. The Proceedings of the 1966 Edinburgh Conference,* Edinburgh.

Malmberg, B. 1945: „Ett barn byter språk", Nordisk Tidskrift 21, 170-181.

McLaughlin, B. 1978: „Second Language Acquisition in Childhood", Hillsdale, N.J.

McNeill, D. 1966: „Developmental Psycholinguistics", Smith, F. & Miller, G.A., 14-84.

McNeill, D. 1970a: *The Acquisition of Language: The Study of Developmental Psycholinguistics,* New York.

McNeill, D. 1970b: „The Development of Language", Mussen, P.H., 1061-1161.

McNeill, D. & McNeill, N.B. 1968: „What does a Child Mean when He Says ‚No'?", Zale, E.M., 51-62. Reprinted in: Ferguson, C.A. & Slobin, D.I. 1973, 619-627.

Meisel, J.M. 1975: „Ausländerdeutsch und Deutsch ausländischer Arbeiter. Zur möglichen Entstehung eines Pidgin in der Bundesrepublik Deutschland", Zeitschrift für Literaturwissenschaft und Linguistik 18, 9-53.

Meisel, J.M. 1979: *Strategies of Second Language Acquisition: More than one Kind of Simplification,* Paper presented at the Symposium on the Relationship between Pidginization and Creolization in Language Acquisition, LSA Annual Meeting, Los Angeles, Dec. 27-29.

Meisel, J.M. 1980: „Linguistic Simplification", Felix, S.W. 1980, 13-40.

Menyuk, P. 1971: *The Acquisition and Development of Language,* Englewood Cliffs, N.J.

Métreaux, R.W. 1964/65: „A Study on Bilingualism Among Children of US-French Parents", French Review 38, 650-655.

Miller, W.R. 1973: „The Acquisition of Grammatical Rules by Children", Ferguson, C.A. & Slobin, D.J., 380-991.

Miller, W.R. & Ervin, S.M. 1964: „The Development of Grammar in Child Language", Bellugi, U. & Brown, R., 9-33. Reprinted in: Ferguson, C.A. & Slobin, D.I. 1973, 355-380.

Mills, A. 1977: *First and Second Language Acquisition: A Parallel Study*, Ludwigsburg.

Milon, J. 1974: „The Development of Negation in English by a Second Language Learner", TESOL Quarterly 8, 137-143.

Molony, C., Zobl, H. & Stölting, W. (eds.) 1977: *German in Contact with Other Languages*, Kronberg/Ts.

Moore, T.E. (ed.) 1973: *Cognitive Development and the Acquisition of Language*, New York.

Mowrer, O.H. 1952: „Speech Development in the Young Child", Journal of Speech and Hearing Disorders 17, 263-268.

Mussen, P.H. (ed.) 1970: *Carmichael's Manual of Child Psychology I*, New York.

Natalicio, D.S. & Natalicio, L.F.S. 1971: „The Comparative Study of English Pluralization by Native and Non-native Speakers", Child Development 42, 1302-1306.

Nemser, W. 1971: „Approximative Systems of Foreign Language Learners", International Review of Applied Linguistics 9, 115-123. Reprinted in: Richards, J.C. 1974, 55-63.

Neugebauer, H. 1914: „Sprachliche Eigenbildungen meines Sohnes", Zeitschrift für Kinderforschung 19, 174-181, 242-246, 360-370.

Neugebauer, H. 1915: „Aus der Sprachentwicklung meines Sohnes", Zeitschrift für Angewandte Psychologie, 298-306.

O'Connor, J.D. 1967: *Better English Pronunciation*, Cambridge.

Ohnesorg, K. (ed.) 1972: *Proceedings of the First International Symposium of Paedolinguistics at Brno*, The Hague.

Oksaar, E. 1970: „Zum Spracherwerb des Kindes in zweisprachiger Umgebung", Folia Linguistica 4, 330-358.

Oksaar, E. 1977: *Spracherwerb im Vorschulalter. Einführung in die Pädolinguistik*, Stuttgart.

Olmsted, D.L. 1971: *Out of the Mouth ob Babes*, The Hague.

Olson, L.L. & Samuels, S.J. 1973: „The Relationship between Age and Accuracy of Foreign Language Pronunciation", The Journal of Educational Research 66, 263-268.

Omar, M.K. 1970: *The Acquisition of Egyptian Arabic as a Native Language*, The Hague.

Park, T.-Z. 1970: *The Acquisition of German Syntax*, Working Paper, Psychological Institute, University of Münster, West-Germany.

Pavlovitch, M. 1920: *Le langage ⟨enfantin: acquisition du serbe et du français par un enfant serbe*, Paris.

Peck, S. 1977: „Language Play in Child Second Language Acquisition", Henning, C., 85-93.

Peck, S. 1978: „Child-Child Discourse in Second Language Acquisition", Hatch, E.M. 1978a, 383-400.

Perkins, K. & Larsen-Freeman, D. 1975: „The Effect of Formal Language Instruction on the Order of Morpheme Acquisition", Language Learning 25, 237-243.

Peuser, G. 1977: *Sprache und Gehirn. Eine Bibliographie zur Neurolinguistik*, München.

Pienemann, M. 1980: „The Second Language Acquisition of Immigrant Children", Felix, S.W. 1980, 41-56.

Pike, K. 1945: *The Intonation of American English*, Ann Arbor, Mich.

Pimsleur, P. & Quinn, T. (eds.) 1971: *The Psychology of Second Language Learning. Papers from the 2nd International Congress of Applied Linguistics at Cambridge*, London.

Preyer, W. 1882: *Die Seele des Kindes. Beobachtungen über die geistige Entwicklung des Kindes in den ersten Lebensjahren*, Leipzig.

von Raffler-Engel, W. 1964: „Die Entwicklung vom Laut zum Phonem in der Kindersprache", Zwirner, H. & Bethge, W., 482-486.

von Raffler-Engel, W. 1970: „Theoretical Phonology and First Language Acquisition", Folia Linguistica 4, 316-329.

von Raffler-Engel, W. (ed.) 1976: Child Language 1975, Special Issue of Word 27.

Ramge, H. 1973: *Spracherwerb. Grundzüge der Sprachentwicklung des Kindes*, Tübingen.

Ravem, R. 1968: „Language Acquisition in a Second Language Environment", International Review of Applied Linguistcs 4, 175-185.

Ravem, R. 1969: *First and Second Language Acquisition*, Paper Presented at the BAAL Seminar on Error Analysis, Edinburgh, April 26-27, 1969.

Ravem, R. 1970: „The Development of Wh-Questions in First and Second Language Learners", University of Essex Language Centre, Occasional Papers 8, 16-41.

Ravem, R. 1974: *Second Language Acquisition*, Doctoral Dissertation, University of Essex.

Redden, J.E. & Bongo, F. 1963: *Twi: Basic Course*. Washington D.C.

Reinecke, J.E. et al. (eds.) 1975: *A Bibliography of Pidgin and Creole Languages*, Honolulu, Hawaii.

Richards, J.C. 1971: „A Non-contrastive Approach to Error Analysis. English Language Teaching 25, 204-219. Reprinted in: Richards, J.C. 1974, 172-188.

Richards, J.C. (ed.) 1974: *Error Analysis. Perspectives on Second Language Acquisition*, London.

Rigault, A. & Chàrbonneau, P. (eds.) 1972: *Proceedings of the 7th International Congress of Phonetic Sciences*, The Hague.

Ritchie, W.C. 1968: „On the Explanation of Phonic Interference", Language Learning 18, 183-197.

Rosansky, E.J. 1976a: *Second Language Acquisition Research: A Question of Methods*, Doctoral Dissertation, Harvard University.

Rosansky, E.J. 1976b: "Methods and Morphemes in Second Language Acquisition Research", Language Learning 26, 409-425. Also in: Papers and Reports on Child Language Development 12, 199-211.

Ruke-Dravina, V. 1963: „Sprachentwicklung bei Kleinkindern. I. Syntax: Beitrag auf der Grundlage lettischen Sprachmaterials", Slaviska och Baltiska Studier 6, Lund.

Ruke-Dravina, V. 1967: *Mehrsprachigkeit im Vorschulalter*, Lund.

Ruke-Dravina, V. 1972: „The Emergence of Affirmation and Negation in Child Language: Some Universal and Language-restricted Characteristics", Ohnesorg, K., 221-241.

Schachter, J. & Rutherford, W. 1979: „Discourse Function and Language Transfer", Working Papers on Bilingualism 19, 1-12.

Schaerlaekens, A.M. 1973: *The Two-Word Sentence in Child Language Development. A Study Based on Evidence Provided by Dutch-speaking Triplets*, The Hague.

Schmidt, R.W. 1977: „Sociolinguistic Variation and Language Transfer in Phonology", Working Papers on Bilingualism 12, 79-95.

Schröder, A. 1979: „Aussprachefehler bei Sextanern im Englisch-Anfangsunterricht im Lichte des natürlichen L2-Erwerbs", Arbeitspapiere zum Spracherwerb 23, English Department, Kiel University.

Schumann, J.H. 1975a: *Second Language Acquisition: The Pidginization Hypothesis*, Doctoral Dissertation, Harvard University.

Schumann, J.H. 1975b: „Affective Factors and the Problem of Age in Second Language Acquisition", Language Learning 25, 209-235.

Schumann, J.H. 1976: „Social Distance as a Factor in Second Language Acquisition", Language Learning 26, 135-143.

Schumann, J.H. 1978: „The Relationship of Pidginization, Creolization and Decreolization to Second Language Acquisition", Language Learning 28, 367-379.

Schumann, J.H. & Stenson, N. (eds.) 1975: *New Frontiers in Second Language Learning*, Rowley, Mass.

Scovel, T. 1969: „Foreign Accents, Language Acquisition and Cerebral Dominance", Language Learning 19, 245-253.

Scupin, E. & Scupin, G. 1907: *Bubis erste Kindheit: Ein Tagebuch*. Leipzig.

Scupin, E. & Scupin, G. 1910: *Bubi im vierten bis sechsten Lebensjahr*, Leipzig.

Selinker, L. 1972: „Interlanguage", International Review of Applied Linguistics 10, 209-231. Reprinted in: Richards, J.C. 1974, 31-54. Reprinted in: Schumann, J.H. & Stenson, N. 1975, 114-136.

Sey, K.A. 1973: *Ghanaian English. An Exploratory Survey*, London.

Sivertsen, E. (ed.) 1958: *Proceedings of the 8th International Congress of Linguistics*, Oslo.

Skinner, B.F. 1957: *Verbal Behavior*, New York.

Slama-Cazacu, T. 1972: „The Study of Child Language in Europe", Current Trends in Linguistics 9, 512-590.

Slobin, D.I. 1966: „Abstracts of Soviet Studies of Child Language", Smith, F. & Miller, G., Appendix, 361-386.

Slobin, D.I. 1970: „Universals of Grammatical Development in Children", Flores d'Arcais, G.B. & Levelt, W.J.M., 174-186.

Slobin, D.I. (ed.) 1971: *The Ontogenesis of Grammar: A Theoretical Symposium*, New York.

Slobin, D.I. 1972: *Leopold's Bibliography of Child Language, Revised and Augmented Edition*, Bloomington, Ind.

Slobin, D.I. 1973: „Cognitive Prerequisites for the Development of Grammar", Ferguson, C.A. & Slobin, D.I., 175-208.

Slobin, D.I. 1975: „The More it Changes . . . .: On Understanding Language by Watching it Move through Time. Papers and Reports on Child Language Development 10, 1-30.

Slobin, D.I. & Welsh, C.A. 1973: „Elicited Imitation as a Research Tool in Developmental Psycholinguistics", Ferguson, C.A. & Slobin, D.I., 485-497.

Smith, F. & Miller, G.A. (eds.) 1966: *The Genesis of Language: A Psycholinguistic Approach*, Cambridge, Mass.

Smith, N.V. 1973: *The Acquisition of Phonology*, Cambridge, England.

Snow, C.E. & Ferguson, C.A. (eds.) 1977: *Talking to Children: Language Input and Acquisition*, New York.

Snow, C.E. & Hoefenagel-Höhle, M. 1978: „Age Differences in Second Language Acquisition", Hatch, E.M. 1978a, 333-344.

Solmecke, G. (ed.) 1976: *Motivation im Fremdsprachenunterricht*, Paderborn.

Staats, A.W. 1971: „Linguistic-Mentalistic Theory Versus an Explanatory S-R Learning Theory of Language Development, Slobin, D.I. 1971, 103-150.

Stampe, D. 1972: *A Dissertation on Natural Phonology*, Doctoral Dissertation, University of Chicago.

Stauble, A.-M.E. 1978: „The Process of Decreolization: A Model for Second Language Development", Language Learning 28, 29-54.

Stern, C. & Stern, W. 1907: *Die Kindersprache: Eine psychologische und sprachtheoretische Untersuchung*, Leipzig.

Stickel, G. 1970: *Untersuchungen zur Negation im heutigen Deutsch*, Braunschweig.

Swain, M.K. 1971: „Bilingualism, Monolingualism and Code Acquisition", Preprints for the Conference on Child Language, Chicago 1971, 208-224.

Todd, L. 1974: *Pidgins and Creoles*, London, Boston.

Tögel, H. 1905: „Sechzehn Monate Kindersprache", *Beiträge zur Kinderforschung und Heilerziehung* 13. Langensalza.

Ufert, D. 1980: Der natürliche Zweitsprachenerwerb des Englischen: Die Entwicklung des Interrogationssystems, Doctoral Dissertation, Kiel University.

Valette, R.M. 1964: „Some Reflections on Second Language Learning in Young Children", Language Learning 14, 91-98.

Villiers, J.G. de & Villiers, P.A. de 1973: „A Cross-sectional Study of the Acquisition of Grammatical Morphemes in Child Speech", Journal of Psycholinguistic Research 2, 267-278.

Volterra, V. 1972: „Il ,no'. Prime fasi di sviluppo della negazione nel linguaggio infantile", *Archivo di Psicologia, Neurologia e Psichiatria*, Fasc. I

Wardaugh, R. 1970: „The Contrastive Analysis Hypothesis", TESOL Quarterly 4, 123-130. Reprinted in: Schumann, J.H. & Stenson, N. 1975, 11-19.

Waterson, N. & Snow, D. (eds.) 1978: *Development of Communication*, London.

Waugh, L.R. & Schooneveld, C.H. van (eds.) 1980: *The Melody of Language*, Baltimore, Mld.

Weiher, E. 1975: *Lautwahrnehmung und Lautproduktion im Englischunterricht für Deutsche*, Doctoral Dissertation, Kiel University.

Weinreich, U. 1953: *Languages in Contact. Findings and Problems*, New York.

Weir, R. 1962: *Language in the Crib*, The Hague.

Weir, R. 1966: „Some Questions of the Child's Learning of Phonology", Smith, F. & Miller, G.A., 153-168.

Wienold, G. 1973: *Die Erlernbarkeit der Sprachen. Eine einführende Darstellung des Zweitsprachenerwerbs*, München.

Winitz, H. 1969: *Articulatory Acquisition and Behavior*, New York.

Wode, H. 1966: „Englische Satzintonation", Phonetica 15, 129-218.

Wode, H. 1968: „Pause und Pausenstellen im Deutschen", Acta Ling. Hafn. 11, 147-169.

Wode, H. 1969: Review of M.A.K. Halliday, Intonation and Grammar in British English, The Hague 1967, Phonetica 20, 229-231.

Wode, H. 1969: „Review of M.A.K. Halliday, Intonation and Grammar in British English, The Hague 1967", Phonetica 20, 229-231.

Wode, H. 1972a: „Zur Erzeugung der Tonhöhe englischer Syntagmata", Acta Univ. Carol. (Philol.) 1, Phonetica Pragensia III, 271-280.

Wode, H. 1972b: „The Intonation of Replies to Wh-Questions in English", Rigault, A. & Charbonneau, P., 1056-1061.

Wode, H. 1974: „Natürliche Zweitsprachigkeit: Probleme, Aufgaben, Perspektiven", Linguistische Berichte 32, 15-36. (Reprinted in this Volume).

√Wode, H. 1976a: „Developmental Sequences in Naturalistic L2 Acquisition", Working Papers on Bilingualism 11, 1-31. Reprinted in: Hatch, E.M. 1978a, 101-117.

Wode, H. 1976b: „Der Erwerb von Fragestrukturen in der Kindersprache", Drachmann, G. 1976, 101-112.

Wode, H. 1976c: „Some Stages in the Acquisition of Questions by Monolingual Children", Raffler-Engel, W.v. 1976, 261-310.

Wode, H. 1976d: „Einige Grundzüge des natürlichen Spracherwerbs", Kühlwein, W. & Raasch, A. 1977, 125-133.

√Wode, H. 1977a: „Developmental Principles in Naturalistic L2 Acquisition". Drachmann, G. 1977, 207-220.

Wode, H. 1977b: „Four Early Stages in the Development of L1 Negation", Journal of Child Language 4, 87-102. (Reprinted in this Volume)

Wode, H. 1977c: „The L2 Acquisition of /r/", Phonetica 34, 200-217.

Wode, H. 1977d: „Lernerorientiertheit im Fremdsprachenunterricht: FU als Spracherwerb", Hunfeld, H., 17-24. (Reprinted in this Volume)

Wode, H. 1977e: „Natürlicher Spracherwerb: der L1- und L2-Erwerb der Interrogation", Kühlwein, W. & Raasch, A. 1978, 5-15.

Wode, H. 1978a: „The Beginnings of Non-School Room L2 Phonological Acquisition", International Review of Applied Linguistics 16, 109-125. (Reprinted in this Volume)

Wode, H. 1978b: „The L1 vs. L2 Acquisition of English Interrogation", Working Papers on Bilingualism 15, 37-57. Revised Version in Indian Journal of Applied Linguistics (IJOSL) 4, 31-46.

Wode, H. 1978c: „Kognition, Sprachenlernen und Fremdsprachenunterricht", Detering, K. & Högel, H., 188-197.

Wode, H. 1978d: „Fehler, Fehleranalyse und Fehlerbenotung im Lichte des natürlichen L2-Erwerbs" Linguistik und Didaktik 9, 233-245.

Wode, H. 1978e: „L1-Erwerb, L2-Erwerb und Fremdsprachenunterricht", Die Neueren Sprachen 77, 452-465.

Wode, H. 1979: „Operating Principles and ‚Universals' in L1, L2, and FLT", International Review of Applied Linguistics 17, 217-231. (Reprinted in this Volume)

Wode, H. 1980a: „Phonology in L2 Acquisition", Felix, S.W. 1980, 123-136. (Reprinted in this Volume)

Wode, H. 1980b: „Grammatical Intonation in Child Language", Waugh, L.R. & Schooneveld, C.H. van, 331-345.

Wode, H. 1980c: „Language Acquisition, Pidgins and Creoles", Arbeitspapiere zum Spracherwerb 21, 20-29, English Department, Kiel University. To Appear in: Studies in Second Language Acquisition.

Wode, H. 1981: Learning a Second Language, Tübingen.

Wode, H., forthcoming: Positional Relationships in Monolingual Children's very Early Syntax.

Wode, H. & Schmitz, T. 1974: „Some Developmental Trends in the Acquisition of Negation in Several Languages", Arbeitspapiere zum Spracherwerb Nr. 3, Englisches Seminar der Universität Kiel.

Wode, H. & Ruke-Dravina, V. 1977: „Why ‚Kathryn no like celery'?", Folia Linguistica 10, 361-375.

√√ Wode, H., Bahns, J., Bedey, H. & Frank, W. 1978: „Developmental Sequence: An Alternative Approach to Morpheme Order", Language Learning 28, 175-185. (Reprinted in this volume)

Wunderlich, D. & Meisel, J. (eds.) 1977: Studium Linguistik 4.

Zale, E.M. (ed.) 1968: Proceedings of the Conference on Language and Language Behavior, New York.

Zwirner, H. & Bethge, W. (eds.) 1964: Proceedings of the 5th International Congress of Phonetic Sciences, Münster, Basel.

Varieties of English Around the World

Editor: Manfred Görlach, Heidelberg

Text Series: Published

IRE BECK

T2 John Holm, et al., *Central American English* (April 1983) 186 pages,
DM 36.00; cassette (90 min.) DM 36.00.

This is the first comprehensive study of some regional varieties of English largely un-
known to the outside world until now. John Holm outlines the region's sociolinguistic
development in a general introduction to chapters on the following varieties:
BELIZE (G. Escure); HONDURAS (E. Warantz); NICARAGUA (J. Holm and B.
Assadi); COSTA RICA (A. Herzfeld); PROVIDENCIA, SAN ANDRES and the
CAYMANS (W. Washabaugh).

Each regional variety is described in a sociolinguistic history with language maps, texts
from field recordings, analyses of the texts' syntax and lexicon, and a comprehensive
annotated bibliography. The accompanying cassette corresponds to the transcriptions in
the volume and represents the largest corpus of Central American English available so far.

General Series: Published

G1 Lanham, L. W. / McDonald, C. A., *The Standard in South African English
and its Social History.* VI/90 pp., paper. ISBN 3-87276-210-9   DM 24.00

G2 Day, R. R. (ed.), *Issues in English Creoles. Papers from the 1975 Hawaii
Conference.* XII + 185 pp., paper. ISBN 3-87276-245-1   DM 38.00

Sole distribution

USA and Canada, Middle and South America:
John Benjamins North America, Inc., Publisher,
One Buttonwood Square, 202, Philadelphia/PA. 19130/USA

Southern Africa: Universitas Books (Pty.) Ltd., P. O. Box 1557, 0001 Pretoria,
South Africa

Australia: River Seine Publications Pty. Ltd., 132 Elgin Street, Carlton, VIC. 3053,
Australia

1804
NULLA DIES SINE LINEA

JULIUS GROOS VERLAG
Postfach ... Heidelberg 1